MW01290777

Disaster and Triumph

DISASTER AND TRIUMPH:
SACRAMENTO WOMEN,
GOLD RUSH THROUGH THE
CIVIL WAR

CHERYL ANNE STAPP

Copyright © 2012 Cheryl Anne Stapp. Sacramento, California.

All rights reserved.

ISBN-13: 978-1467906289
ISBN-10: 146790628X

LCCN: 2011960313

Permissions for use of illustrations are noted beneath the illustrations.

Printed in U.S.A.

2/20/2012

DEDICATION

To all of the pioneer women who made Sacramento their home, and

To the memory of my late grandmother Lola Helvick, who always wanted to be a writer but raised seven children instead, and

To my husband Murry, for his loving support and encouragement.

Acknowledgements

Researching and writing this saga of Sacramento's pioneer women occupied two years. Throughout the process, I have been fortunate to receive assistance from many people who love to delve into the past.

I wish to express my gratitude to Greg Voelm, who serves on the Board of Directors of the Sacramento County Historical Society, for his advice, encouragement, and personal efforts to bring this history "to light." My editor Stephanie Robinson, the California State Military Museum's librarian, helped immeasurably with her thoroughness and valuable suggestions which improved the work. Many thanks also to Dr. Ken Umbach, fellow writer/researcher, member of both the California Writers Club and Northern California Authors and Publishers boards of directors, who gave the manuscript a final page-by-page edit.

For their patient and expert help with research I would like to thank Karen Paige and Janet Clemmensen at the California State Library, Pat Johnson and Dillon McDonald at the Sacramento History Center (formerly Sacramento Archives and Museum Collection Center), Nancy Jenner at Sutter's Fort Archives, Neil Roby and Mark Michalski at James Marshall Discovery State Park, the staff at Community Memorial Museum of Sutter County, and most of all Jennie Wimmer's descendant Judy Lopez, who so graciously furnished me with family materials collected by her late father, Bert Hughes. Special thanks go to Georgia historian Anne Dismukes Amerson, for her sources on Jennie Wimmer and for her enthusiastic support. I would also like to thank Teresa Gonsolis at the California Rail Road Museum, Peggy Norris with the Bergen County, New Jersey, Historical Society for supplying valuable information about the Zabriskie family, and Steve Beck at Sutter's Fort State Historic Park for sharing his considerable knowledge of early Sacramento.

If there are any technical errors in this book, they are solely the responsibility of the author.

Contents

Illustrations

1. Northern California, Circa 1850s

By Author

Author's Note on Prices and Costs

Equating 19th century costs to current market values is a challenge, for several reasons. California's prices during the Gold Rush years were incredibly inflated, the classic result of overwhelming demand meeting a severely limited supply, with the added burden of high transportation costs. Except for private orchards and vegetable gardens, and the few tradesmen who worked for the self-sustaining *rancheros* or John Sutter's Sacramento Valley compound, California had no developed agriculture and no manufacturing. Most items were delivered by merchant ships at a substantial mark-up. The most common complaint found in old diaries is the miners' anger and incredulity at the price of potatoes and onions: $1.00 *apiece* when they were accustomed to paying pennies per pound in their home towns.

As gold-rushers poured in, the cost of land in Sacramento spiraled upward, its prices driven by merchants out-bidding one another for desirable waterfront lots, and speculators who feverishly sold and resold until, inevitably, the bubble burst. Property values shrank 30 percent after the 1850 Squatter's Riots, and remained low for some time afterward. Land has traditionally been valued according to location and use. Much of the Sacramento land that constituted desirable locations for Gold Rush merchants and settlers lies beneath state-owned freeways or city-owned parcels today. In the meantime the city has expanded, resulting in high values to lands formerly considered below prime. Construction modes, equipment, and materials have changed for housing and office buildings.

Road, bridge, and levee construction are special categories for which there is no over-all equitable comparison. Early Sacramentans repaired or re-built their river levees many times, accomplished by individual men wielding shovels of fill trucked in by mule-powered wagons, at costs well below $500,000 per occurrence. As of 1999, new technology and more sophisticated tools have raised levee improvements costs to upwards of $2 million. We no longer use planks or cobblestones to cover our roads, and we incur a plethora of costs the pioneers never had to contend with: right of ways, licenses, union salaries, environmental specialists, high-powered machinery, and more costly—albeit more durable—materials that were unknown to them.

One solution to equate the costs of goods and services is to use a formula based on the average price of gold per ounce in pioneer days, $20, compared to 21st century prices per ounce. Using a middle ground of $1,000 since the year 2000 produces a multiplier of 50. This formula doesn't hold true in all cases, due to our own present-day fluctuating marketplace. For example, front row live-theater tickets cost $2 in 1850. Today performances can be enjoyed from the same vantage for 25 percent less than the formula would have it.

Prices, costs, and expenses are shown as they were in 1800s money. Selected comparisons or explanations of those amounts versus current values can be found in the End Notes for each chapter.

The Time, the Place, the Culture: Stories of Decent Ladies and Fallen Women

C ontrary to cherished sentimental beliefs, the California Gold Rush created Sacramento, not the hospitable pioneer-in-the-wilderness sometimes fondly credited as the city's founder. Indeed, Swiss immigrant John Augustus Sutter, who built a fortress compound in the Sacramento Valley, rejected the low lands so vulnerable to flooding at the confluence of the Sacramento and American Rivers as a potential town site.

Instead, it was gold that goaded the rapid rise of stores and saloons and warehouses on the Sacramento River waterfront, where signs of prior inundations were blithely ignored by merchants who sold picks and pans and shovels and foodstuffs. The location, a natural debarkation point, was ideal for profit-making. The fastest way to get to the interior for gold rushers coming by sea through the port of San Francisco was via the San Joaquin or Sacramento Rivers, and the Sacramento River enjoyed advantages and a type of fame that could be exploited. John Sutter had an established wharf that provided access where the water was deep enough to allow sea-going vessels, and his inland outpost, two miles east, was already a well-known destination. Further, the gold discovery site at Coloma was a mere forty miles away. By the summer of 1849, an immense trade had developed between Sacramento and the now far-flung mines, stimulating city growth north, south, and east from the river levee.

Before the January 1848 gold discovery in northern California's foothills, the whole countryside was pastoral. California had perhaps five hundred massive cattle ranches owned by the

1

descendants of Spanish Dons, a few coastal towns, and John Sutter's self-sustaining wilderness compound, known to all as Sutter's Fort. Currency was scarce and seldom used. *Ranchero* owners traded hides and tallow with passing merchant ships for furniture, tableware, clothing, sugar, flour, and other necessities or luxuries. The capital city was Monterey, where merchant Thomas O. Larkin served as the United States consul to Mexico. Prior to 1840, Mrs. Larkin was the only known American wife in the province.

By contrast the East Coast boasted a robust economy, railroads, fire departments, water transport systems, the telegraph, stagecoach lines, regular mail service, newspapers, and factories. They had lovely, substantial homes, schools, hospitals and churches, fancy goods for ladies (corsets, gloves, laces, parasols and such), ice, and champagne. They had women in adequate proportions to the male population.

In no time at all after the gold discovery, champagne was flowing in Sacramento's hastily erected tent-saloons. The women slowly trickled in. Their scarcity is a common theme in miners' diaries and newspapers of the period.

The handful of American and European women at Sutter's Fort before 1848 is rarely mentioned in histories. Some were the wives of Sutter's hired craftsmen. Others were members of intermittent wagon trains that stopped there to recuperate from the arduous cross-country journey before scattering about the surrounding flatlands to found farms and villages elsewhere. California was just another frontier—albeit much farther away— for a restless populace that had already pushed the boundaries of the original thirteen colonies to the Missouri River and into the Republic of Texas, driven by a search for something better: a land hunger that had created thirty united states.

For a decade wagons had traversed the plains carrying families of men, women, and children to Oregon Territory, attracted by an agricultural paradise jointly occupied, until the mid-1840s, by British and American interests. The California Gold Rush was a different migration altogether. It was the largest peacetime migration the world had ever seen—and its makeup was almost exclusively male.

The gold mines that eager prospectors swarmed to were not "mines" at all in the sense of a hole or tunnel. California's gold mines were simply the mountain watercourses, ravines, and gulches on public domain lands, discovered in the limbo period between the Republic of Mexico's absolute ownership and Yankee triumph in the Mexican-American War. The treaty granting Alta California to the United States was signed in Mexico in the month following the January 1848 gold discovery. Both factions were ignorant of the other's information. In an era when news traveled by ship, the discovery was yet unknown to the outside world, and the Treaty of Guadalupe Hidalgo documents had not yet reached the American military governors stationed in California during the war. Undermining these *de facto* governors' authority, however, Congress—embroiled in slavery issues—neglected to organize America's new acquisition as an official territory subject to the laws of the United States. No federal troops would interfere with prospectors' claims, as had happened in the state of Georgia's gold rush twenty years earlier.

By the end of 1848 *everyone* knew the gold fields were rich and California was a minimally governed region, which meant, on a practical level, that the gold was anybody's for the taking.

The men who arrived in California in 1849—then and evermore dubbed the '49ers—the 89,000 individuals who were the first wave of Americans and Europeans lured by gold, were mostly young. Future railroad baron Mark Hopkins, a thirty-five-year-old bachelor from New York, was considered old by his gold-rusher contemporaries. Many were married, others betrothed; adolescent males too young to consider matrimony set out for the adventure of their lives. All were anxious to get there before the thousands who lived closer and had invaded the rivers and streams in 1848 *took all that free gold.* Most of them never intended to stay in California. In a few weeks, a year maybe, they would have their own pile to bring home to pay off their debts, add more acreage to the farm, or start a lucrative business. They traveled mostly unencumbered by wives, children or parents who would slow them down. Greybeards with their wives and daughters were so sparse around campfires that their presence was specifically noted in other men's diaries.

About forty percent came by ship. The San Francisco harbormaster counted more than 41,000 Americans and foreigners who disembarked there in 1849—of which just 599 were women.

In June 1849 American military governor Bennet Riley called for elected representatives from all over California to draft a constitution in anticipation of statehood. Sacramento District (there were no counties yet) sent eight delegates, John Sutter among them, to Monterey for the September convention. For six weeks the forty-eight convention members hammered out important issues like the state's eastern boundaries and citizens' fundamental rights. They agreed on a traditional American government of three branches, made provision for a system of public schools and taxes, and chose San Jose as the capital.

Every man at this conference knew the state-to-be was short of women, particularly marriageable women of good moral character able to provide a man with well-raised children who would honor his name and legacy. Nevertheless, grumbling and dissension greeted the unorthodox proposal that married women be allowed to own property separate from their husbands. Delegate Henry Halleck from Monterey (later General Halleck in the Civil War) finally urged the bachelors in the group to approve the measure on the grounds it would induce women of wealth to come to California.

He meant it as a little joke. They passed it anyway.

The next year 35,333 men and 1,148 women sailed into the Bay. Statistics for overland emigrants are not as precise because not every wagon caravan traversed the same routes or stopped at the same places. Conscientious efforts to count the Golden Emigration, as the phenomenon was quickly dubbed in the nationwide press, soon became policy. Tallies at Fort Laramie during 1850 counted 39,560 men, 2,421 women, and 609 children.

California was admitted to statehood on September 9, 1850, and the subsequent 1850 Federal Census revealed that women composed only eight percent of the total California population. Less than one percent of these females lived in the remote mining regions. Thus the Gold Rush spawned a uniquely masculine world free from the constraints of traditional society, where men could drink and forsake church services and gamble and curse if they damned well pleased, without suffering women's reproaches.

Mid-nineteenth century America was a patriarchal society to begin with. Wives were subordinate helpmates; young children "belonged" to their fathers; spinsters were pitied and dismissed as irrelevant in the grand scheme of things. Educated men knew that women—from Cleopatra of Egypt to Isabella of Spain to Elizabeth of England—had ruled nations. But these queens had been monarchs by birthright, a political tradition from which Americans had successfully fought to free themselves not too long past. As for the current queen of America's Mother Country, men were content with the fact that Victoria had a husband and male advisers to tell her what to do, and, moreover, were smugly aware that the Queen herself had declared "We women are not made for governing."

This is not to say Victorian-era women were not loved, respected, and adored as individuals by their men or that their advice and personal wants weren't taken into consideration. Generally, though, women were viewed as delicate creatures to be protected and above all, *guided.*

The California Gold Rush gradually changed that perception as pioneer women displayed considerable initiative in proving their mettle as capable decision-makers and breadwinners.

An enormous number of the 1849 immigrants passed through Sacramento. Of these, a few dozen had come specifically to import American culture and civilization, men who envisioned California as a plum acquisition for the United States, gold notwithstanding. Their efforts were successful: Sacramento became California's first incorporated city on February 27, 1850. Hundreds more who were unlucky in the gold game had the good sense to quit searching for buried treasure and resume their former occupations. Sacramento quickly acquired more merchants, skilled craftsmen, manufacturers, wholesale grocers, and freighters. The flow of newcomers ebbed in 1850 as the bulk of overlanders halted their wagons in the northern or eastern mines before reaching town. Nonetheless, according to the *Sacramento Transcript*, the city's growth continued unabated. Women's faces remained largely absent, however, as verified by the first census.

Admitting that his preliminary findings in the 1850 Census for Sacramento County were flawed due to the constant moving about of the city's inhabitants and the cholera epidemic which had just erupted, the census marshal nevertheless published his findings in the *Sacramento Transcript*: near 6,000 residents, maybe another 1,500 if one considered the number who had fled in fear of cholera, plus an additional "floating" population of 2,000. Out of the more or less solid 6,000 Sacramento County citizens, 460 were females.

Those females had spunk and determination and skills today's women have no reason to learn: how to recognize and harvest deposits of saleratus (baking soda), make candles, churn butter, or coax a recalcitrant mule. They worked hard from before sunrise to after dark tending to their families. Often they worked jobs outside the home to help feed the family while their husbands mined upriver or took whatever low-paying jobs were available in town.

In Sacramento women worked as laundresses, shop girls, dressmakers, milliners, and hotel housekeepers. One married lady advertised herself in city directories as a dealer in fancy dry goods. Women *owned* saloons, restaurants, boarding houses and hotels. They sold the pleasure of their fleeting company at gaming tables; some grew well-to-do by selling their bodies. After 1854, a few taught school. None in those early years was a lawyer, banker, real estate agent, or newspaper editor.

Mrs. A. P. Petit announced the opening of her private boarding house on L Street in the December 29, 1849 *Placer Times:* "A few gentlemen with their wives, or single gentlemen can be accommodated with furnished rooms and good board, on reasonable terms." Clearly, she wanted no rowdies. The same issue carried an ad from a tailor with the postscript "Two good seamstresses will find employment by applying [to the] above." A month later the *Times* published a letter from an unnamed lady to her friends in Maine. She had ten boarders, who occupied one end of an open chamber divided by a cloth curtain while the family occupied the other. She did all her cooking "by a very small fireplace, no oven, [I] bake all my bread and pies in a Dutch oven." Her little store room was "about as large as a piece of chalk." She was making money, though, collecting $189[1] per week and clearing $75 after expenses, an income verging on riches by 1849 standards.

The upside was that the scarce pioneer women were looked upon with a certain bedazzled awe. Luzena Stanley Wilson lived in Sacramento only a short time before moving on to Nevada City and from there to Vacaville, where she is considered one of that city's founders. Her memoirs entitled *My Checkered Life* relates how hard she worked running a boarding house and also the gallantry displayed by the lonely miners who ate at her rough-plank table: ". . . always at my coming the loud voices were hushed, the swearing ceased, the quarrels stopped, and deference and respect were as readily and as heartily tendered to me as if I had been a queen. I was a queen."

Luzena was so busy with her children, chores, and cooking that she claimed she saw only two other women during her six months in Sacramento. As time went on and genuine houses replaced tents and cabins, domestic help became common among the swelling middle-class. City dwellings often sheltered extended family members, so tended to be large two story structures surrounded by flower beds and home vegetable gardens. Hiring help relieved the lady of the house and provided employment for new immigrant women or widows who needed it.

It wasn't very long before those oh-so-free gents began to sorely pine for a woman's voice, her smile, her tender loving care, her cooking. In the spring of 1851 the *Sacramento Daily Union* editor somewhat wistfully reported "sightings" of newly arrived women he fervently hoped might become permanent residents. His April 18 City News Column voiced many a man's sentiments:

> Among the arrivals we were glad to observe a large number of females composing members of families who must be looked on as the principal agents of civilization and refinement among the community of California. All this speaks well for our progress and permanency.

Respectable ladies seldom saw their own names in print in Sacramento newspapers from the Gold Rush through the end of the Civil War; nor were they normally the subjects of news items, except in extraordinary circumstances. Sacramento's first newspaper, the *Placer Times*, devoted a long paragraph to Sacramento's first wedding in December 1849. The editor opted to report the dress coats, vests, and kid gloves the gentlemen wore, adding only a general statement that the twenty female guests were attired fashionably. He made no mention of the bride, other than her name.

San Francisco newspapers, after 1851, and specialty publications like the *California Farmer* were more liberal with ladies' names, but Sacramento publications adhered to a journalistic style meant to protect the "sensitive feelings of modest wom[e]n." If a woman signed public, published letters for charity appeals, editors simply inserted "Mrs." in front her husband's full name and title, for example: Mrs. Judge John Jones. Women who organized church bazaars and wished to promote the fund-raising affair or report success afterward were identified in the press as "the Lady Managers." Occasionally an editor employed the very coy "Mrs. (or Miss) J___" format. These practices make research efforts of individual women's activities difficult. Now and then, women's first names appeared in advertisements for private schools they were forming. There were no Ladies Pages and no gossipy "society news" columns until the mid-1870s. Meantime, printed mention of women's names or any other overt singled-out references to women's views or activities remained scarce.

One remarkable exception occurred during the May 1851 Whig Party Convention. A procession of delegates marched grandly down K Street to Front Street to J Street bearing their flags and pennants amid cheering crowds and blazing bonfires. At Seventh Street the parade came to a halt, for this was where the Whig Ladies of Sacramento City were to present their hand-sewn banner to the Committee. Women's suffrage was a long way off; the Whig Ladies were merely the wives of committee members, who had come together to lend support to their men folk. The banner itself, rich satin elaborately embroidered with symbols and mottos, was unfurled to, as the *Sacramento Daily Union* crowed, ". . . such exulting and terrific cheers as went up for the fair donors, we have never heard." Fannie Kewen—wife of delegate Colonel Kewen—made the formal presentation followed by a short address to "the breathless stillness of the multitude." The gentlemen were in fact so thrilled with these pronouncements from

9

a lovely woman that they insisted on publishing the text of her speech in the *Union*. As might be expected, Mrs. Kewen's words were a masterpiece of feminine decorum laced with patriotism and the charming disclaimer, "It is not the province of woman to mingle in the political foray . . . [but] our sympathies are entwined around the creed you profess and our hearts are kindled with the same enthusiastic hopes . . . ." Her own full name appeared at the end.

Another extraordinary circumstance was Sacramento's great fire of November 2, 1852. Reporting in the breathlessly lurid prose of the day, the *Union* chronicled the ravages of the fire over several issues. Three days after the conflagration they printed a woman's story of the event. Mrs. M. A. Acherson was part of the fleeing throng when flames broke out inside the Crescent City Hotel, becoming separated from her six-year-old daughter in the dash to the street. She heard the child crying out for help, in agony for her little girl's life yet unable to save her as the hotel's eastern side quickly became engulfed. The hero of the story was the named gentleman who risked his life to deliver the child to her mother's arms.

The 1852 fire devoured nearly ninety percent of the town—devastation so absolute that San Francisco's *Daily Alta* devoted many issues to the conflagration and also noted Sacramentans' swift re-erection of 761 buildings by December. Several men perished, but no women or children. Since the fire started in Madame Lanos' millinery shop, she was first assumed dead until days later when the *Union* happily declared that she was alive and well. Madame Lanos, about whom nothing else is known, listed her business in city directories for many years afterward. Mrs. Acherson and daughter apparently left Sacramento before the ashes cooled.

Fannie Kewen, Mrs. Acherson, and Madame Lanos were re-spectable ladies. Bad girls' names were dragged into stories that blatantly broadcast their private lives, as per this item:

> SUICIDE. A coroner's inquest was held on Saturday upon the body of Mmlle. Caroline, well known to all frequenters of the Polka Saloon. The unfortunate young woman came to her death by taking strychnine. The act was caused by some love affair in which she had been engaged, and the verdict of the jury was in accordance with the above facts. —*Sacramento Daily Union November 6, 1852*

Sacramento's naughty ladies apparently held to certain standards despite being known to indulge in distilled refreshments. No Sacramento lass harbored a wanted stage robber as did a Nevada City woman of low virtue, nor did any copy the antics of tobacco smoking, whiskey swilling "Dutch Kate" of Marysville, who disguised herself in men's clothing to rob stage coaches *herself.* Sacramento was still a young, raw place where violent death was not uncommon, when a pretty young prostitute named Ida Vanard plunged a knife into the torso of a rival she thought had stolen her man's affections. She was arrested and tried for murder, and all the evidence condemned her until her lawyer's closing remarks captivated the spectators and the judge advised the jury of twelve men that Ida's gender, alone, was sufficient to doubt any "real depravity of heart in the bosom of the defendant." She was acquitted.

Sometimes women's daily tribulations were relieved by a bit of humor. This article appearing in the October 13, 1852 *Saint Joseph Gazette*, reprinted from an unidentified California newspaper, surely forced a hoot of laughter from women who had endured the overland trails:

> A man from Illinois has just arrived from Independence having driven the entire distance 2,000 turkeys, all hale and heavy. They cost him about 50 cents apiece in the States and the cost of feeding them on the way—nothing; they fed themselves. He has

11

been offered $8.00 apiece.[2]

Obviously, this unnamed entrepreneur was immune to the blood-boiling frustrations commonly experienced by the majority of men and women who drove herds of cattle, horses, sheep, milk cows and the occasional pig across country beside their wagons. Though unstated, one can reasonably guess that the turkeys were caged atop flat-bed, mule-powered carts for much of the journey.

Statistics of the 1852 immigration across the plains, as presented in the *Daily Alta California* that November, noted 16,362 men, 3,242 women and 4,266 children, with the disclaimer that the count did not include those who departed from Council Bluff, Iowa. Not all of these, of course, settled in Sacramento. California authorities took their own in-state census that year to update and hopefully correct the admittedly flawed 1850 federal census. Published 1852 census data for Sacramento County listed 10,430 men and 2,020 women, numbers somewhat skewed because not all elements of the ethnically diverse population, although counted, were included in the official total of 12,589. Of that number 8,530 lived within the city limits, not broken out by gender.

Still, Sacramento's female population was rising, and so was women's gentling influence. Aside from providing enthusiastic emotional support to elected or politically aspirant husbands, women had no official say in political affairs except for those suggestions they made at home—an influence that simply cannot be quantified.

However, one politicized movement that drew and welcomed women members was the Sacramento temperance leagues—two in 1850, and three by 1853. These were organized to combat the heavy drinking occasioned by the gold rushers' homesickness and sudden social freedoms, abetted by truly astonishing amounts of liquor received at San Francisco's port-of-entry. For just the three months ending September 30, 1852, San Francisco's *Daily Alta* reported the intake of almost 400,000 gallons of whiskey, brandy, gin, rum, and claret, plus thousands more casks of assorted alcohol. This translates to slightly less than 1.5 million gallons annually for a reported state-wide population of 200,000 males. The resultant alcohol-fueled fist fights, reckless shootouts, and general moral turpitude quite naturally offended the straightlaced.

Good women—those protectors of home, hearth, and morals—were generally not known to imbibe. Disreputable women were another cut of lace, as this finger-wagging article by a shocked and affronted editor attests:

> It is lamentable in a Christian country, to witness the extent of depravity to which even woman sometimes renders herself a subject. On Saturday evening a prostitute belonging to that class which dresses finely, rides spirited palfreys (with feathers in their caps) and who, among other accomplishments, boast a large share of personal beauty, was arrested in the public streets for being drunk . . . As a general thing, this frail class of community—the victims of man's deceit and seductions—are more to be pitied than condemned; but, in Heaven's name, let them keep their shame within doors, that the virtuous may not be shocked by their vileness, nor those who sympathize in their fall, be forced to loathe them!

—*Sacramento Daily Union, August 15, 1853*

By the same standards it was hard not to notice that when respectable women appeared in towns, the streets became passable, clean and quiet, and pistols were less frequently fired.

By the end of 1853 Sacramento had six churches and one synagogue, but no public schools existed until February 1854. Two attempts to open schools had been made by concerned gentlemen in late 1849, the first a prominent merchants' agent and the second a Congregational pastor. Their schoolhouse on I Street was a one story, 14- by 28-foot structure having old sails for its walls and roof, and no floor save the ground. Neither drew more than twelve pupils, and neither lasted more than a few weeks, partly due to inclement weather. Unfortunately, all we know of the early public schoolmarms are their last names and the schools where they taught. Miss Griswold ran the "female department" of the first public school that opened on February 20, 1854, presiding over seventy girls. Two primary schools opened within the next eighteen months with lady teachers. Educational boards decreed that only male teachers could be employed as principals—so a Miss Doyle no doubt considered her 1860 appointment as assistant principal of Franklin Grammar School a coup. At the end of 1866, 1,524 children were enrolled in the public schools' lower grades with a smaller number attending high school.

Private schools filled the gap. Women enjoyed greater opportunity in these institutions, often unabashedly declaring themselves as school principals in print advertisements. However, if these ads are an indication, they also experienced less job security and greater risk. Shoestring finances, retirement from teaching upon marriage, and competition probably all contributed to the rise, demise, and staff changes in several private girls' schools through the end of the 1850s.

James Stratton and his wife opened the Sacramento Academy and Female Institute in 1853, with two female assistants. By year end one of the assistants, Miss M. S. (Mary) Bennett had replaced Mrs. Stratton as Preceptress, or head instructor. On March 30, 1854 the *Sacramento Daily Union* announced the opening of a boarding and day school for young ladies from the residence of Reverend and Mrs. Wheeler of the Baptist Church, under the charge of Principal Miss Mary Doty, an experienced teacher from Illinois. The following February, the *Union* lamented Miss Doty's loss when she accepted a teaching position at a Napa Valley girls' school. Meanwhile, Mary S. Bennett opened her own Young Ladies' Seminary in 1854, which proved so popular that she built and moved to larger quarters a year later—a move approved and applauded by the *Union* as an ". . . enterprise so successfully consummated by a lady." However, by late 1856, Mary Bennett was featured as a teacher of French and painting in an advertisement for the same school under the supervision of a different lady preceptress. Miss Kennedy and Madame Heritier opened their Union Academy for the Education of Young Ladies in January 1857. Eleven months later Pauline Heritier had a new partner. These young ladies' academies all advertised classes in music. Evidently seeing a need, Mrs. Ehrich from Georgia advertised her expertise as a private teacher of the piano, harp, and guitar. The longest lasting private school in Sacramento, St. Joseph's Academy, was established in 1860 by the Roman Catholic Sisters of Mercy, originally as a day and boarding school for girls, regardless of their religious affiliation.

Another educated lady who saw a need in Sacramento and filled it was Elizabeth Thorn Scott Flood, a black woman from New Bedford, Massachusetts. The full picture of her life is unknown, and her arrival in the gold fields at Placerville, where her husband Joseph Scott was a gold miner, is undocumented. On the 1852 Census Elizabeth specified her birth place as New York and her age as twenty-four. Joseph Scott's date and cause of death is not known, but it is believed Mrs. Scott was already widowed when she left Placerville.

Elizabeth and her young son Oliver were living in Sacramento when she opened her home as the first California school for black children on May 29, 1854. Fourteen black children enrolled; she received $50 per month as teacher, collected from the one dollar per week tuition fees paid by the students' parents. Soon Mrs. Scott's classrooms were open to Native American and Asian children as well, and as the number of pupils increased, the class location was changed to the basement of St. Andrews African Methodist Episcopal Church on Seventh Street between G and H, where Elizabeth was an active member. It is thought that Elizabeth Thorn Scott met her second husband Isaac Flood, a man active in many civic and social causes, through fellow church members, but the date of their marriage is uncertain. In 1856, Elizabeth moved to Isaac Flood's home in present day Oakland, California. There, in 1857, she pioneered another school for black children from her home. Elizabeth Scott Flood died in Oakland in 1867.

Mrs. Flood's school was a private facility. After her departure, the African American Public School was taught by Jeremiah B. Sanderson in a schoolhouse near Fourth and K Streets, on property purchased by Priscilla Yantis and three other black women determined to provide an educational facility for their children. Sacramento's public schools were segregated until the mid-1880s.

Sacramento changed with each passing decade. As the 1860s dawned and the thunder of approaching war-clouds could be heard across the nation, magnificent homes with elegant porticoes reclined on well-tended lawns in exclusively residential areas. Sleekly coiffed, big-skirted ladies "took the air" beneath elegant chapeaux and sun-shading parasols. Quilting and sewing groups were, no doubt, still an important part of women's social lives just as some of the more intrepid ladies slowly but surely moved ahead into previously male-dominated occupations.

The years surrounding the Civil War were not yet the font of opportunity women would find in the 1890s. Still, Sacramento's 1868 city directory listed a lady photograph gallery owner, a female artist, two women nurses, an inventor (Patent Stamping Powder for dressmaking), an undertaker, and a smattering of other women business owners. These lady entrepreneurs likely took advantage of a stunning bit of legislation passed by California law-makers in 1852: the Sole Traders Act, which authorized married women to transact business in their own names. In May 1853, Sacramento resident Mary E. Miller published the requisite notice in the *Sacramento Daily Union* declaring her intention, as a married woman, to transact a fruit, nursery, and vegetable garden business for which she would individually be responsible for all debts, acknowledging before a notary public that she did so "without fear or compulsion or undue influence of her husband." Mrs. Elizabeth Cooper published the same legally worded declaration to establish a general provision and grocery business in August 1861. She might not have been a successful business-woman. A later city directory has no listing for Elizabeth Cooper's grocery, though it does list her husband George as a whiskey dealer.

Women became litigants, too. Perhaps emboldened by pro-gressive legislation, they asserted their rights as citizens despite having no right to vote. In February 1857 private boarding house owner Miss Mary S. Bennett—evidently the same Miss Bennett who taught school—filed suit against merchant Mark Hopkins over the care and boarding of his dog Chevalier. The action quickly dissipated into a farce. The press had a wonderful time expending ink and editorial scribbling hours on this "Important Suit" for $125,[3] chronicling an entire afternoon's testimony in the "Black Dog Case" including Mr. Hopkins' counter-allegation that the plaintiff *requested* the dog's presence to keep pigs and cows out of her yard. With barely restrained glee, the *Sacramento Daily Union* informed its readers of Hopkins' complaint that his animal was fed on scraps and crumbs, countered by Mary Bennett's assertions she gave the animal pies, custards, cakes, choice cuts of meat and creamed coffee. By the time "a thousand and one questions were asked [of one witness] relative to all points of a dog, their habits, peculiarities . . . cross-examined with extreme minuteness . . . " Judge Jenks must have been very weary indeed. His ruling (printed verbatim in a rather long column) was $57.71 for the plaintiff.

Of a more serious nature, divorces, spousal support, and

property settlements were awarded to wives of errant husbands. James and Anne Warner's suit against a steamship line for breach of contract reached the California Supreme Court. In two separate actions, two married women successfully claimed that their sole and separately-owned farm lands could not be confiscated by their husbands' creditors despite the fact, in both cases, that the husbands had used the wife's property. In their rulings, the courts cited the California constitutional delegates' original intent in granting separate property to a wife was to protect her against the improvidence of a husband, and that such separate property could not be held to answer for his debts.

Sacramento's post-Civil War directories show an increase in the listings of marriageable women, single and/or widowed. The 1860 Census documented that the number of women had risen to thirty percent of the California population compared to just eight percent in 1850—still not enough for every man who wished to marry. In California, white women were outnumbered by white men three to one. The numbers for minorities were just as dismal for bachelors: 1,259 black women for 2,821 men; 1,784 Asian women for 33,149 men; 7,211 Indian women for 10,587 men. These census statistics, however, don't say how many were already married. The phenomenon of "mail order brides" for California bachelors, after disappointing efforts in the 1850s by Eliza Farnham and others to import East Coast women of virtue, came into acceptance in the 1870s. The *Matrimonial News*, published weekly in San Francisco and Kansas City, Missouri, ran personal ads placed by their many subscribers. No statistics exist to say how many of these women accepted Sacramento men as husbands.

The women, few as they were, had accomplished more than was realized at the time. Theodore Hittell's *History of California* says:

> But when respectable women became numerous and
> miners in general became married men, there was a

very great change in the appearance of things all over the [state]. Everywhere and in every respect the change made itself manifest. Tastes and habits altered; there was less low conduct and less coarse conversation; less drinking and less gambling; more neatness of dress and more refinement of manners; more civilization and more culture. . . . Nowhere in the world, perhaps, were women . . . treated with more respectful attention or consideration than in California . . . Without them of course the country never could have advanced in the path of progress or amounted to anything worth the name.

The six women whose lives and times appear in the following pages all lived in Sacramento, or the pre-statehood Sacramento District, between 1848 and 1869, a period of tumultuous transition from a Far West frontier to maturity as a city. Three remained Sacramento residents for a while after the end of the Civil War in 1865 and the completion of the transcontinental railroad four years later—events that forever changed America.

Not all lived here at the same time. Some relocated, as their own lives and the mobility of the times led them. Except for one who died young, their lives didn't end in 1869, and their stories continue in abbreviated form after they left Sacramento. Two remained in Sacramento many years beyond the transcontinental railroad tie; their life-stories continue until their deaths.

Their stories are told here because, except for Donner Party survivor Dorothea Wolfinger Zins, these ladies' descendants and other interested parties donated enough personal information about them to libraries and other institutions to facilitate further research. What details there are of Dorothea's life came from various Donner Party chronicles, monologues about her second husband, and old newspapers. The length of each individual woman's chapter is no reflection on her personal life or interests or influence, but merely a function of available information. Almost nothing more is known of the women who have cameo roles in the narrative—instead of their own chapters—other than what is presented in these pages. None of the women left diaries of their lives in Sacramento. Margaret Frink kept a journal of her trek across country with no further daily entries after her first year as a settler.

These six ladies and the others noted in sketches are some of the women who lent their talents and energies to the making of California's capital city, ladies who built a community by their very presence.

End Notes, The Time, the Place, the Culture

[1]The lady from Maine was collecting approximately $819 per month, or $9,828 annually. Using the gold-ratio multiplier discussed in the Author's Note, her income in modern dollars translates to $491,400, and she was renting rooms, not apartments. By comparison, business facilities rented for as high as $5,000 per month in Gold Rush days, or $3 million annually in current dollars.

[2]The gentleman sold his turkeys (presumably live) for $8.00 in 1852, or $8 x 50 = $400. While some buyers undoubtedly consumed the birds, others might have purchased a pair to start their own flock.

[3]By the same formula as above, $125 then = $6,250 now; however, such a minor complaint today would be heard in a California Small Claims Court, whose upper limit for damages claimed is $7,500.

The Gold Discovery:
Jennie Wimmer

Sacramento, the Capital City of California, owes its beginnings—in part—to a woman with a discerning eye and a pot of simmering home-made laundry soap. That woman was Elizabeth Jane Cloud Baiz Wimmer.

Jennie, as she was called, was employed as the camp cook and laundress at Coloma, the little wilderness valley on the South Fork of the American River where carpenter and jack-of-many-trades James Marshall and his crew, including Jennie's husband Peter, were building a sawmill for their mutual employer, Captain John Sutter. Sacramento did not yet exist, nor was there any other town or village in either the Sacramento Valley or the mountain foothills. The only inland outpost was forty miles downriver from Coloma, where Swiss immigrant John Augustus Sutter's high-walled adobe fortress and agricultural empire sprawled over acreage at the confluence of the Sacramento and American Rivers, a hundred miles northeast of San Francisco Bay. Captain Sutter had named his fiefdom, acquired by Mexican land grant, New Helvetia (New Switzerland). Most people simply called his holdings Sutter's Fort.

Marshall and the Wimmers must have realized they were working for an ambitious man. Sutter had great plans to improve his farm/ranchlands, and he also fondly dreamed of someday establishing his own colony in what was then Mexican-owned California. For that he needed good lumber for beams, flooring, fences, and dozens of other uses, but the cottonwoods, sycamores, and white alders surrounding his fortress had proved disappointing—and the valley oaks were necessary for shade and their acorns for substitute coffee. His solution was the lovely Coloma site in the foothills that James Marshall found, filled with stands of ponderosa pine. It was deemed the perfect location for a sawmill. That John Sutter had no legal claim to this location was no deterrent. Almost all of northeastern California was empty of other settlers, and neither the Republic of Mexico nor its Spanish Crown antecedents had journeyed that far into the interior. In short, there was no one to dispute his use of the land—and apparently none of these issues were of concern to either Marshall or the Wimmers. The sawmill design was simple and common: a waterwheel, powered by a flow of water through a channel, pushed a seven-foot saw up and down while a cog system pushed logs into the saw. The mill's estimated capacity was about 1,000 board feet a day.

As the project neared completion, Marshall noticed a problem with the tailrace (the ditch through which the water flowed to the wheel) and he ordered his crew to dig this channel deeper. On the icy-cold morning of January 24, 1848, while inspecting the tailrace, he spotted "something shiny" and picked up some particles of this material, not entirely confident whether it was truly gold or merely iron pyrite or yellow biotite, two metals that were common in Sierra Nevada river streams. Then and later, Jennie would say either her husband Peter or her son Martin was the first to notice the glimmering metal, although the Wimmers conceded that Marshall was the first to lean over and retrieve the pea-sized pieces and smaller flakes from the ditch. That evening Marshall discussed his find with his men, whose immediate responses to the question of genuine gold were statements like "I reckon not," and "No such luck."

But Jennie Wimmer thought she recognized gold when she saw it, from her experience in the Georgia gold camps several years before. She happened to be making a large kettle of laundry soap, a days-long process that melded tallow with the very caustic ingredient lye. She had just tested the lye water with a feather and knew it was ready for the next ingredient. Jennie told Marshall she would boil his specimen in her soap kettle all day as a test, knowing full well that genuine gold would not dissolve in the harsh chemicals.

"I finished off my soap that day and set it off to cool and it stayed there 'till next morning," she recalled later. "A plank was brought for me to lay my soap unto [sic] and I cut it in chunks but [the gold] was not to be found. At the bottom of the pot was a double handful of potash, which I lifted in my two hands, and there was my gold as bright as could be."

Unknown to anyone at the time, the gold Jennie plucked from the powdery potash was an event that changed the world. The resultant stampede to the gold fields from everywhere in both hemispheres would lift San Francisco from a mud-flat harbor to an international port. Within a year, Jennie's bright gold would create Sacramento City whole out of John Sutter's private wharf on the Sacramento River.

Before and after Jennie's test, James Marshall employed other measures: he bit into the metal, hammered a specimen flat between two stones, and threw a piece in the fire. Those satisfactory effects and Jennie's results filled him with growing excitement. Four days after his discovery, on the dark and rainy afternoon of January 28, 1848 a swift-riding, rain-soaked and mud-splattered Marshall burst into John Sutter's office at the Fort, demanding to see his sawmill partner alone. More tests followed. The specimens were weighed on an apothecary scale and then subjected to a dousing of nitric acid. Nothing disturbed the sample. Sutter consulted his *Encyclopedia Americana:* the seed-sized particles tied in Marshall's handkerchief were gold, estimated to be of twenty-three carat purity.

J. W. Marshall and Mrs. Wimmer Testing Gold in Boiling Soap.

2. James Marshall and Jennie Wimmer Testing Gold in Boiling Soap

Courtesy California History Room, California State Library, Sacramento

Jennie recalled years later that "Sutter came right up with Marshall." She was mistaken, or perhaps she didn't think a few days' lapse was important. James Marshall had returned to camp, but Sutter, having other business matters to detain him, did not leave his fort until February 1, four days after Marshall's visit. Jennie indeed saw Sutter and Marshall arriving together, because Marshall (who may have ridden out more than once hoping to intercept Sutter) encountered him about half-way en route and accompanied him the rest of the way. No doubt the two were deep in conversation as they rode, because the master of New Helvetia—the only established inland community in northern California—was becoming increasingly worried.

John Sutter would ever afterward claim that from the day of Marshall's unexpected visit he experienced fearful premonitions of how this gold discovery might ruin him and his 150,000 acre agricultural domain. If indeed the foothills and upper reaches of the Sierra Nevada east of his enclave held rich gold deposits, the workers he depended on to sow and harvest his grains, herd and shoe his livestock, forge farming tools, grind his wheat into flour, and dozens more tasks he needed done to make his New Helvetia compound self-sufficient and profitable—would leave him and he would not be able to recruit replacements. Without workers, he was doomed. It is unknown whether Sutter's fearful premonitions included the vision that gold rushers would trample his valley crops and rustle his livestock—as they surely did. James Marshall had an ownership agreement in the mill with Sutter; both realized that easy gold that could be picked out with pocket knives could halt construction. Sutter's and Marshall's first imperative was swearing the Coloma crew to secrecy, at least for six weeks, until both his sawmill and a grist mill then under construction on the American River closer to the Fort should be in operation. His workmen agreed, especially since Sutter told them they could prospect on their own free time and also because none were yet prepared to relinquish the steady wages Sutter was paying for the less certain occupation of gold-gathering. Jennie, who never left camp, supposedly had no one outside to tell.

But the secret was altogether too intoxicating to keep for long, and it escaped via different informants.

The first was a teamster. In compliance with his agreement to provide provisions to the Coloma encampment, Captain Sutter had sent his heretofore reliable employee Jacob Wittmer to the mill site around February 9 with a wagonload of supplies. Strolling about the area after his delivery, the teamster encountered one of Jennie and Peter Wimmer's young sons, who boasted, "We've found gold up here!" The child was seven-year-old Martin Baiz, Jennie's son with her deceased first husband. Jacob Wittmer laughed at the boy and so ridiculed the very idea that Jennie became angry enough to divulge the details and give the man a sample or two to prove her son was telling the truth. Wittmer whipped his ox team back to Sutter's Fort. Right outside the fort walls was a combination general merchandise store and *cantina* named C. C. Smith & Company, just opened the previous October, where Wittmer occasionally tried to buy a drink with promises of later payment. Now he marched up to the counter and demanded to buy a bottle of brandy with the gold dust Jennie had given him. The day was February 14, and Sutter happened to be in his office at the fort. Mr. Smith's suspicions about Jacob Wittmer were allayed after a private audience with Captain Sutter, and Mr. Wittmer got his brandy. Smith, in turn, passed this information on to his partner Sam Brannan—a man not to be underestimated when it came to opportunities that fell in his lap.

Jacob Wittmer repeated his story to everyone who would listen, although initially most brushed it off as barely believable. It isn't known whether Jennie felt abashed after Wittmer left camp and her ruffled mother-hen feathers smoothed back into place—or what, if anything, James Marshall said to her afterward. Captain

Sutter's inability to stifle Wittmer's talk made him even more nervous. Sutter knew he needed protection for his investment in this sawmill—the wages and supplies already expended, plus his anticipated profits when he sold the extra lumber—erected on land he did not own. Coloma was part of the enormous Sacramento District in the province of Mexican California, but the area itself was miles outside the eastern boundaries of his land grants. To hold trespassers at bay, Sutter felt he needed a pre-emption (a right to acquire certain property in preference to any other persons) for the quarter section of land on which the mill stood.

Accordingly, in mid-February Sutter dispatched Marshall's trusted associate Charles Bennett to Monterey for an audience with military governor Colonel Richard Mason, chief representative of the United States government in California. In his saddlebags were six ounces of gold samples in a buckskin bag and documents for Colonel Mason to sign. En route to Monterey, Charles Bennett was unable to resist showing his samples and blurting out some tantalizing tidbits in a combination store and saloon at Benecia.

Down the coast at Monterey, Colonel Mason examined the gold samples but denied Sutter's request for a pre-emption. The Treaty of Guadalupe Hidalgo that ended the Mexican American War had been signed on February 2, 1848, but word of this peace treaty had not yet reached Colonel Mason. Under the terms of the agreement Mexico relinquished California, Texas, Nevada, Utah, and parts of Arizona, New Mexico, Colorado, and Wyoming to the United States for a payment of fifteen million dollars in gold and silver. Unaware of this, Colonel Mason refused to grant a land title to Sutter, citing as his reason that California was still a Mexican province to which no laws of the United States applied. Purportedly the colonel and his staff attached little importance to this discovery, since gold of little value was known to exist in southern California at San Fernando, but his decision would prove monumental—for both Captain John Sutter and the hordes that

29

sped to this new discovery site that spring and for years afterward.

Without a land title, the area remained in the public domain and the gold found at Coloma would be anyone's to take. Sam Brannan, co-owner of the mercantile where teamster Wittmer spent Jennie's gold sample, would see to it that the cautiously excited gossip circulating about from Wittmer's and Bennett's show-and-tell stories turned into excited action.

Not yet thirty years old but already a Mormon Elder, Brannan had sailed on the *Brooklyn* from New York to Yerba Buena (later San Francisco) in 1846 leading 238 men, women, and children of the faith to investigate possible settlement opportunities outside of American jurisdiction. Other churchmen were looking too: a year after Brannan's ship anchored in California, Brigham Young led a flock of Latter Day Saints overland to his own chosen Zion in Utah Territory. A printer by trade who seemed to be blessed with an unerring sense of business opportunity, Brannan brought a printing press with him aboard ship. Soon after landing he established a general business store named Sam Brannan and Company and founded *The California Star*, a newspaper for the faithful. Quickly ascertaining that Sutter's Sacramento Valley New Helvetia settlement was the only inland bastion of any importance or promise, he opened another store outside the fortress walls in partnership with fellow Mormon Charles Smith. Upon hearing Smith's story of Wittmer's gold dust, Brannan may have thoughtfully stroked his fashionable sideburns for a few hours before quietly buying up every pick, pan, and shovel he could find to stock his stores in San Francisco and Sutter's Fort.

Jennie did not yet know Sam Brannan, but she knew Wittmer and Bennett and was well acquainted with sawmill crew member Henry Bigler. Toward the end of February Bigler wrote to some of his former Mormon Battalion comrades working at Sutter's new grist (flour) mill, also under construction. He told them about Marshall's find, asking them to keep it a secret. A week later, several of his friends came to Coloma to investigate. These men found more color downstream on a river bar opposite a little island that quickly became the superbly rich gold mine and well-populated community known as Mormon Island, today submerged beneath Folsom Lake.

Yet despite all this early publicity, skeptics continued to outnumber enthusiasts until April.

As Sutter bitterly complained years later in an interview given to *Hutchings' California Magazine*, Jennie Wimmer and her children babbled the secret to a man who was delivering supplies to the camp. To another, he groused, "Women and whiskey let the secret out." Perhaps he was conveniently forgetting his own slip, when early that February he broadcast the news in a letter to his impatient creditor Mariano Vallejo, the *patron* of a vast estate named Petaluma. In the end, it was easier to blame all the loose tongues on Jennie and her boy.

As for the nugget Jennie boiled in lye, she always maintained that James Marshall gave it to her as a gift, an assertion she would have to swear to before a judge several months before her death. That, though, happened much later. On the day Jennie retrieved the nugget from the bottom of her kettle she was twenty-five years old, the mother of several children and pregnant with another. She was a woman who had already traveled far and seen much.

Jennie was born Elizabeth Jane Cloud in Franklin County, Virginia, the second-born child and oldest daughter of Martin and Polly Dickerson Cloud's three boys and three girls. The teen-aged Jennie is described as a pretty, auburn-haired, blue-eyed young woman with a reasonably good education for the times. Martin Cloud was a prosperous tobacco planter until 1836 or so, when he was swindled by an unscrupulous partner and forced by both the economics of the times and his own Methodist conscience to sell his land and holdings to meet his obligations. In an attempt to recoup some of his losses, Mr. Cloud loaded his family into an ox-driven wagon bound for Lumpkin County, Georgia, where gold mines were operating. According to one source they arrived there in August 1837. In the gold camps Jennie operated a restaurant and boarding house with her mother, spending some of her off-hours prospecting in the red clay while her father and brothers worked as miners.

There is some confusion and contradiction about the dates of Jennie's birth, her family's move from Virginia to Georgia, and her marriage to Obadiah Baiz. Some sources (including the 1880 Census) note a birth year of 1820; others claim June 18, 1822. The 1850 Census taken at Coloma lists her age as twenty-eight, which would be correct for a birth date of 1822. Similarly, the Cloud family relocation date of 1837 raises questions, because Jennie supposedly met and married Obadiah Baiz in Georgia in April, 1840. However, evidence has surfaced of an application for a marriage license—along with a note giving Martin Cloud's consent—in Patrick County, Virginia, both dated August 4, 1838, when Jennie was just sixteen. No marriage certificate has yet been found in either state, but it seems more likely that Jennie and Obadiah actually married in Virginia and then both accompanied her family to Georgia in 1838, not 1837.

Whatever the date of Jennie's marriage to Obadiah Baiz, the couple, along with Jennie's parents and siblings, sold out their disappointing mining claims and left northern Georgia before May 1840. Jennie and Obadiah's first child, Martin Dickenson Baiz, was born in Virginia that year. After the birth, the young Baiz couple relocated to the new frontier in Missouri; Jennie's parents decided to remain in Virginia. Certainly by 1843 Jennie and Obadiah were living on a farm in Lexington, Missouri with their two children, three year old Martin and another son. Their neighbors on an adjacent farm, with whom they became well acquainted, were Peter and Polly (Mary Ann) Harlan Wimmer and their five children. In the autumn of 1843 a chilling fever called "the ague"—probably malaria—swept the area. Both Obadiah Baiz and Polly Wimmer were afflicted and died. A year later on June 20, 1844, widow Elizabeth Jane Cloud Baiz married her neighbor, the widower Peter Laboyteaux Wimmer. He was ten years her senior and said to be a decent, courageous man with little book learning. California census takers would later check the column "cannot read or write" next to Peter's name.

This 1844 marriage, when Jennie had just turned twenty-two, made her the instant mother of Peter's children Elijah, aged fourteen; John, thirteen; George, eleven; Sarah, six; and William, four, in addition to her own two young sons.

They had been married eighteen months when a relative of Peter's looked them up on his way farther west. George Harlan, the late Polly Harlan Wimmer's brother and at forty-four the Harlan family patriarch, had become enthralled with the wonderful land beyond the Rockies as described in *Hasting's Work on California and Oregon.* He was taking his family to California and the Wimmers were welcome to come along. George Harlan was already an experienced pioneer, as was Peter Wimmer, and both men knew enough of the Indian languages to get by. After his marriage to Polly Harlan in 1828, Peter moved from Indiana to Michigan to Illinois—the latter two still relative wilderness areas—before moving his family to Missouri. Jennie was an experienced traveler, too. She may have read, or heard about, Richard Henry Dana's recently published *Two Years Before the Mast,* another book that created excited talk of California as it passed from hand to hand. Jennie and Peter decided they wanted to go see this new land of promise for themselves. In early 1846, they began building wagons with good tent-cloth covers and gathering supplies and livestock. The seventeen-member Harlan family group, joined by the Wimmers and other families, made their way to Independence, Missouri to await the new spring grasses that would provide feed for their animals as they crossed the Plains. However, these grasses appeared late that year and so delayed their departure. Among the assembled emigrants headed west were brothers George and Jacob Donner and their families from Springfield, Illinois. It's possible that Peter and Jennie met the individuals who later perished in the Sierras in the famous saga of the Donner Party. In mid-May about five hundred wagons rolled out of camp herding cattle and saddle horses alongside, many of them headed to Oregon. The word "California" was gaily painted on each wagon cover of the Harlan entourage.

Soon the large train broke apart into smaller, more manageable groups for greater traveling ease. Each new group traveled at its own pace with some wagons being several weeks ahead of, or behind, the rest. There was no road, just a trail. It was a journey fraught with unforeseen obstacles, hardship, and loss, yet Captain Harlan's party managed to cross the Sierra Nevada before early snowstorms blocked the passes. They were the last wagon train to make it safely through that season. After resting at Johnson's Ranch (today's Wheatland) for several days, they pushed ahead to Sutter's Fort, arriving November 15 or 16, 1846. Most of Peter Wimmer's in-law relations departed from there for the Mission Santa Clara area. Peter decided to remain at the fort and find work with Captain Sutter.

The Mexican-American War, overtly declared over the disputed Texas-Mexico border (and unofficially over President James Polk's intention to acquire everything between Texas and the Pacific Ocean), was in full swing. Almost immediately, Peter Wimmer enlisted in one Captain Aram's company. Jennie complained that her husband "enlisted before they got the oxen unyoked," leaving the family dependent on the good will of others at the fort. Captain Sutter gave them lodging but, as she further stated, she and the children "drew rations like common soldiers" while Sutter's beloved compound was under the command of the

United States Army.

During Peter's absence, Jennie—without her husband's assistance or solace—had to endure the pain and sorrow of losing a child.

New Helvetia Cemetery was not so named until 1850. During the years 1839 through 1849 the area was simply known as the burial grounds a short distance from the Fort at today's northeast corner of Alhambra Boulevard and J Street. However, Sutter's Fort State Park officials believe a Wimmer child was buried in this graveyard in January 1847. Surely this was Jennie's youngest boy with Obadiah Baiz. This child, whose first name is unknown, was probably three or four and thought to be alive when the overland journey from Missouri commenced; Jenny herself said she arrived in California with seven children. Martin Baiz appeared on census reports for decades while his little brother disappeared from official records.

Peter Wimmer's army service ended after he was injured in a wagon accident. When he returned in February or March, Captain Sutter hired him as a carpenter's assistant to James Marshall.

Between February and April 1847, the surviving Donner Party members were rescued from the Sierras where they had been trapped for the winter and delivered into Captain Sutter's care. In her memoirs, Eliza Donner Houghton speaks of the kind and tender treatment she and her sisters received from the women at the Fort. She remembers the cup of fresh milk given to her by a tall, freckle-faced, red-haired boy who came out of Mrs. Wimmer's lodging with a milk pail on his arm. Since the boy tells little orphaned Eliza that he, too, lost his mother, he was one of Peter's sons Elijah, John, or George Wimmer, all teenagers at the time. At some point that spring, Peter and three other men took wagons into the mountains to retrieve the Donner Party's personal effects.

Jennie spent those early months in 1847 caring for her own brood, happy to have her husband back safe and sound at the Fort, giving aid to the Donner children even as she mourned the loss of her own little boy. The gold discovery in which she would take part was still in the future.

Summer was approaching, actual fighting in the Mexican-American War on California soil ended, and Jennie's host Captain Sutter again considered his many improvement projects to make his lands more profitable. He had already transformed a wilderness area into a flourishing rancho filled with livestock, crops, orchards and vegetable gardens. His adobe fortress contained living quarters and various shops that produced or manufactured foodstuffs, tools, and other necessary items. River craft lay at anchor at his docks. Almost all of it, except the land, was obtained on credit. Sutter wanted a bigger gristmill to produce more flour, which he could use to repay his debts. To build this gristmill he needed a quantity of board lumber, then scarce and expensive. Previously he had obtained redwood from the areas around the coast, harvested by whip-saw and transported in his river vessels, but this method was costly. Years earlier he had (some said rashly) purchased the livestock and buildings at Russian-owned Fort Ross near Bodega Bay when the Russians decided to abandon their settlement. Sutter increased his herds and dismantled the lodges and out-buildings for their lumber. The lumber he had thus acquired (on credit) had long since been used. Sutter decided to build his own sawmill near a good supply of timber, and so, at various times until the Mexican-American War interrupted these forays, he sent exploring parties into the mountains. When hostilities subdued, he resumed the search.

Jennie Wimmer later stated that she readied her family and household effects in June 1847 to accompany a crew to a proposed sawmill location at Battle Creek, about one hundred twenty-five miles north of the Fort. Instead John Sutter chose another, closer site discovered by James Marshall in mid-May. "Colloomah" (beautiful vale) as the native Nisenan Indians called this little valley on the American River filled with pine, balsam, and oak, was just forty miles distant from the Sacramento Valley flatlands.

Part of the delay interfering with Sutter's proposed sawmill, new gristmill and other projects was his lack of skilled labor. During the last week of August 1847, a contingent of discharged Mexican-American War Mormon Battalion soldiers on their way home to Utah camped on the American River near Sutter's Fort. Several had decided to remain in California until the next traveling season and they needed employment. Among them were experienced carpenters, wheelwrights, and millwrights—the answer to Sutter's prayers. Six of these men—Henry Bigler, Alexander Stevens, James Barger, Azariah Smith, William Johnson, and James Brown—hired on to build the sawmill; others accepted employment to construct the gristmill. A partnership arrangement between Sutter and James Marshall, partly written and partly verbal, was negotiated around August 27, 1847. (Jennie told the eminent historian Hubert Howe Bancroft that she thought their deal was fifty-fifty ownership; the actual agreement was more complex. Ownership of various rights depended on whether the peace treaty awarded California to Mexico or the United States.) Marshall's job was to build and run the mill; Sutter's responsibility was to pay the crew and furnish supplies. Peter Wimmer, with his frontier knowledge of Indian languages, was to supervise the Indians Sutter hired to dig the mill channel. Jennie was hired as camp cook and laundress. The amount of Jennie's wages, or Peter's, is unknown.

Marshall set out with his party of ten white men (the six Mormons and Charles Bennett, William Scott, himself, and Peter Wimmer) and eight Indians, plus Jennie and the children. The little caravan of people, wagons, oxen, and riding stock carried tools and supplies on Mexican ox-carts, two-wheeled conveyances valued for their sturdy construction of ox hide flooring, massive solid-block wheels, and plenty of straw for springs. The party drove a small herd of sheep for food and probably took a milk-cow for the children's meals and fresh butter. The trip, slowed by the need to hack a road for the wagons through trees and brush, took them a week. At night they slept in tents or bedrolls, listening to the night singing of frogs and insects. Jennie probably guided her young ones in their bedtime prayers as she tucked them in, reciting the words of the Methodist faith in which she was raised. They arrived at the prospective mill site sometime in the first ten days of September.

Their first priority was to build a double cabin to house the mill workers. This structure was formed of two log cabins, side by side, with a "breezeway" between acting as a buffer and space for storage and utensils, with a single roof over the whole of the two buildings. The Wimmer family occupied the west side and the other hired men slept in the opposite end. Marshall put up another cabin for his own private use.

Jennie felt dismayed at having to cook three meals a day, seven days a week for nearly twenty people over a crudely dug, unvented pit—and said so. The fact that Jennie complained, instead of dutifully keeping quiet when presented with such primitive accommodations, seems just another indication of her spirited (and maybe willful) personality. "Grub" in those early weeks was mostly mutton, and salmon fished from the river. Flour for biscuits and flapjacks, peas, tea, and coffee were furnished from Sutter's stores. Jennie cooked outdoors while the weather permitted but was forced to cook inside on inclement days. Her indoor cooking apparatus is not described; it was possibly a small tin stove of the type overlanders strapped to the backs of their wagons to use during the cross-country journey. Since Jennie told an interviewer that the hired Indians scrubbed her cooking pots and swept her dirt floors, evidently the cabin had no flooring and the stove would have been set directly on the ground. When the billowing smoke became intolerable indoors, the mill hands built a stone hearth and chimney for her.

Soon the woods rang with the sounds of mill construction. While the Indians dug out the tailrace, the others felled trees and hewed lumber. At first all were cheerful, laughing and bantering. James Marshall worked among them, picturesque in his habitual garb of buckskin leggings over white linen trousers, moccasins, Mexican sombrero, and sashes.

The workmen liked Marshall, considering him honest and fair. Apparently he was free and friendly with them as he usually was with associates and subordinates—in contrast to the marked surliness and ill temper he often displayed to the world at large. He was moody and mercurial, an eccentric with ideas linked to spiritualism. Jennie's relationship with Marshall was cordial, perhaps even mutually affectionate, dating from the time she nursed him through an illness after he returned from the Mexican-American War. Her relationship with the Mormons wasn't so tranquil.

Exactly what incident—if there was a particular one—lit Jennie's fuse on Christmas Day is unknown. By the end of December she had been pregnant for the greater part of that month, and perhaps hormonal changes were influencing her attitude. The delicate topic of her condition would never have been discussed with the mill hands, either by Jennie or her husband. Yet even before her outburst, an antagonism had already developed between Jennie and the Mormon workers (and perhaps non-Mormons Bennett and Scott as well), who accused her of saving the best provisions for her own family. She countered that if they didn't get the choicest morsels it was because they were always late for meals. The reason for her explosion appears not to be liquor. According to a later newspaper interview, it seems Jennie was tolerant of the workers' drinking—and might even have enjoyed a wee nip herself from time to time. For Christmas Captain Sutter had sent a dozen bottles of brandy packed in a barrel of dried peas, six for the mill hands and six specifically tagged for Jennie. She says: "After they had drank up their six bottles they wanted mine, and they got them."

Whatever her reasons, on Christmas morning Jennie angrily announced she would not cook for them anymore. She later relented and prepared a fine Christmas dinner of meat, bread, and pies, although she must have missed having her oldest step-sons at her table. An entry in Captain Sutter's journal dated December 24, 1847 states that Peter Wimmer's sons left the fort that day to deliver livestock to Sutter's Hock Farm near present-day Marysville. Jennie's capitulation failed to calm the gathering storm, though. An equally angered Mormon composed a derogatory poem about her and read it aloud to the others:

> On Christmas morning in bed she swore
> That she would cook for us no more
> Unless we [come] at the first call
> For I am Mistress of you all

The mill workers began building another cabin for themselves on Christmas Day, moving into it about a month later. They took on their own cooking too, stubbornly foregoing Jennie's stews and pies for meals of salt salmon and boiled wheat.

No doubt Jennie was relieved by this development, still having plenty to keep herself busy with laundering, cooking for the others in camp, and supervising six children. From sunrise to sunset every frontier woman's days were filled with ordinary household chores: mending or sewing family clothing, educating their children, butter-churning, and a dozen other tasks. Soap making, the activity that let her test Marshall's gold nugget, was an important job given Jennie's role as camp laundress, and took hours spread out over several days.

Making lye took the longest time in the process. Jennie meticulously gathered only the white, paper-like flakes from a cooled fire of hardwood and tramped them down into a wooden container with a small hole drilled at the bottom. She then hung the filled ash bucket above another catch-basin container and slowly poured boiling water into the upper bucket to let it leach through the ashes into the pot below, creating lye water. Jennie might have assigned the collection of white ashes to the teen-aged children. Pouring boiling water over the packed ashes created a bubbling, spitting, splashing reaction, and she probably did this herself. She had to repeat the process several times over several days by boiling the lye water in the catch pot and slowly leaching it again through the ash bucket. Jennie knew the lye was strong enough to make soap when a bird's feather dipped into the lye water dissolved. She used beef or mutton fat from butchered animals for tallow, cooking the pieces for several hours until the fat was rendered, a smelly chore best done outside. Next she strained the softened white fat and carefully mixed it with the lye. After a few hours to simmer, cool down, and set up, the mixture was ready to pour into molds or, in Jennie's wilderness home, a trough or plank, where it was cut into chunks.

The men's decision to build another cabin for themselves did not deter them from their paid duties. The mill frame was raised on New Year's Day of 1848, a Saturday. Yet by early February work on the structure would take a decided second place in the minds of the crew, whose free-time prospecting was garnering from three to eight dollars a day[1] just by using their knives. The sawmill was eventually completed on March 11, 1848.

A month after Marshall's discovery—and Jennie's confirming lye-water test—the outside world was still largely ignorant of California's gold, although a few visitors began trickling in. Mill-hand Henry Bigler's friends showed up February 27, lured by Bigler's earlier "secret-sharing" letter. Sutter's employees and hangers-on at the Fort, many of them men Jennie knew, came to check out teamster Jacob Wittmer's wild tale. On March 15 *The*

Californian, a San Francisco newspaper, reported the discovery in a small article that drew little interest. At least one outsider was curious enough to find out for himself, though he was drawn more by Sutter's courier Charles Bennett's saloon talk than by a back-page news article. This was Isaac Humphrey, an experienced Georgia gold miner, who arrived April 1 with his rocker, a sophisticated piece of mining equipment, compared to knives and pans. Word began seeping through coastal towns, mostly falling on disbelieving ears while at the same time sending a tingling thrill coursing through men's hearts and fingertips. Outbound merchant ships carried the news to the next port—news that began spreading more rapidly as gold hysteria took hold. On May 5, merchant Sam Brannan rode into camp, with a stop-over at Mormon Island fifteen miles downstream. A week later he galloped through the streets of San Francisco flamboyantly heralding the American River's astoundingly rich gold deposits—shrewdly stirring up business for his stores. Brannan's action was the spur that finally goaded the Rush.

The first wave of gold-seekers from California, Mexico, South America, Hawaii, Oregon, and other west-coast locales began pouring into the region by June, quickly fanning out from the Trinity River in the north to the Tuolumne River south of present day Stockton. Eventually, the whole of the gold-rich Sierra Nevada foothill region became known as the Mother Lode. This prospecting area became so large that it was easier for men's minds to divide the region into the northern, central, and southern mines. When Sacramento City surged to life toward the end of 1848 it was as supplier and outfitter to the northern mines that were accessed by the Sacramento, American, Feather, and Yuba Rivers.

In mid-June 1848, Colonel Richard Mason—the man who had refused John Sutter's request for land title at Coloma—left Monterey for the gold regions to inspect the ever-escalating reports of fabulous discoveries. He brought with him his adjutant, Lieutenant William Tecumseh Sherman, later General Sherman of Civil War fame. Surely Lt. Sherman met and spoke with Jennie, if for nothing more than gathering information, though his memoirs merely state that "Wimmer's family of wife and half a dozen children were there." Colonel Mason prepared and sent a long and detailed report to Washington dated August 17, 1848, estimating that upwards of 4,000 men were mining along the riverbeds, creeks, streamlets, and ravines. He sent his report and specimens via special courier, allegedly packing more than two hundred ounces of gold inside a tea caddy.

Few of these 1848 gold miners Colonel Mason saw brought their wives. Jennie claimed she was the only white woman in Coloma for the first nine months she lived there. As the Gold Rush progressed wives did come to the mines, but their numbers weren't more than one percent of the entire far-flung, out-back mining region's population for at least the first two years.

As Jennie's pregnancy advanced, another woman arrived from Sutter's Fort, an educated woman of similar age whom Jennie already knew. Some suppose Elizabeth (Eliza) Gregson was sent by Sutter to assist Jennie with the cooking and laundering, although this is not certain. She does report in her own memoirs that Jennie was glad to see her. Eliza was an Englishwoman who came to America with her parents, and married fellow English immigrant and blacksmith James Gregson in Rhode Island. Two years later, in 1845, the Gregsons emigrated to California, arriving at Sutter's Fort in October. James cut lumber for Sutter, and also did some blacksmithing. Their daughter Anna was born in the spring of 1846. Like Jennie, Eliza remained at the Fort when her husband volunteered to fight in the war. James found $3,000 in gold at Coloma but the Gregsons' luck ran out when he became ill, and within two years they moved to Sonoma.

In July 1848, another woman Jennie knew moved to Coloma.

Peter's niece-by-marriage Mary Ann Harlan Smith, her husband and some friends—as excited as anyone by the glowing reports—set out from present-day Oakland in June only to find themselves held up for ten days at the Martinez ferry by a throng of people ahead of them. Mary Ann's memoirs are filled with exclamation marks in the telling of "Aunty Jane's" soap kettle story. The Smiths made a permanent camp under a big oak tree. They found gold, both in the soil and in trading merchandise. More Harlan family members followed in July and August.

By late July, Jennie was growing big with child. Some sources say Jennie's son Benjamin Franklin Wimmer was born in the spring; the historian Hubert Howe Bancroft gives the date as early August, 1848.

Jennie's family was growing and so was Coloma. At the time of Benjamin's birth there were only three stores (one of them Sam Brannan's), a situation soon remedied. The treaty with Mexico released hundreds of men from their military duties, and those who had not yet started for their homes swarmed to the discovery site. Sailors deserted merchant ships anchored in San Francisco Bay. On August 19, 1848, the *New York Herald* printed an item on the discovery of gold in California, and in early December, President Polk verified the news in his fourth annual message to Congress. The first ship with gold-rushers aboard left the East Coast in November, marking the start of the 89,000 Americans and foreigners who would pour into California during 1849 by land and by sea, consequently dubbed the "49ers."

At John Sutter's boat landing on the Sacramento River west of his fort, the scene was bustling with the earlier '48ers and the new '49ers coming up river from San Francisco, where a good number stopped to buy supplies before heading into the foothills. Sacramento was in the making as a hub city. Coloma burgeoned into a town filled with hundreds of tents and shanties, replaced with more substantial structures, including a few opulent hotels and restaurants, as it developed into a regional trading center for the more remote mines. A post office was established in 1849.

Within four years churches and schools graced the landscape. Businesses included Little's Emporium, the three-story Crescent City Hall Hotel, a soda and candy shop called Virginia Saloon, a number of liquor-serving saloons and gambling halls, the Coloma Theatre, two book stores, and at least one brothel: The Lone Star Texas, run by a woman calling herself Texas Ellen. She died when a jealous admirer fired a gun through her window and accidentally hit Ellen instead of his rival.

Meanwhile, the sawmill stood unused at the river's edge. James Marshall tried to continue operating it, varying this occupation with mining, but labor costs of sixteen dollars[2] a day combined with his harassment by greenhorn miners who followed him everywhere in the belief that he knew exactly where every sparkling flake lay beneath the surface, rendered the enterprise hopeless. Coloma became the county seat when El Dorado County was formed in 1850. At that time, officials were swamped with requests to record deeds for town lots already claimed and improved.

Did Jennie and Peter Wimmer find a fortune in gold? The record shows they had enough means to invest in local opportunities. It appears they had determined to make Coloma their settled home for themselves and their children. They grew wheat and vegetables. Their peach and apple orchards are said to be the first fruit trees planted in Coloma. They raised pigs, likely the progeny of the six hogs John Sutter had sent to the mountain camp the day before Marshall's startling revelation at his fort back in January 1848. According to one source, Peter formed a partnership in 1849 with two other men to operate a store, with Peter contributing $4,000[3] in merchandise and agreeing to handle purchasing and drayage (transport). The 1850 Census lists his occupation simply as "Hotel," a description that could mean he was either an owner or manager, but there is no evidence that he owned a hotel in 1850. There is no evidence Jennie operated a boardinghouse in Coloma either, although it is known that certain individuals boarded with the family from time to time—James Marshall, for one. In 1851 the Wimmers sold a lot across from the courthouse for $275.[4] They built a house in Church Block, a clapboard sided, whitewashed home with double-hung sash windows. Their barn and orchard stood on land directly across an intersecting street.

There are no property deeds confirming that the couple owned a mining claim, although they may have mined in the ditches that curved through their residential and orchard properties. Considering the Wimmer's business ventures and farming pursuits this activity would have been part-time. Jennie had less and less time as their family kept growing. Martha Wimmer was born in 1852.

At some point after Martha's birth, the Wimmers left Coloma to visit family in the East. Their mode of travel is unknown, but by then passenger ships bringing eager new gold-seekers to California—and carrying the disappointed ones home—were abundant. They returned about two years later; county records verify that Peter and Jennie Wimmer appeared before the clerk to record a sale of land on November 21, 1854. It appears that Jennie's brother accompanied them home, because a sale the Wimmers recorded five years later was for land originally held by M. V. Cloud, purchased in 1854.

In 1855 the couple celebrated the birth of Peter Wimmer, Jr. In May 1856, the Wimmers purchased a parcel with existing buildings described as being near the village of Coloma on the Sacramento Road, for $500. Jennie had another baby in 1857, named Charles. That same year they deeded a property to Emanuel Church for $50, substantially less than the prices they had formerly charged other buyers for other lots.

Writer Bret Hart reported in his *Overland Monthly* magazine that seedling peaches from the Wimmer gardens at Coloma were shown at the 1858 Agricultural Fair. The 1860 Census in El Dorado County, which describes Peter as a gardener, lists Martin Baiz and the younger Wimmer children residing with their parents. Peter's children with his first wife were grown and living elsewhere. John, who was about twenty-nine in 1860, had moved to Hawaii sometime during the previous decade to attend a missionary school. Rupert Ira—the Wimmer's combined tenth and last living child—was born in 1860 after the census data was collected.

Sometime in the early 1860s the family left Coloma for good. They lived in Potter Valley (Ukiah) before moving on to Sonoma County, and by 1870 they were residing in Santa Rosa, San Luis Obispo County. From there they moved to various places in southern California. Around 1882 they relocated to San Diego County where, on July 27, 1883, they filed a homestead claim for 164.87 acres in today's Valley Center. Wherever they went they never escaped the controversy over the nugget James Marshall had given Jennie in 1848, although when they settled at Valley Center she no longer owned it.

In 1874, nine years prior to purchasing the Valley Center property, Jennie and Peter granted an interview to news reporter Mary P. Winslow, who knew the couple was in San Francisco to apply for aid from a pioneer society. She found them at a run-down hotel and invited them to dinner at her home. Mrs. Winslow described Jennie as a large woman of perhaps sixty years (she was fifty-two) with an intelligent, kindly face. She described the gold piece as "rather flat and filled with indentations, like a piece of spruce-gum just out of the mouth of a schoolgirl." After dinner, Mary offered Peter a smoke and Jennie said she wanted one too. The hosts offered both a pipe and a cigar. Which one Jennie chose was left unsaid. Mary Winslow sold the story to the *Daily Evening*

Bulletin. Three years after this interview, the Wimmers sold the nugget to W. W. Allen who, according to his flowery-phrased disclaimer, purchased it "in consequence of such neglect [of a government pension] and the actual want of Mrs. Wimmer [and her husband] . . . that the first nugget of gold discovered passed into [my] hands . . . ." He paid them $5,000; $250,000 in today's gold values.

Allen proceeded to exhibit the piece in several venues over the next several years. Both Jennie and Peter signed depositions in San Diego Superior Court in April 1885, attesting that the gold piece then in Allen's possession was the same one tested in her soap kettle. Eight years later Mr. Allen published *California Gold Book: First Nugget, its Discovery and Discoverers, and Some of the Results Proceeding Therefrom* co-authored with R. B. Avery. This book, largely a promotional work justifying his purchase, devotes many pages to Jennie's life—not all of them accurate. The Wimmer depositions give January 19, 1848, as the date of the gold discovery—the date Marshall himself originally fixed on, although Marshall admitted he didn't actually know the exact date. However, chroniclers and historians of the period, by analyzing Marshall's and others' oral testimonies together with several journals and diaries of participants at the scene, have determined the correct discovery date to be January 24, 1848.

Jennie lived a little more than thirty-seven years beyond the discovery date. She died in 1885, the same year she signed the deposition. She was about sixty-three; her cause and exact date of death are unknown. She is buried in Valley Center Cemetery, San Diego County. A replacement headstone installed in the 1940s was a simple concrete block merely marked "Weamer" (misspelled). In 2003, the order of E Clampus Vitus provided a new headstone for her grave with appropriate ceremony. After Jennie's death Peter returned to San Luis Obispo County, where he died on August 17, 1892, at age eighty-two.

3. Elizabeth Jane (Jennie) Wimmer, Undated.

Courtesy of the Bert Hughes Family Collection

The so-called "Wimmer Nugget"—a one-third-ounce piece valued at $5.12 in 1848—resides in the Bancroft Library at the University of California, Berkeley. Today the gold piece is worth about $300, if it were not for the fact that its historical significance renders it priceless.

Coloma's gold deposits gave out early. By the time Jennie and Peter moved away, the town was changing from an exciting mining center of 1,000 inhabitants to a peaceful village with a couple hundred citizens. Other mining towns in the vast Mother Lode region also rose and diminished over time as fresh strikes provoked mass movements of prospectors from one watercourse, hill, or canyon to another.

Down in the great valley Sacramento City, geographically located as a gateway to the northern mines, continued to expand and flourish.

Gold fever drew thousands of would-be prospectors through the fledgling city, where profit-minded merchants seized the strategic Sacramento River banks to capitalize on the trade they knew would come upriver from San Francisco Bay. For overlanders, the Mecca was Sutter's Fort, two miles east of the riverfront. From 1849 forward, hundreds of disappointed miners moved to Sacramento to settle down and practice other occupations, many becoming prosperous pillars of the community by catering to the mining trade. Before Sutter's sawmill project led to a totally unexpected outcome, there was no Sacramento—and Sutter had no plans to build a town at the flood-vulnerable confluence of two rivers. Jennie's precious nugget is but a symbol of the major historical event she touched off the day she proved Marshall's "find" was the real thing. If not for the gold discovery—and Jennie's part in it—today's Sacramento might not exist.

End Notes, Jennie Wimmer

[1]Based on gold-per-ounce ratios, $3 to $8 prospected gold in 1848 is $150 to $400 in modern money.

[2]Nineteenth century laborers generally earned between $1 and $1.50 per day in the East, but could command almost anything in inflationary Gold Rush California. Based on the gold ratio, $16 then is $800 now.

[3]The nature of Peter Wimmer's contributed merchandise is unknown, although the term "drayage" implies that the goods were heavy. It must also be considered that Gold Rush prices reflected the fact that California had no manufacturing facilities in 1849 and therefore the price of goods was inflated by scarcity, high ocean transport costs, multiple middlemen, etc. Given California's industrial progress, the current value of Peter's $4,000 in merchandise might be substantially different than the $200,000 derived by formula.

[4]Coloma developed as a commercial center for the very remote mines, in a small valley, and because of its geography was inaccessible via river by the major shipping lines. Land prices in Coloma during the 1850s appear to be less than land values in Sacramento for the same period; however, these values have no equivalent market price in today's economy because Gold Rush era downtown Coloma is now part of James Marshall Discovery State Park.

Bricks for the Young City:
Dorothea Wolfinger Zins

Dorothea Wolfinger Zins' contribution to the growth of Sacramento was quite literal: with her own hands she aided her husband George Zins in the manufacture and transport of over 140,000 kiln-fired bricks to build homes, boarding houses, and hotels in the area between 1847 and 1849.

She was a Donner Party survivor, a woman who had endured months of starvation, extreme cold, and desperation in the Sierra Nevada. Vainly hoping rains would wash away the unexpectedly early snows so they could cross the mountain passes, the emigrants had exhausted their provisions too early, and the rescue was late. No one even realized the group had not safely descended the Sierras until late October 1846—when heavy snows already thwarted an initial relief effort. Military actions in the Mexican-American War were occurring on several fronts; scores of strong young men who might have volunteered as rescuers had already left the Sacramento Valley to fight at the Battle of Santa Clara and other places down the coast, to win California for the United States. Finally, in February 1847, a small group of men were induced to go, motivated both by their own altruism and the exorbitant pay of three dollars a day.

By then, those members of the Donner Party who were still alive were reduced to walking skeletons in tattered clothing. Dorothea was chosen to accompany the under-equipped First Relief Party when they left the Donner campsites on February 22, 1847 because she still had the strength to walk out over the formidable peaks and chasms, as the rescuers themselves had been

4. Front Street, December 1849.

Courtesy California History Room, California State Library, Sacramento

forced to enter on foot, through ten- to thirty-foot snowdrifts too deep for horses and mules.

Dorothea Wolfinger had another reason to be afraid and desperate; even before the emigrants were snow-bound she knew her husband was dead, and his sudden absence left her alone and vulnerable with no other family to support or protect her. Needing to lighten their wagon for the arduous climb over steep peaks and boulder-strewn ravines, Mr. Wolfinger and two trail companions had stopped somewhere near present day Wadsworth, Nevada to bury the couple's valuables while the rest of the party moved ahead. When these two men caught up with the others they claimed that Wolfinger had been killed by marauding Indians who had burned his wagon. A very frantic Mrs. Wolfinger almost collapsed at this news. Foul play was suspected when a search party found his wagon and peacefully grazing oxen but no sign of him. The wagon and two yoke of oxen were brought to Dorothea, who hired one of the teamsters to drive it over the mountains. But there was no time for an investigation. Already short of provisions and knowing the season was growing late to safely traverse the Sierra before snow fell, the group anxiously moved on.

The snowstorms came early that year during mid-to-late October instead of the second or third week of November, and despite early efforts to cross the summit the Donner Party found themselves trapped. Most of the emigrants found shelter in some rough cabins near Truckee Lake (Donner Lake today). Six or so miles back at Alder Creek, George Donner was unable to go farther as infection flared in a hand he had severely injured while repairing a broken axle. The two Donner brothers, their families, and others—twenty-two people in all including Mrs. Wolfinger, who had been taken in by kindly, charitable George and Tamzen Donner after Mr. Wolfinger "disappeared"—remained there with him. Dorothea helped gather materials and build the crude shelters that the Alder Creek campers made from tents, quilts, buffalo robes, and pine boughs.

By the time she was rescued after a hellish four months in the mountains, she knew that at least one of the party's hired teamsters, a man named Joseph Reinhardt, who died from exhaustion or exposure at Alder Creek, had murdered Mr. Wolfinger for the money he was thought to be carrying.

Mr. and Mrs. Wolfinger were a German-speaking couple who apparently conversed mainly with the several other Germans in the group during the overland trek and didn't mingle much with the English-speaking American Midwesterners who comprised most of the wagon train members. So far as is known, Dorothea spoke no English; it can be surmised she learned a few words essential to survival from George and Tamzen Donner while in their camp. All that is recorded of Dorothea in the diaries and memoirs of other survivors is that Mrs. Wolfinger was a tall, queenly-looking lady of good birth and much refinement who wore elegant clothes and beautiful, costly jewels at the start of the trip. There is no description of Mr. Wolfinger's wardrobe or demeanor; her attire tells of a couple who were completely unaware of the ordinary harsh conditions and potential daily dangers inherent in traveling across vast miles of wilderness.

Various social, political, and economic factors in Europe had prompted both German nationals and German-speaking peoples from other countries to sail to a new and better life in America during the 1840s. It is thought the Wolfingers came as a couple directly from Germany, her birthplace, but questions of when they arrived from Europe, exactly where they lived in the United States before joining the wagon train, how they lived, or why they chose to go to California are all unanswered. Nothing at all is known of Mr. Wolfinger, including his age, family origin, or occupation; even his first name is disputed among historians. Her first name appears in various documents and reports as Dorothy, Dorethy, Dorothy, Doris, and more. The 1850 Federal Census in Sacramento lists Dorothea's birth country as Germany and her age as twenty-three; however, the special census taken two years later by the State of California shows her age as thirty-three. Based on later data, her birth year might be 1816 or 1817 and her birth month was in or before August, which means she was twenty-eight or twenty-nine when she began the journey to California. The date and place of the Wolfinger's marriage remains a mystery as does Dorothea's maiden name. Names that keep surfacing now and then are Muller or Mueller, although these have never been substantiated.

The rescue of the Donner Party (there were four relief parties between February and April 1847) was as harrowing and life-threatening as their entrapment. The widow Wolfinger, like the others with the First Relief Party, trudged through snowdrifts and slept in the bitter cold with little food for more than a week, finally stumbling below the snowline into Bear Valley. Two days later they reached a camp at Mule Springs, thirty miles above William Johnson's Ranch (today's Wheatland) where mules were waiting to transport them to the ranch and from there into the Sacramento Valley. Along their escape route death claimed a man and two children. At Johnson's Ranch the starving sufferers were well, but sparingly and carefully, fed. Mrs. Sinclair, the wife of Sacramento Valley ranch manager John Sinclair, sent up some women's clothing for the "poor half-naked" refugees. Undoubtedly, Dorothea's garments were as worn and shredded as the other women's.

Most of the Donner Party refugees—only forty-eight of the eighty-one trapped in the Sierras that winter lived through the entire ordeal—were remanded to the care of Captain John Augustus Sutter, whose well-provisioned agricultural domain New Helvetia was the only establishment large enough to accommodate and shelter the survivors. Camped in around the fort environs at New Helvetia—known by most as simply Sutter's Fort—were several women with their families. Many were denizens of wagon trains that had crossed the Sierras ahead of the winter snow storms, some of them German-speaking, but nothing was recorded specifically about Mrs. Wolfinger's care and lodging.

One of the women who remained at Sutter's Fort with her children while her husband was away with a volunteer Army regiment was Jennie Wimmer. Given the time frame and the relative smallness of the Fort's population, particularly the women there, it is quite likely Dorothea Wolfinger and Jennie Wimmer knew each other, but, as neither left a diary or other personal papers, the idea remains mere supposition.

It was a busy time at Sutter's Fort, referred to in those months as Fort Sacramento. The fort was then under the official command of United States Army Captain John Fremont's aide Lieutenant Edward Kern, while a humiliated John Sutter was relegated down the chain of command in his own establishment. Insofar as northern Californians knew, the Mexican-American War was still in progress, and a steady stream of men, wagons, and supplies trundled in and out of the compound almost daily. Several of the recently-arrived overland men were still away with their battalions, leaving their women and children in the care of Sutter and his military usurpers. Captain Sutter might have asked some of these families to board Dorothea in their tents and temporary shacks or cabins while they waited for their men to return.

Alternatively, Dorothea might have roomed with Sacramento District's civic official John Sinclair in his home on Rancho del Paso, where Sinclair and his wife were Captain Sutter's closest neighbors. Rancho del Paso was a near-50,000 acre property across the American River from Sutter's lands, and the Sinclair ranch house was located at the approximate intersection of today's Howe Avenue and Hurley Way. Dorothea must have been housed in or nearby Sutter's fortress because she eventually met her future husband there. What skills or talents she had or what tasks she employed to earn her keep are unknown.

She would find that her new home was blessedly snow-free and sheltered from harsh storms. Rain fell regularly from November through February, and mists rising from the ubiquitous tule-filled marshes often fogged the landscape, but temperatures rarely dropped below freezing. At the time of her arrival the trampled grounds about the fort compound were still slickened with mud from the winter rainfall. In July those same grounds would be dry, cracked, and sun-baked. Summer temperatures routinely exceeded 100 degrees—neck-dampening heat even amid the dense clusters of oaks, sycamores, elms, alders, and cottonwoods that shaded the acreage west of the fort. Captain Sutter cut a wagon road through these woods and dense underbrush to a point below the confluence of the Sacramento and American Rivers to Sutter's *embarcadero* (Spanish for landing place) at the waterfront, where tall trees stood sentinel above his moored schooners and other river craft bobbing on the Sacramento River. This rut-filled road became J Street when Sacramento City was platted near the end of the following year. All manner of bugs, ants, and flying pests plagued both Sutter's hired hands and incoming settlers, nuisances that were somewhat mitigated by clear skies and abundant water.

Captain Sutter was already known far and wide as a gracious host and great provider to all who came to his wilderness outpost for aid. Following some drought seasons, 1847 was a good year for his providence. His wheat fields, vegetable gardens, salmon fishery, and cattle and sheep herds were well established. His tannery—strategically located on the banks of the American River a distance away from the fort to escape the smell—was busily processing hides. He was progressing with the construction of a gristmill upriver. His fortress, a parallelogram of high adobe walls with loop-holes and bastions at the angles, housed in its interior a collection of granaries, warehouses, living quarters, a bakery, a blanket factory, a distillery, and several workshops. He built almost all of his empire by borrowing and had limited liquid funds. Sutter's legendary generosity was proffered in goods and services, in compassion rather than cash.

In May 1847, Dorothea Wolfinger was summoned to testify as a witness for the plaintiff at the trial of Louis Keseberg, a fellow Donner Party survivor, who filed a defamation of character suit for damages of $1,000—a princely sum equivalent to three year's wages for a skilled laborer—against certain men who were involved in the Donner Party rescue efforts. The cause of the action in *Keseberg vs. Coffymere* (Edward Coffeemeyer) was the rescuers' accusations that Keseberg had murdered Tamzen Donner. Mrs. Wolfinger's summons must have been as a character witness, since Tamzen Donner was still alive when Dorothea left the mountains with the First Relief Party.

Sacramento City didn't exist, nor did any county designations in what was still a province of Mexico. Instead there was the Sacramento District, an enormous jurisdiction encompassing all of the area from the Coast Range to the Sierra Nevada and the entire length of the Sacramento Valley from the San Joaquin River northward. For law and order, the District relied on a sheriff and an *alcalde,* a Spanish title conferred on a rather unique, in American eyes, functionary at the local level. The *alcalde* was usually elected by his community, subject to approval by the province's Spanish (and later, Mexican) governor, to whom he was ultimately answerable. His office encompassed that of judge, justice of the peace, mayor, and other unspecified civic duties, among them trying criminal cases, presiding over town meetings, and issuing licenses and passports.

The Sacramento District's *alcalde* in 1847 was John Sinclair, a Scotsman held in high esteem by his peers, who had come to California via Honolulu six years earlier. As *alcalde*, he played an important administrative role in the rescue of the Donner Party. Sinclair's papers relevant to the Keseberg case were either lost or destroyed and there were no newspapers in the Sacramento Valley at that time, so almost nothing is known about the trial except the outcome: one dollar awarded to the plaintiff, Keseberg. The details of Dorothea's testimony and others' do not survive, but there can be little doubt this case was a very stressful episode for Dorothea Wolfinger.

At the time of this trial she most likely already knew her future husband, although there is no record of her introduction to or courtship by George Zins, an ethnic German born in Searburg, Lorraine, who was about her same age. George immigrated to the United States in 1843, working on farms around Galena, Illinois, until he joined Heinrich Lienhard's group of Swiss and German friends traveling from St. Louis to California in 1846. Lienhard, Zins, Valentine Diel (or Diehl), Heinrich Thomen, and Jacob Rippstein are known to history as the "five German boys," all bachelors in their twenties and thirties, who felt they could make better time by forging ahead of that season's wagon caravans. (They were not, however, the first party to make it into California that year.)

Crossing the Sierra in early October, the "boys" found Johnson's Ranch on Bear Creek, the first outpost of civilization west of the mountains, albeit just a couple of crude buildings, cattle, and some fenced areas. They remained there for a few days eating huge chunks of beefsteak and recuperating. At the time, Dorothea Wolfinger and the Donner wagon train were still far behind on the deserts of present-day Nevada. The friends finally rolled into Sutter's Fort in the latter half of October 1846, shortly after the official Call to Arms for the Mexican-American War was sounded on October 17 by United States Navy Lieutenant Joseph Revere, a grandson of American Revolutionist Paul Revere. Lienhard, George Zins, and two of their comrades volunteered for duty in Fremont's California Battalion for a march on Los Angeles and left almost immediately, according to a memo preserved in the

Fort Sutter military papers dated October 20, 1846. This memo, addressed to Fort Sutter Commandant Edward Kern, was from mountain-man-turned-war-recruiter William Fallon, the same man who would lead the fourth Donner rescue party the following April.

When he returned from the war, Heinrich Lienhard became a close confidante of John Sutter and the overseer of Sutter's Mimal and Hock Farms south of the site where Marysville was later founded. George Zins received his discharge in Los Angeles probably in early 1847 (no date is given) but remained there a few weeks working for a vineyardist to earn enough money to return to Sutter's Fort. Once back at the enclave the quick-learning, mechanically adept George is said to have "made himself useful" to Captain Sutter—and he met Dorothea Wolfinger.

In his *From St. Louis to Sutter's Fort 1846* journals Heinrich Lienhard describes his cross-country traveling companion George Zins as a short, bow-legged man who was strong for his size, with a broad face, big nose, and small eyes. He had thick, straight black hair. He liked to sing (oblivious, says Lienhard, to his lack of a good singing voice), was clever and often entertaining. Yet, Lienhard laments, George displayed arrogant behavior and was often prone to angry outbursts. These character flaws notwithstanding, he won the heart of the tall, queenly, and refined widow Wolfinger.

The two were married by *Alcalde* John Sinclair at Sutter's Fort. Sinclair's Marriage Register (he spells her name Doriss with a double 's') preserved at Sutter's Fort Archives reads:

> *Territory of California*
> *Sacramento District*
>
> *I do hereby certify that on Sunday the twentieth day of June A.D. 1847 George Zins and Doriss Wolfinger both of this District personally appeared before me and by me were lawfully joined together in the Holy Bonds*

of Matrimony.
In witness whereof I have here unto set my hand and
seal this twentieth day of June A.D. 1847.

John Sinclair
Justice of the Peace

Not having a genuine seal of office at hand, Sinclair drew a small, square, spiral-outlined facsimile of one beneath his signature with the initials "J. S." in the center.

The newlyweds didn't settle at the fort, however. Despite the addition of many rooms, there weren't enough structures to house all the new arrivals, and John Sutter—who hoped for and expected continuing immigration from Europe and America—conceived the idea of a new town. Realizing that the low lands about his Sacramento River embarcadero were unsuitable for a town site because of their vulnerability to flooding, he surveyed and mapped a township in early 1846 on higher ground three or four miles southwest of his fort in the approximate area of today's William Land Park. His plan included a grid of streets with spaces for city parks, a city plaza, a commercial or market area, and some two hundred plots for homes. Sutter's intention was that this settlement would become a trading post, while the wharf closer to his fort would remain just a river-port. He wanted to name it Montezuma; the name Sutterville quickly came into popular usage and stuck. Construction activity was earnestly underway by the month of the Zinses marriage. George and Dorothea set up housekeeping in a tent in this community of tents and make-shift shacks where Captain Sutter had recently erected the first "real" house, one he may never have occupied.

At this time George was most likely still in Sutter's full-time employ, difficult to verify because many of Sutter's documents were destroyed when his farmhouse at Hock Farm burned in 1865. The journals that remain reveal Sutter's constant need for competent men experienced at a number of trades and crafts that were essential to maintain and expand a frontier outpost, but specific references to George Zins are sparse. Certainly George had frontiering skills. Heinrich Lienhard's journal chronicling their overland journey attests to George's expertise at repairing wagon tongues and driving ox teams. George could have worked in any of several mechanical shops at the fort. Or, because of his farming experience from his years in Illinois, he might have been assigned duties at Sutter's hog and sheep farm located south of Sutterville, thought to be near the present-day intersection of Fruitridge Road and Freeport Boulevard. Employee or no, George built a kiln near his tent-home and began making bricks in 1847, hoping to serve a growing demand for substantial building materials in San Francisco.

His first kiln produced 40,000 units of fine red brick, the first kiln-fired common bricks made in California. Of these 10,000 went to Captain Sutter for the construction of a large oven at the fort in anticipation of the flour that his new gristmill farther east on the American River would supply. The reason for this rather magnanimous gift is never explained. It could have been in exchange for ground flour and corn, a horse and saddle, simple household furnishings, vegetable seeds, et cetera, items every frontier married-man settler needed. The couple used the remaining 30,000 units to build an 18- by 35-foot, tiled-floor house for themselves. The Zinses' was the third house built in Sutterville, on a lot that, according to records at Sutter's Fort Archives, Sutter gave to George Zins in lieu of wages.

The Zinses' house in Sutterville is often touted as the first brick home erected in California, although there is a rival for that distinction from another brick home also built in 1847 by the Dickenson family in Monterey. Unquestionably, George and Dorothea's home was the first brick house in the Sacramento Valley.

Dorothea's rescue, her marriage, and the newlyweds' brick

house all occurred in the year preceding the gold discovery. The couple envisioned the brick-making business as a profitable enterprise to be marketed in the fledging but growing Pacific port city of San Francisco and other coastal towns. Elder Sam Brannan had arrived from New York just a year earlier aboard the *Brooklyn* with a shipload of 238 Mormon men, women, and children who needed building materials for housing, schools, and businesses. In addition, John Sutter's enthusiastic promotion efforts and promises of generous gifts of Sutterville lots to his friends gave the Zinses good reason to anticipate an eventual local market for their product.

However, George's plan crumbled when enterprising, opportunistic Sam Brannan flamboyantly provided visible confirmation of the January 1848 gold discovery at Coloma. Naysayers, men who considered the notion of a rich, massive gold find delectable but not quite credible, still existed. Brannan rode through the streets of San Francisco on May 12, 1848, waving his hat over his head and flourishing a bottle of gold pieces in the other, shouting, "Gold! Gold from the American River!" to excite interest and draw customers to his recently stocked mercantile outlets. This shrewd act effectively launched the Gold Rush, the beginnings of the city of Sacramento, and Brannan's own fortune. The stampede to the inland rivers immediately obliterated anyone's notion of wasting time erecting permanent structures around the Bay when pure gold lay about the inland river beds, just waiting to be picked up with a man's fingers! As United States Consul to Mexico Thomas Larkin expressed in May 1848, "The improvement of Yerba Buena [San Francisco] for the present time is done." Real estate values dropped one half or more, and all non-mining merchandise declined in price. Labor rose tenfold in price—if employees could be held at all. Within months San Francisco's docks, merchant shops, and newspaper offices emptied of all able-bodied men. And it wasn't just San Francisco. Men from Monterey, San Jose, Sonoma, Sutterville, San Diego, Santa Barbara, Mexico, South America, Hawaii, and other places along the Pacific Coast all abandoned their towns for the gold fields.

In August 1848, a San Francisco newspaper reported there were more than 4,000 workers engaged in the mines. The market for George Zins' bricks collapsed. Captain John Sutter's crews deserted him, leaving unharvested grains in his fields and hides rotting in his tannery.

If George Zins and his wife abandoned Sutter for the gold regions, their names don't appear among those who struck it rich. Moreover, there is a brief entry in the New Helvetia Diary dated March 5, 1848—five weeks after the discovery—noting that Sutter took a ride with Mr. Zins to the Cosumnes [Indian] Rancheria to find workers, an indication that George was still on the payroll around the time that Sutter's other employees were slowly but surely trekking upriver to Coloma. Certainly Sutter's friend and neighbor John Sinclair staked a successful claim on the American River's upper North Fork. His net take was $16,000[1] in gold for five weeks' work, fourteen pounds of it obtained in just one week using pans and closely-woven Indian baskets. Three men who held responsible positions at Sutter's New Helvetia formed a gold mining partnership. Jared Sheldon and William Daylor, ranch owners on their own land grants on the Cosumnes River, with their friend Perry McCoon, who had married teenaged Elitha Donner just nineteen days before the Zins-Wolfinger nuptials, found riches in the summer of 1848. Mining with knives and shovels in Weber's Creek several yards below the crossing of the road from present-day Diamond Springs to Placerville, the partners netted a reported (and possibly exaggerated) $17,000[1] *each.*

With gold fever quickening the heartbeat of everyone within easy riding distance of the Sierra foothills it is easy to suppose, although impossible to prove, that George and Dorothea gave the "diggings" a try. If so, their time spent must have been short and their results meager because they were back making bricks at Sutterville in the fall of 1848.

As word of the fantastic gold discovery spread far and wide, the Russian government, which had sold its Fort Ross buildings and equipment to Sutter some seven years earlier on credit, now assumed he was a very wealthy man when in truth he had been unlucky in the gold fields. They began pressing for payment, threatening foreclosure against New Helvetia, on which they held a mortgage as guarantee of their terms of sale. To escape the escalating demands of the Russians and other creditors, the now quite beleaguered Captain Sutter transferred his properties to his recently arrived twenty-one-year-old son John Augustus Sutter Jr., who was called August, on October 14, 1848. August, in turn, was convinced that selling portions of this real estate was the only way to raise enough money to liquidate his father's debts. If this transfer of land titles included Sutterville to the south of Sutter's riverfront embarcadero, that settlement's properties soon became irrelevant.

Sutterville, situated behind a slough that required bridging, had no river landing and therefore was doomed as a trading post; the market instead developed around John Sutter's wharf four miles north. This location was preferred by Sam Brannan and others, men who were much craftier than young, malleable, well-intentioned August Sutter, for it was the natural debarkation point for men in a hurry to get to the gold country. Sutterville was eclipsed as a trading and population center (but not without some vigilant campaigning by its citizens) after Sacramento City was surveyed and mapped during December 1848. Sam Brannan took credit for the name. The surveyor August hired at Brannan's urging was Captain William Warner, a U.S. Army topographical engineer who was aided by then Lieutenants Edward Otho Cresap Ord, for whom California's Fort Ord is named, and William Tecumseh Sherman.

With some exceptions, the layout of Sacramento City was a grid of rectangular blocks of north-south streets numbered One to Thirty-one—except that the avenue bordering on the Sacramento River was called Front instead of First Street—intersected at right angles by east-west streets given letters from A to Y. Each block contained eight lots divided by an interior alley. A public auction was held at the Fort on January 8, 1849, selling the new Sacramento City lots for around $250. Six months later, the same or similar plots were commanding as much as $3,000. George Zins purchased eight lots at the edges of the town's eastern limits, in the squares between Twenty-eighth, Twenty-ninth, Thirtieth, J and K Streets for $800 total as recorded January 10, 1849. In May 1849, Captain Sutter granted a west-side, 60-by-150 foot parcel in the square between Front, Second, M, and N Streets to George and Dorothea Zins as a belated wedding present.

By July throngs of goldseekers were arriving by sea, coming up the Sacramento River toward the gold regions, with more expected by overland routes. Driven by speculation, land prices in the new city continued to escalate. John Sutter's wedding gift was not officially recorded until November 29, 1850, and included the verbiage "pursuant to a bond for title dated May 14, 1849." The document notes consideration paid of $500 when by that time the property was easily saleable at four times that much. Acknowledgment of consideration received for land is a legal requisite, and doesn't have to be money. As the parcel was supposed to be a gift, it is unknown if actual cash changed hands.

Prior to receiving the Front Street property, George and Dorothea had burned another kiln of 100,000 bricks at Sutterville in the late fall of 1848, trying again for San Francisco sales. Finding that the demand for building materials was still suspended, the Zinses used this inventory to erect the first brick house in Sacramento City, hauling the bricks four miles by ox-drawn wagon to their new lot.

The two-story structure, completed in October 1849, measured 35-by-60 feet and fronted on the river. The Zinses originally intended for this to be a family residence upstairs with two stores on the ground floor. The inflated prices on property rentals likely convinced them to rent the second floor in late 1849 to John Winters, who used the space as a hotel/boarding house he named the Anchor House. The dimensions of the building, plus the fact that Winters operated a hotel, argue against the idea that the Zins family lived in Anchor House along with John Winters' guests. They may have remained in their Sutterville residence, assuming they still owned it, or moved to the property George had purchased earlier near Sutter's Fort, considered far out of town when most of the population lived west of Twelfth Street. Their dwelling in 1849 can only be guessed since no city directory was published for that year, and early property records for Sutterville no longer exist.

George and Dorothea sold a portion of the river-fronting parcel to Henry Schoolcraft, then second *alcalde* for the District of Sacramento, for $2,000[2] per a deed recorded November 15, 1849. The city's land ownership was already subject to some confusion and dissent, and it probably was this transaction that prompted the belated recording of Sutter's wedding gift, recorded in 1850 as an 1849 sale, to clear the title for Schoolcraft's benefit.

In the 1848 brick-making endeavor as well as the first effort in the prior year, Dorothea Zins proved herself an extraordinary helpmate. As one chronicler phrased it, "In the manufacture of the brick and their transportation to Sacramento Zins was most effectively aided by his wife." Another, a reminiscence appearing in the *Sacramento Daily Union* many years later recalls: "Mrs. Zins, with an energy worthy of imitation by many men, went at really hard work, and the venerable Binninger house [formerly Anchor House] on Front Street, between M and N, exhibits bricks which are the result of her handiwork at that early day. Excellent bricks they are, too, and only excelled by the pioneer lady herself."

These accolades to Dorothea Wolfinger Zins have been repeated and paraphrased in several places, yet only one provides any detail of the very hard work she performed. According to the *Stockton Democrat,* "It is said that Zins and his wife did most of the work in building the [Anchor] house, she making the mortar, carrying the hod, etc. while he laid the bricks . . . ." Brick making in 1840s California meant mixing the clays and other ingredients by hand and shaping the mixture into wooden molds which, when set, were lifted, perhaps on broad paddles, into kilns to be fired. The kilns themselves were anything from bonfire pits to rectangular ovens formed with bricks from a previous firing. The ovens had openings at the top for venting the hot gasses formed inside. Sacramento's summer sun must have burned Dorothea's face while the vapors from the vent offended her nose. Certainly the hours she spent holding a hod aloft, mixing mortar, or lifting finished bricks into wagons for transport tortured her arm and shoulder muscles and raised painful blisters on her hands.

As Anchor House rose on Sacramento's Front Street facing the river, Dorothea Zins was heavy with child. Her daughter Rosa was born September 19, 1849, a month or so before the building was complete. Around September 1, after Dorothea had probably retired from public mixed-gender gatherings as was the custom, her husband was up on the scaffold when Sam Brannan and a group of other men walked past. "That Dutchman up there," Sam remarked—pointing to Zins—"is the richest man in all California. No other man is able to build a brick house at this time." Hyperbole or otherwise, aiming to impress his friends or not, the already financially powerful Sam Brannan would shortly be proven wrong about George Zins' wealth.

Dorothea gave birth to an infant who thrived, an event to be celebrated in a frontier environment of high infant mortality. Before and after the birth she witnessed many improvements to

Sacramento City in the years 1849-1852—considering that at the close of 1848, only twelve simple tent-structures stood near the river. Construction of Sam Brannan's mercantile outlet on the levee at the foot of modern K Street was almost complete that December. Moored at the foot of the I Street landing was a goods-laden, dismantled ship brought from San Francisco. River traffic, however, was already high. In January 1849, another frame building went up at the corner of Front and I Streets, followed by some merchants' log-cabins and "cloth-houses," wood frames overlaid with canvas or sailcloth sides and ceilings.

From that crude beginning Sacramento City grew exponentially as hordes of men poured into a settlement located at the gateway to the mining camps springing up along the upper American and Sacramento Rivers and their tributaries: to Coloma, Hangtown (Placerville), Rattlesnake Bar, Mormon Island (today submerged beneath Folsom Lake), Texas Hill, Yankee Jim's, and hundreds more colorfully-named places. By mid-1849, just weeks before Rosa's birth, the somewhat fluid population of less than three hundred persons in and around Sutter's Fort swelled to 2,000. One hundred canvas and frame buildings and tents now stood interspersed between the tall oaks and sycamores at or near the waterfront. Hundreds of tents were pitched south of the emerging city center at Front, J, and K Streets. Later that year, some forty-five wooden buildings and three hundred cloth houses dotted the landscape.

Sacramento's first newspaper appeared in April 1849. The *Placer Times* began publishing from a hut outside Sutter's Fort as a 13-by-18- inch newspaper, moving to new quarters on Front Street in July, where it continued publishing weekly until it was finally succeeded, after some merging and jostling, by the *Sacramento Transcript* and two other short-lived newspapers published during 1850-1851. A more enduring newspaper, the *Sacramento Daily Union*, presented its first issue on March 19,

1851. None of these newspapers were printed in German and it is not known if Dorothea learned to read English. However, she could have enjoyed the German-language newspaper *Staats Zeitung*, published in San Francisco and doubtless available in the Sacramento bookstores that advertised supplies of newspapers from all over the States.

As more gold rushers poured in, dozens more high-priced merchants and transporters, liquor distributers and cardsharps—and those few who sought to import stability—followed close on their heels. Religious leaders came with the intention of forestalling any withdrawal from the Atlantic States' established church and family values, determined to salvage any souls who had already succumbed to immoral temptations. Yet, diaries and journals record witnessing some of these ordained spiritual guides prospecting in the gold fields and gambling shoulder to shoulder alongside the less enlightened in Sacramento's infamous drinking and gambling parlors the Stinking Tent, the Diana, the Gem, the Empire, and many others. A saloon called The Plains adorned its walls with frescoes depicting scenes Dorothea would have recognized in the very unlikely event she ever entered the place: Independence Rock, scenic mountain passes, and other trail landmarks. The always-crowded saloons and gambling dens clustered about the waterfront and the main commercial streets. Cigar smoke and the smell of spilled whiskey permeated the air; robust singing and fiddle playing throughout the night disturbed those few who were trying to sleep. Nevertheless, certain upstanding, dedicated men of the cloth prevailed, and by the end of 1849, a handful of churches were organized in Sacramento City, most getting their start from Sunday services held beneath oak trees.

In response to so much hard drinking, temperance leagues sprang up all over the mining districts. They were popular yet ultimately unsuccessful at influencing lawmakers to curb "the evil" in a territory where liquor was such an important commercial factor. Dorothea's views on temperance and her religious preferences are completely unknown. Her husband must have had a relaxed attitude toward the benefits of alcohol; he would establish a brewery within another year.

A post office opened in mid-1849 on board the bark *Whiton* anchored on the river (later moved to a downtown building), but this facility proved no less unreliable or aggravating to the miners than the San Francisco Post Office. Several enterprising men looking for gold found it when they put down their picks and shovels and set themselves up as expressmen who delivered mail by canoe or muleback to the outlying camps for $1 or $2 per letter. Sacramento's City Hotel, three stories high and built with wood scavenged from Sutter's abandoned flour mill at Brighton (east of the Fort and south of the Jackson Road) rose on Front Street between I and J. Down the block the flimsy, canvas-sided Eagle Theatre opened in the fall of 1849 to capacity crowds who whistled, stomped, and cheered their appreciation of the melodramatic *The Bandit Chief* on opening night.

Vessels clogged the waterfront. The Horse Market at Sixth and K, where immigrants traded their trail-worn draft animals for fresh livestock, held busy auctions daily. A ferry service operated between the city and Washington on the west side of the Sacramento River (today's West Sacramento). There was a bowling alley and twenty-five or thirty stores, but it was still a city of tents, lean-tos, and shanties scattered around the many unfilled blocks stretching eastward from Front Street. After sunset, only open camp fires and the full moon alleviated the nighttime darkness. Sickness was rampant, particularly among the recent immigrants who were afflicted with scurvy and other maladies in addition to sheer exhaustion and exposure from arduous travel. Some days the death toll was as high as twenty people. A hospital had been established at the fort in the early part of the summer.

After the rains set in, Doctors Morse and Stillman succeeded in getting sufficient backing to erect another hospital on the corner of Third and K Streets. Their announcement in the December 29, 1849 *Placer Times* also touts a drug store connected to their Home for the Sick. Their terms: $10 per day for the main ward, $20 for a private room occupied by one person, and $15 each for two.[3] Rates for care and medicines, though lower at this new hospital, were still so high that only a small number of the sick could afford to be treated.

It is not known whether George or Dorothea ever had need to avail themselves of general medical services. Babies were born at home; the *Placer Times* had no advertisements by midwives or obstetric practitioners in 1849, when the Zinses' daughter Rosa came into the world.

By the end of Rosa's birth year, the swarm of predominantly male gold rushers had increased California's population ten-fold. Sacramento boasted a population of 4,000, about half of them transients camped south of the business district. In a raw frontier society where women cooked, laundered, baked from scratch, and kept house using labor-intensive methods, it doesn't seem likely that Dorothea met very many women or had much leisure time to enjoy their company if she did.

One source estimates that for several months before Stockton and Marysville became competitive "hub" cities, nine-tenths of the fortune hunters passed through Sacramento to purchase their mining implements and provisions. The city was booming, and gold paid for everything: whiskey, $1 a glass, boots up to $32, pickaxes $12, lumber $1 per foot; bread the size of a six-penny loaf in New York sold for fifty cents, flour $50 a barrel, onions $1 each. Butter and cheeses sold from $1.50 to $3 per pound. To put these prices in perspective, skilled laborers in the Atlantic States typically earned $1 a day. Gold dust, measured by a varying finger "pinch" equating $16 per ounce, wasn't dust at all, but formed of scales or lumps of all shapes and sizes. Rents for business property, payable in advance, went as outrageously high as $5,000 per month, the equivalent of many years' pay for an ordinary worker in the States.

Not all was dawn-to-dusk toil. The community observed the Fourth of July in 1849 with fireworks and a Grand Ball at the yet unfinished City Hotel. Townsmen undertook an immense effort to locate and cajole into attendance every female for miles around, and the result was 200 men and eighteen women who danced and toasted each other with imported champagne. Unstated is whether the ball was only for the unmarried. The Zinses would have declined to attend anyway because Dorothea was seven months pregnant. The following year Rowe's Olympic Circus came to town featuring pantomimes, comic dances, tight rope performances, snippets of operatic arias, and a dancing horse. The *Placer Times* announced that several barrels of peanuts had arrived for the spectator's enjoyment, and reported capacity crowds.

On August 1, 1849, a handful of responsible men were elected to organize a city government. The people voted in favor of a revised proposed charter on October 13, 1849, after rejecting the Council's first effort. Opposition to the first charter largely stemmed from the gaming entrepreneurs who opposed any infringement of their freedoms or profits. George and Dorothea had no say in the matter. Unlike a handful of other states or territories, California did not extend suffrage to non-citizen male residents, and women had no voting rights anywhere in America.

The burgeoning city had its drawbacks. The thermometer reached 114 degrees at noon the second week of July, while winter nights were raw. Swarms of flies, mosquitoes, and fleas tormented sweltering or chilled-to-the-bone flesh, depending on the season. Pioneer women had to wage resourceful, vigilant war against these irritating pests. One remedy women used to eradicate flies was to set out a plate of well-mixed black pepper, brown sugar and cream.

The town smelled of garbage, offal, dead animals, and human excrement. Increased river traffic brought rats that jumped ship, scampering everywhere. Scores of immigrant men, misled by myths of easily accessible gold and ignorant of the distances between San Francisco, Sacramento, and the Sierra foothills, had not thought to bring money. Others were destitute because they had been forced to abandon their wagons east of the mountains. Without resources to buy food or mining supplies, they stood in line to beg for the few wage-paying jobs. More than a few slaughtered Captain John Sutter's cattle. By the fall of 1849 an overwhelmed John Sutter, heretofore the main source of employment in the area, sold his fort (after paying off the Russians with the proceeds of city lots sales), and relocated to his Hock Farm near Marysville.

Respectable women fared better, partly due to their scarcity. Some prospered by serving daily hot meals to homesick miners, while others sold pies baked in Dutch ovens, took in mending and laundry, or ran boardinghouses.

It can be hoped, though not assumed, that the Zins family enjoyed a better standard of living than other immigrants. They lived sheltered from the elements in a roofed brick house in Sutterville (and later on the site of their brewery), and were, presumably, receiving rental income from the two first floor stores of their Sacramento building plus the upstairs Anchor House Hotel. Likely, they owned a cow for milk and chickens for fresh eggs, as did many other town residents. Churning fresh butter didn't take long and was far preferable to paying premium prices for the aged, brownish article brought around Cape Horn. Dorothea probably made her own bread and pastries even after professional bakeries came to town, and laundered her family's clothing herself instead of paying the inflated price of $6 to $12 per dozen garments that entrepreneurial washerwomen charged wifeless gold miners.

Pioneer Luzena Stanley Wilson's memoir tells of laundering

her family's clothing and also speaks of Sacramento's "town crier," who rode about the streets on a thin pony, clanging his bell as he called out his news and announcements. It was this crier's warning, Luzena relates, that alerted Sacramento's occupants of the river levee breach just before Christmas 1849. The breach was hastily fixed, but with years of light rainfall thus far experienced combined with enormous profits at the waterfront landing uppermost in mind, Sacramento's citizens chose to relegate the native Indians' warnings of prior inundations as a tall tale to be ignored. Therefore everyone was stunned when the Sacramento and American Rivers, swollen by weeks of rain, overflowed on the night of January 8, 1850, submerging the entire city beneath a lake of water more than four feet deep.

People came floating out of their tents and wooden shacks on cots and boxes. A quick escape was impossible; cries of help were answered, but many drowned or died from exposure. Untethered merchandise of all kinds—wood from toppled shanties, uprooted tents, and the carcasses of drowned livestock—swept past those lucky enough to grab a particle of wood for a raft or climb on their rooftops. Uncounted sacks of grain burst. The fragile Eagle Theatre collapsed. The second floor of the Zinses Anchor House (reportedly, one couple spent their honeymoon stranded there) and Sam Brannan's City Hotel became crammed with refugees. The few spots of high ground quickly filled with people, livestock, and dogs. Much of the floating merchandise was bottles of liquor, retrieved and consumed by men bobbing about in whatever type of hastily procured lifeboat that would keep them from sinking. As Sacramento's first historian, Dr. John Morse (who was on the scene), put it, "the city seemed almost mad with boisterous frolic, with the most irresistible disposition to revel in all the joking, laughing, talking, drinking, swearing, dancing and shouting that were ever patronized by the wine-drinking son of Jupiter. . . ."

Regardless of the prevailing revelry and frivolity, the flood was a major calamity in terms of lives, property, and merchandise lost—and not at all hilarious to women with babies such as Dorothea Zins. If George and Dorothea and their infant daughter were still residing in Sutterville during the flood—or even, at that time, already living in temporary quarters on Twenty-ninth Street near the fort's location—they were on higher ground away from the deepest floodwaters at either place, although not entirely unaffected. Their floors, bedding, clothing, and sacked foodstuffs would have been dampened or soaked by rain and seeping water.

The flood shut off access to the outlying mining areas, greatly compromising Sacramento's premier role as outfitter to the gold regions. When freight wagons and mule train traffic finally resumed in February, thousands of miners found that their provisions had greatly increased in price. Work to raise the river levees about the town was completed the following summer at a cost of $170,000,[4] but their new height of between three and twenty feet (depending on location) would ultimately prove inadequate. In the wake of the inundation Sacramento stank even worse than before. Interest in Sutterville was renewed, but too many citizens chose to rebuild and restore at the established profit centers. Sutterville held tight for a few more years and then gradually began to decline.

Even as the flood waters receded another disaster was brewing, this one man-made. A growing faction of would-be homesteaders took the view that city land already purchased by others from John Sutter wasn't his to sell.

There was, indeed, a surveyor's error on Sutter's original Mexican land grant, but Sutter's buyers staunchly refuted the idea that the lots they had bought, paid for, and often improved were, as the newcomers claimed, properties in the public domain. The newcomers called themselves "settlers" and their foes "speculators." The titleholders of Sutter's former lands called themselves "landholders" and their opposition "squatters." Both groups held angry meetings, nailed up inflammatory broadbills, and instigated legal actions. Squatters interfered by force with owners' attempts to build, and landholders forcibly ejected those who attempted to take possession. An out-and-out war, still bloodless, erupted. A series of shameful, destructive, escalating acts by both sides finally came to a violent confrontation known as the infamous Squatter Riots over a stretch of days in mid-August 1850.

The major showdown took place at Fourth and J Streets, where Mayor Bigelow was severely wounded and Assessor James Woodland, who was unarmed, was shot and killed. Three squatters died, also from gunshots. Several other men were wounded to varying degrees, and a child was wounded in the leg. The following evening Sacramento County's first Sheriff, twenty-something Joseph McKinney, was killed while attempting to apprehend some squatters who had fled to a roadhouse in Brighton. There, four more were killed or wounded. Armed men roamed the streets; women stayed in their homes. Fearing renewed attacks, Governor Peter Burnett demanded military intervention from the California Militia. On the day of Sheriff McKinney's burial, the California Guard and Protection Engine Company arrived from San Francisco, one hundred-fifty strong, to enforce the peace. The riots were over.

George and Dorothea were undoubtedly as horrified and frightened by the months-long fiery confrontations (verbal assaults had begun in 1849) as their fellow townsfolk. Perhaps more so— they were foreigners who held land titles amid a storm of several hundred angry native-born Americans demanding their "rights." There is no indication George took any part, either as a jeering, laughing spectator before things got out of hand that awful August afternoon on J Street or as an armed, patrolling town citizen in the days that followed. The aftermath, though, affected the Zinses and everyone else. Suddenly, titles were contested along with the general value of properties. This land-value crash in turn contributed to a business panic in September, causing overextended banks and inexperienced merchants to declare bankruptcy. Sacramento's financial conundrums were righted shortly, and happily, by increased trade with the mines in the fall.

But George Zins wasn't a merchant, nor was he employed in the resurgent freighting activities. With Captain Sutter removed from the scene and his brick-making endeavors unrewarding, George needed a way to make a living. Why the couple chose to abandon this business just when demand for building materials was on the rise can only be surmised. Perhaps they were unwilling to again endure such intensive labor. Or maybe Dorothea didn't want to commit so many daily hours of concentrated attention when she was rearing a toddler. (Other entrepreneurs rose to meet the challenge. When brick machines became available in the mid-1850s Sacramento boasted thirty brickyards manufacturing more than 250,000 bricks a day.) Whatever the reason, George's interest was sparked by the notion that a brewery would be an advantageous acquisition for the young city, as well as a profitable enterprise for his family.

At the time there was only one such business in Sacramento, the Galena Brewery operated by German immigrant Peter Cadel. It was located near Sutter's Fort at Twenty-eighth and M Streets in a "neat frame house" constructed for that purpose. Peter Cadel announced the opening of his brewery in the February 9, 1850 *Placer Times*, giving "notice to the public that P. Cadel & Co. were making the best quality ale and beer." The Zinses owned eight full-sized lots just two blocks north of Cadel's establishment. The original ledger *City or Town Lots Assessment Roll for the Year 1849* has an entry in the elegant handwriting of the period attesting to George Zins' ownership of lots one through eight, blocks J – K, between Twenty-eighth and Thirtieth Streets, valued at $9,600,[5] with no improvements noted. And they still owned Anchor House;

the same page shows this second property with a land value of $15,000 and improvements of $8,000.[2]   Evidently, permanent structures for living quarters and a brewery building on the J and K Street parcels were constructed during 1850, probably after the flood receded.

Zins founded his brewery in partnership with fellow German immigrant George Weiser, of whom little is known, sometime during 1850. The partners hired an experienced brewer named Koester as their brewmaster. The 1851 Sacramento City Directory, compiled from information gathered in late 1850, lists Zins & Weiser, Brewers, at Twenty-Ninth Street between J and K. Below that is another line indicating a residence that reads, "Zins, George, at Zins & Weiser's." His partner George Weiser's separate residence listing also shows that address. At least by November 8, 1850, when the census was taken in Sacramento City, George, Dorothea (her name here is spelled Dorithy or Dorethy), and little Rosa shared their home with three adult men, two of them German natives and one born in Switzerland, all designated as laborers. These men were possibly employees of the brewery or friends partaking of the Zinses' hospitality; none of their names are listed separately in the city directory. Weiser and his wife lived adjacent to the Zinses, and both men's occupations were described as brewers.

Unlike their competitor Cadel & Company, Zins & Weiser did not announce the opening of their business, nor did they advertise, in Sacramento newspapers. Like Cadel's, their brewery's capacity was most likely six to eight barrels.

Establishing a brewery requires considerable capital. It would seem logical that to raise funds George and Dorothea sold or mortgaged their brick house in Sutterville, although there is no extant evidence they did so. However, no further mention of this property occurs in later accounts of Zins' life and career. It is known that George signed notes for business loans to finance the

81

brewery, for which he was the personal guarantor, from either a bank or private party. In addition to building the structure, equipment and ingredients needed to be built or purchased. While water was abundant and barley could be purchased from valley farmers, there were no hop fields in Sacramento; this essential ingredient was only available from Europe or from a limited number of growers in upstate New York. As a pioneer brewery, Zins & Weiser had little choice but to accept and pay market price for a variable quality of hops further degraded by long sea voyages.

In November 1850, the *Sacramento Transcript* published preliminary census information gathered by Assistant Census Marshall William Neely Johnson, the brother of a future California governor. Admitting his labors were incomplete, Johnson listed four hundred stores and shops, three mills, eight cabinet shops, sixty-five blacksmiths, five soda or lemon syrup manufacturers, eight livery stables, close to a hundred each physicians and lawyers—and just two breweries. They were not named. Surely one was Peter Cadel's. The second was most likely Zins & Weiser, although another brewery of short duration did open in 1850 on Front Street.

George and Dorothea's second child, a boy named Albert, was born in 1851. But aside from joyously welcoming a healthy son, 1851 was a disaster for them. Purportedly the brewery burned down that year, suddenly leaving them broken financially.

Zins & Weiser's operation, like Cadel's Galena Brewery, was likely a crude affair consisting of a frame building filled with wooden barrels. Also likely is that both made use of steam engines to generate power and high temperatures during the brewing process. Whether misuse of this potentially volatile engine or accidental mishap led to the fire isn't known. Nor is it known if just the brewery structure was destroyed or if the fire consumed their living quarters as well. Curiously, the Zins & Weiser fire was not reported in the newspapers, therefore making the 1851 date a generally accepted estimate culled from other somewhat vague facts about George Zins. Explanations, then, are mere conjecture. Perhaps the brewery was too far distant from downtown or the story was eclipsed by news of another major happening the day it occurred. Like other frontier towns crowded with canvas and clapboard structures menaced by chimney wastes, open flames and kerosene lamps, Sacramento suffered many fires big and small. Most were quickly doused, but in April 1850 a not-so-easily-controlled fire consumed eight to ten buildings on Front Street. The first volunteer fire department appeared in 1850, followed by the formation of more volunteer companies through the end of the decade. Cisterns were installed in mid-1851, but only in the business district.

The downtown cisterns were of no use to far-distant Zins & Weiser, though. The brewery was ruined and, if obituaries written by friends can be relied upon, so were George and Dorothea.

The Zinses sold the eight east-side lots *and* Anchor House to Jacob Binninger for $5,000 total in a sale recorded October 14, 1851—affirmation of just how far property values had dropped following the Squatter Riots the year before. Binninger was already a hotel operator who owned other Sacramento properties, notably the Fourth Street House. He renamed the Zinses' Front Street building Green Tree Hotel in honor of the large oak tree that stood in front of it, and under which incoming immigrant wagons often rested. Jacob Binninger and George Zins had somewhat common backgrounds and almost certainly knew each other personally in small-town Sacramento before this transaction. Jacob, several years George's elder, was a German who had lived for a time in George Zins' first American home of Galena, Illinois, had traveled overland to Sacramento three years after George's arrival, and like George Zins was a man of several talents.

George and Dorothea probably used the proceeds of this sale to pay some creditors. Even so, it is said they still owed $15,000,[6] a staggering sum in 1851, with no provenance to both feed and shelter themselves and repay their outstanding debts. In desperation, George Zins applied to Sam Brannan—now well on his way to becoming California's first millionaire—for help. Reportedly, Brannan was so impressed with George's honesty and proven past industriousness that he offered to let the Zinses move to his ranch near the town of Nicolaus, a bustling trading post and ferry crossing in Sutter County on the Feather River, forty miles or so north of Sacramento.

One source asserts the family moved to Nicolaus either in late 1851 (right after the brewery fire) or early 1852. However, the actual date could not have been before the fall of 1852. George Zins became a naturalized citizen of the United States on May 21, 1852 in Sacramento County District Court, when—were they already living in Nicolaus—established district courts in Sutter County were closer. There was no citizenship test. After residing in the United States for two years an alien, males or females "of good moral character," could file a declaration of intent, in any court of record, to become a citizen. After three additional years the applicant filed a petition for naturalization, not necessarily in the same court. When the petition was granted, an oath of allegiance and renunciation administered and court fees paid, the alien was issued a certificate of citizenship. There was no need for Dorothea to apply. Wives of naturalized men automatically became citizens, and besides women couldn't vote and typically didn't appear as "persons" before the law. Dorothea's proof of citizenship was a combination of her marriage certificate and George's naturalization record.

Furthermore, the special 1852 California Census shows the family still residing in Sacramento County in July of that year. Rosa's age is given as three, Albert's one. Dorothea is listed merely as Mrs. Zins with no first name, but her birthplace on this report is further narrowed to Hanover, Germany, and she gave Illinois as her place of residence prior to California, in the first census that asked this question. On this document George's occupation is given only as "Hotel," indicating that he either owned or managed one, in this case presumably the latter as he sold Anchor House the year before. The mystery is why, according to a published statement by the City of Sacramento, George Zins was assessed a license fee of $25 for the period April 1852 to March 1853 while Jacob Binninger only paid $10. This suggests that a private agreement was reached regarding fiscal responsibilities and/or Jacob Binninger offered George and his family a business share and shelter in one of his other hostelries. The great fire of November 1852 spared Anchor House/Green Tree Hotel, but damaged Binninger's other properties.

The Zins family reportedly left for Brannan's ranch with barely enough funds to pay their passage and freight bill on the *Governor Dana,* a sternwheeler that traveled the Sacramento River between Sacramento City and the Feather River districts.

Sam Brannan's ranch wasn't actually in Nicolaus, a village that was established in 1843 as a ferry launch on the east bank of the Feather River, on the road between Sutter's Fort and Captain Sutter's Hock Farm. The town's founder was Nicolaus Allgeier (also spelled Niklaus Altgeier), a German-born trapper who had accompanied John Sutter from New Mexico to the Pacific Coast back in 1838. The township grew: Nicolaus town lots were advertised for sale in the February 16, 1850, *Placer Times.* When the Zins family relocated there, the settlement had grown into a major stopping point for gold-rushers needing to cross the river. It already had a post office; not long after they arrived a school was established in the Philip Drescher residence. Many, if not most, of the town's residents were German immigrants, a factor that must have given the German-speaking Zinses much comfort.

Brannan's ranch lay on the west bank of the Feather River across from Nicolaus, a two-square-mile tract he purchased in June 1849. The following year he erected a large, pre-cut house, known as the "White House," on this land, and had plans for a pear orchard. The Zinses might have lived on the edges of this ranch as caretakers, converting an outbuilding into a home. A short article in the May 31, 1854 *Sacramento Daily Union* reporting Jacob Binninger's reconstruction of the south end of his Green Tree Hotel on Front Street, informed readers that George Zins was then farming successfully on the Feather River, *opposite* Nicolaus. The piece also gave credit to Dorothea: "The Pioneer Brick—the first brick building erected in this city . . . commenced by Mr. George Zins in the spring of 1849 . . . bricks manufactured by himself and wife at Sutterville, the latter doing no small share of the work."

Brannan's ranch was indeed opposite Nicolaus, but there is another possibility. In 1850 Sam Brannan and some other investors acquired another, much larger area farther west in Sutter County. Originally known only as "Lot 8," most of this acreage fronted on the east bank of the Sacramento River. According to descriptions of the Zinses' efforts to tame and develop the plot or patch they were "given" by Brannan's largess, the latter seems just as likely.

Whatever the exact location, their first residence was merely a rude cabin. Once again George and Dorothea shouldered hard work, renovating their living quarters and cultivating the land. They bought cows and chickens on credit and established a small-scale dairy operation. Here again, Mrs. Zins was commended in print by George's eulogizer, for "not alone by his but by his wife's industry also" the couple saved enough, after paying off old debts, to purchase 160 acres on August 10, 1855. This purchase from Sam Brannan is known to be a portion of the sixty-six lots resulting from Brannan's subdivision of Lot 8. On this land George and Dorothea built a comfortable house and several outbuildings.

The family enjoyed their new prosperity for only a short time before they lost wife and mother.

Dorothea Wolfinger Zins died in August 1861, when Rosa was almost twelve years old and Albert only ten. Her death notice in the August 26, 1861 *Sacramento Daily Union* reports her date of death as August 23, noting her age as "in her 46th year," with no cause of death cited. Her tombstone in Nicolaus Cemetery, which spells her name with an "a" is carved with a different date and age at death:

DORATHEA
WIFE OF
GEORGE ZINS
AGED 44 YEARS
DIED AUGUST 22, 1861

Etched at the bottom of the stone are the words "She is not dead but sleepeth," the tribute and epitaph of a grieving husband and children. This quotation is from Luke 8:52, and although not an uncommon epitaph on nineteenth century gravestones, it does suggest that George and Dorothea read their Bibles. Like so many other things about their personal lives, their faith and church membership remain open questions. Her gravestone is a two-inch thick, flat marble rectangle two feet tall and fifteen inches wide, flaring to eighteen inches at the top into an intriguingly curlicued, carved design that very much resembles a queen's crown. Whether this stylized "crown" is a deliberately chosen homage from an adoring husband to a queen of a wife, or just a lovely, catalogue-variety design can only be wondered—and the stone may well have been installed some years later to replace an original, decaying wooden marker.

Nicolaus Cemetery is located on grounds that were originally part of the Herman Minden Ranch. Dorothea's grave is set apart in a back expanse of grass, yet nearly toe-to-toe with the remains of German-born Andrew Sallantier, who died in 1863 at age thirty-one. Both graves are canted together at an odd angle. No records exist to either prove or refute that Dorothea and Andrew were related.

George Zins married again on December 7, 1863, in Sutter County. His second wife was Christiana Schlichting, who died in 1870. Rosa Zins married Conrad Schuler in 1875, when she was in her mid-twenties. She died in December of that year, seven days after giving birth to a daughter, also named Rosa. Dorothea's granddaughter Rosa Schuler died, unmarried, in 1945. All that is known of Albert Zins is that he later worked as a machine shop engineer, possibly for the railroad, and died without issue. According to his obituary, George Zins moved to Oakland in 1885 to be near an old friend. He died there October 24, 1885, aged sixty-six.

A few of the red clay bricks George and Dorothea Zins formed and fired by hand so long ago in young Sacramento City still exist. Whether the couple did it as a merchandizing design or pride in the hard labor they endured making them, they marked their bricks with the initials "G Z." Some of their handiwork was found during a 1960 excavation near Capitol Avenue (M Street in pioneer days) and Front Street.

One of their bricks is embedded above the mantle in the Courtyard Grill dining room fireplace of the Firehouse Restaurant in Old Sacramento.

5. Gravestone in Nicolaus Cemetery, Dorothea Wolfinger Zins.

Photo by Author

End Notes, Dorothea Wolfinger Zins

[1] Using the gold ratio formula, $800,000 and $850,000, respectively.

[2] The land between Front, Second, M and N is state-owned land between the river and Interstate 5, directly south of Old Sacramento Historic State Park. As property owned and maintained by the state, it has no publicly available assessed value and no current resale value.

[3] $600, $1200, and $900 in modern money.

[4] Nineteenth century expenditures for piecemeal levee construction and repair have no adequate correlation to current costs, due to modern technology and different materials.

[5] George Zins purchased this property in January 1849 for only $800, at the first public auction after the city was surveyed. He may have been the only bidder. The land, situated directly northeast of Sutter's Fort, was two miles east of the developing town, and therefore undesirable to most as a business or residence. Its assessed value of $9,600 just a few months later reflects the highly inflated values engendered by subsequent land speculation. At present these once fringes-of-town parcels, which now lie beneath commercial development abutting sections of Sutter General Hospital, are collectively worth millions.

[6] This figure first appeared in George Zins' 1885 obituary, and has been repeated in various histories. There are no other documents to confirm or deny this amount, which might have been a misprint in the original. Fifteen thousand dollars in the early 1850s translates to $750,000 in modern money, a sum few ordinary workingmen today could repay in a short time, if ever. George Zins was an ordinary man who repaid his debt within five years with farming income, suggesting the debt was far lower than stated in the original source.

The Governor's Wife:
Mary Zabriskie Johnson

As the ship heaved itself across the ocean waters into the great bay, the day was warm and sunny and clear, another typically lovely fall day appreciated by San Francisco's settled and transient inhabitants alike. To Mary Brevoort Zabriskie it was a wondrous sight given her growing-up experience of muggy, sometimes rainy October weather in her hometown of New Brunswick, New Jersey. Standing on the deck and looking out, she could see sand-colored hills in the distance and what looked like a forest of denuded trees in San Francisco harbor until, drawing closer, she realized they were the stick-like masts of abandoned sailing ships. Activity at the wharf became more discernable as the steamship *Carolina* at last anchored at Rincon Point on October 7, 1850. The passengers and crew were very anxious to depart from that particular vessel.

The weeks-long voyage from New York had mostly been tedious. Shipboard mealtimes were a regiment of beans, salt pork, corned beef, and pilot bread broken by leaden tea-time cakes. Worse, passengers were often fed an odious dessert called Indian Pudding—molasses poured over bread. What Mary thought of this fare can only be imagined. There was nothing for ladies to do in crowded quarters except fill their hours between meals with conversation, card games, reading, needlework, walking the decks for exercise, or staring out to sea where, occasionally, whales exuded a bushy stream of misty air and vapor or a school of porpoises joyfully leaped in the sunlit waves. But all that was in the first, benign part of the trip. The *Carolina*, carrying $12,000 in specie (coined money) and a large amount of mail, stopped in New

6. J Street Circa 1854-55.

Courtesy California History Room, California State Library, Sacramento

Orleans before rounding the stormy South American Cape Horn. She had put into port at Panama, Acapulco, and San Diego to take on wood for the boiler, fresh water and supplies, and new passengers.

It was the last leg of Mary's voyage that turned terrifying.

The dreaded cholera had insidiously invaded the *Carolina*—that horrifying, contagious scourge of no known cause or cure with its repugnant symptoms and all-but guaranteed swift death. This spectral enemy emerged in 1849 to haunt East Coast cities, flaring across the Missouri River frontier settlements and the vast prairies to the Pacific Ocean as the excitement over California gold drew thousands of overlanders into close contact. In just that one year, cholera claimed more lives than had been lost during the two year duration of the Mexican-American War. Its spread was exacerbated by thousands more of otherwise rational men too impatient for a longer sea voyage or plains crossing, who willingly traversed meso-American jungles rife with disease of all kinds for a hazardous but quicker route between the Atlantic side and the Pacific port at Panama. The cholera deaths on the *Carolina* began September 19, three days after departing the Isthmus of Panama. Fourteen men perished and were given hasty burials at sea.

Twenty-three year old Mary, her step-mother, and her eighteen year old sister Lizzie plus ten other women numbered just thirteen adult females among the vessel's male passengers and crew of over two hundred. Their numbers would be added to the 5,950 men and fifty-seven women that San Francisco's harbor master tallied between August 1 and September 13, 1850.

Although it is highly unlikely the lady passengers aboard ship were permitted anywhere near the afflicted, the disease was highly contagious, its exact transmission unknown, and a ship afforded no escape. It's easy to imagine that once the shipboard deaths began the women ate little and slept less, fearful of touching table utensils or sleeping lest they or one of their young children exhibit signs of

93

illness in the night.

THE CHOLERA! The words were rent in bold headline type above the *Daily Alta's* report of the *Carolina's* entry into San Francisco Bay. The 210 passengers still living disembarked in the early morning light. Their relief at escaping cholera, if indeed that's what they felt as they hurried down the gangway, would prove to be mistakenly premature.

Mary's step-mother Mary Hancock Zabriskie and the children—Mary Brevoort, Lizzie, fourteen year old Alexander, and James Albert and Anna, both under ten—were escorted from New Brunswick by Mary's thirty-something uncle Albert. They were coming to join husband and father Colonel James C. Zabriskie, who had sailed to California the year before, accompanied by Mary's uncle Dr. Christian Zabriskie, her oldest brother William, and Dr. Zabriskie's son Elias.

The men departed New York in February 1849 on the steamship *Crescent City* just as California's gold discovery—the event of the century—lured multitudes west. Their ship set sail amidst the firing of cannon and loud cheers from a large crowd at the docks, who were doubtless intoxicated with gold fever and wishing they too were going. Mary, her step-mother, and siblings likely said their good-byes in private and remained at home in New Brunswick safely away from the milling, shoving, shouting crowds on the New York docks. Unlike their fellow *Crescent City* passengers, the Zabriskie brothers and sons were not making the difficult passage in search of shining metal to gather up and bring back home. James and Christian Zabriskie were going to California to build viable communities, to create a new life in a new land that promised untold new opportunities for their children's futures. They landed in San Francisco July 4, 1849. Within two weeks the brothers were in Sacramento, where James set up his law practice in a shanty under an oak tree at Second and K Streets with just one volume as a law library. Before the year was out, he was selected

94

as second magistrate and penned Sacramento's first city charter, approved by the voters October 13, 1849.

By the time Mary's ship the *Carolina* anchored in the Bay in October of 1850, the Zabriskie brothers had established themselves as leaders and professionals in the boom-town atmosphere of newly-chartered Sacramento City. Most likely they and their sons were in San Francisco to greet Mary's steamer as it docked, for a joyous family reunion after a year apart—a joy tempered by the frightening news that a dreaded scourge had just arrived in California's major port city. It was not wise to linger; James took his wife, children, and younger brother Albert home to Sacramento where it was deemed safer.

Mary, a vivacious young woman by nature, must have felt her excitement and curiosity rise as she viewed this so-called City of the Plains. Sacramento was busy and prosperous, with shops of all descriptions and hotels lining Front Street from I Street south to O and stretching eastward to Third Street along J and K. An immense and profitable trade between miners and merchants had resurged following a devastating year: January's deep floods, a fire in April that gutted eight buildings along Front Street, the August Squatter's Riots that claimed the lives of Sacramento's city assessor and young sheriff, and September's business panic which prompted the closure of three banks and several merchant establishments. Not all in this new strange country was raw and unfamiliar. New Brunswick was a river-port city, with ships leaving daily for New York. Sacramento was a river-port city, with ships leaving daily for San Francisco. Sacramento already contained seven churches, a small library, four well-attended theatres that boasted professional performances, a post office, restaurants, a private school, book stores, house painters, and a number of other tradesmen.

The bustling scene would change within the month, for the reunited Zabriskies had not escaped the terrors of the *Carolina* after all. Another ship was blamed for bringing the disease to Sacramento, despite reports that cholera was already present in other inland settlements.

Just two weeks after Mary came ashore, the steamer *New World* dramatically arrived at Sacramento's *embarcadero* at three-thirty in the morning of Saturday, October 19. The ship's rapidly booming cannons awakened citizens to the electric news from Washington D. C. that California was admitted as the thirty-first state on September 9, 1850. The *Sacramento Transcript's* Monday, October 21 issue excitedly reported the whole story: the firing cannons, a horse rider who dashed up and down the streets shouting the news, the bonfires that swiftly lit the pre-dawn skies; the celebratory crack of guns and pistols, the brilliant candles and lanterns blazing top to bottom from the Crescent City Hotel, the hubbub of the thousands who collected for a mass meeting on the river levee at the foot of J Street. A young lawyer named J. Neely Johnson was appointed chairman of a swiftly formed committee to organize a formal, public celebration of the great occasion. Speeches, of course, dominated the Saturday night ceremonies, eloquently delivered by judges, city aldermen, the mayor, and Mary's very prominent father Colonel James Zabriskie.

James Zabriskie was a seasoned lawyer, forty-six years old in 1850. He was a former long-tenured municipal and probate judge in New Jersey, a commissioned officer in the New Jersey militia, involved in national politics before he was thirty, and a friend of United States Senators. Known to be a stern disciplinarian with his militia unit, he doubtless raised his children in a similar fashion—with high standards, mitigated by love and pride in his offspring. Mary grew up to be self-assured, indicating an environment of fatherly affection and protection. In 1845, Colonel Zabriskie was First Assistant Marshall at the inauguration of President Polk—the president who declared war on the Republic of Mexico to successfully bring Texas, and ultimately California, into the Union.

Further, James was a close personal friend of Commodore Robert Stockton, a fellow New Jersey native who had played a major role in the military take-over of California during the Mexican-American War, a man who fervently advocated statehood for the nation's new acquisition. Accomplishing this meant settlement by like-minded Americans who possessed the skills to make it happen. James Zabriskie and other civic-minded men of substance and influence decided they would be those individuals.

Now that goal of California statehood was finally realized. Mary and her family had every reason to be proud as they listened on the sidelines, clapping and cheering with the other revelers. Excitement of another kind eclipsed the celebration almost overnight.

Early on the morning of October 20, an unidentified immigrant purported to have been a *New World* passenger was discovered on the Sacramento levee, dying of cholera. Four days later the *Sacramento Transcript* published a short list of cholera deaths and reported the city's efforts to forestall an epidemic by burning immense quantities of street rubbish. The cause of cholera would not be known until 1883, when German scientist Robert Koch isolated and named the water-borne bacteria *vibrio cholera asiaticae,* which enters the mouth and creates a chemical reaction in the intestines that quickly depletes the human body of all its fluids and salts. Medical consensus in 1850 was that the malady only struck those of "intemperate and irregular habits," a view that had to be retracted when it became obvious that industrious citizens with careful habits were just as vulnerable. The afflicted violently expelled vomit and excrement until death mercifully claimed them, usually within eighteen hours from the onset of the first symptoms.

With no known cause, there was likewise no known cure, and no one understood the necessity of replacing lost fluids or sterilizing hands that had come in contact with the afflicteds' person or clothing. Treatments consisted of doses of peppermint or other stimulants, packing hot bricks or water bottles at the extremities, camphor pills, rubbing the victim with spirits, and administering perfectly legal laudanum, powdered opium mixed with whiskey. This bottled substance was a staple of every household's medicine chest, used for pain relief for everything from toothache to broken bones, and sometimes as a palliative for "melancholy," as depression was termed.

The camphor did nothing except mitigate the smell. Heat on the limbs may (or may not) have comforted the sufferer. Alcohol rubs unwittingly aided the care-givers by sterilizing their hands but did little for the patient. The only effective treatment was opium—again unwittingly, rendered as it was to alleviate pain—because it stopped the bowels from further expulsion of body fluids and gave the victim a chance to rally their own bodily defenses, if such was still possible.

Now the scourge was in Sacramento. Mary and her family were once again exposed to potential death.

As the days wore on, the *Transcript's* lists of deaths attributed to cholera grew longer. Justifiably panic-stricken, so many fled Sacramento that the population was reduced by an estimated eighty per cent. There weren't many places to hide; cholera was rife in other major cities including San Francisco, Stockton, and Marysville. Among those who remained to aid the sufferers and bury the dead in this reign of terror—and afterward awarded highest accolades—were the city's dedicated physicians, and men who belonged to the Order of Odd Fellows or the Masons. Before it abated around the middle of November, the epidemic claimed the lives of hundreds, but an accurate tally proved impossible because too many died too fast to count them all. Given James' position as a community leader, it is likely the Zabriskies remained in town during the epidemic, although surely nonessential social visits and excursions ceased.

On November 19, 1850, the rainy season began with a violent storm that blew down several unstable buildings. Refusing to be crushed by these disasters all of one year, Sacramento's citizens, with characteristic resolve and energy, set about restoring their town. Experience guided certain improvements. In anticipation of the knee-deep mud winter rains created downtown, they planked K Street from Front to Eighth by the end of December.

With the arrival of his wife and children, Colonel Zabriskie also had need of improved circumstances. Many Sacramento merchants and professionals in a nearly exclusively male environment—men who were unmarried or men whose families had not yet moved west—lived in boarding houses or quarters above their offices. The Zabriskie men followed suit by renting bachelor accommodations when they became residents. November 1849 advertisements in the *PlacerTimes* offered the services of Dr. C. B. Zabriskie as a physician and surgeon and James Zabriskie as an attorney specializing in deeds, mortgages, and land surveying. Both listed their offices "at the rear of Mr. Gates's boarding house." No address is shown; the town was small enough that the location of boarding houses, eateries, stables, and saloons were well known by most. In the first city directory published in January 1851, James, Christian, and Mary's brother William Mann Zabriskie (also a lawyer) were listed with offices on Second Street, with no residence specified, although by that date the family was living on their own property in an area southeast of the downtown grid on much higher ground than the sloping floodplain beneath the city's business district.

Commonly known as The Ridge, this location was the only hill in the flat landscape, an evolutionary hold-over from millions of years of erosion. As the city expanded it became enclosed by Nineteenth, Twenty-Second, R, and W Streets and, despite its later lavish mansions, was dubbed Poverty Ridge or Poverty Hill because of the disheveled, disordered tents that appeared each time flood waters rose and the poor, dispossessed flatlanders took refuge there. In 1850 the area was an oak-studded region with few inhabitants, but before long real estate agents placed newspaper advertisements promoting desirable Oak Ridge for private residences.

James Zabriskie purchased two large lots on The Ridge in July 1850 in the square between U and V, and Twenty-first and Twenty-second Streets, for $1,000.[1] The seller was Sacramento's first Mayor, Hardin Bigelow. In December of that year, he purchased two more 80- by 160-foot lots adjacent to the first ones, from another party. For many months city auctioneer J. B. Starr & Co. had been advertising "framed houses" for sale in various sizes, from single story 11- by 16-foot homes to 20- by 40-foot, two-story versions. These were prefabricated structures with each element—doors, walls, roof, moldings and window sills—pre-cut to size for quick and efficient assembly, then stacked and shipped around Cape Horn. No description remains of Mary's first home in Sacramento, except as noted in James Zabriskie's property deeds for land with no existing dwellings. It is within the realm of possibility that her father bought one of these prefabricated houses, in style and size simpler than the decades-old, stately, multi-windowed, shutter-trimmed, solid two-and three-story dwellings that lined New Brunswick's cobbled streets. As was common practice the family gave their home a name: Oak Cottage.

Settling into her new home, perhaps helping to choose furnishings with her two sisters and stepmother, exploring about town as soon as the cholera danger passed and meeting new people, must have been welcome activities to Mary, who left a lifetime of friends and extended family a continent away. She was born July 26, 1827, in New Brunswick, the firstborn of James Cannon Zabriskie and his first wife, Elizabeth Mann Zabriskie. Mary's middle name Brevoort came from her paternal grand-mother, whose maiden name was Maria Brevoort. Mary's parents were married April 20, 1826, in Hackensack, New Jersey and had six children together, one of whom did not survive infancy. Mary Brevoort's surviving siblings from both parents were William Mann, Elizabeth (Lizzie), Alexander, and James Albert. A family letter states that Mary's mother died from failing health after so many pregnancies but the exact date is unknown; presumably, it was soon after she gave birth to James Albert in 1840. Mary's father remarried in mid-December 1842, in Philadelphia, when Mary Brevoort was fifteen. His second wife was Mary Hancock. Mary Hancock Zabriskie presented her husband with two more children: Anna, called Annie, and another daughter who died before 1850.

As she matured into a young woman, Mary Brevoort was considered quite beautiful, charming, and gracious. She and Lizzie were both educated, likely only through secondary-school graduation, as college for women still seemed a radical idea. True, a woman named Elizabeth Blackwell defied all odds by graduating from a New York medical college in 1849, but female education was primarily understood to be a vehicle to provide young women with the skills needed to become useful and accomplished wives and mothers, not a path to political or economic equality with men. Which school Mary and Lizzie attended is not known, but New Jersey historian Lucia McMahon confirms that from the early 1840s there were many private young ladies' secondary schools throughout New Jersey, as well as others in Philadelphia, Connecticut, Massachusetts, and New York, that catered to the daughters of the well-to-do. Miss Hannah Hoyt's prestigious young ladies' academy operated right in New Brunswick. Curriculums varied, but most schools included courses in grammar, arithmetic, elocution, astronomy, geography, natural philosophy, chemistry, botany, mineralogy, and geology. The study of a foreign language was often a proffered option; students were also given instruction in music, needlework, and painting.

Two gentlemen who were her father's peers praised Mary for her accomplishments, but without specifying the nature of these achievements, in an age when the ideology of separate spheres dominated thought about gender roles. They might only have meant her education, although the compliment suggests Mary had talents or proficiencies beyond that. Womanly accomplishments that nineteenth century men admired were in the realms of music and painting, plus nurturing activities such as teaching small children or aiding the poor. Men approved of women's expertise in botany, and the propagation and habits of butterflies and song-birds, because they felt these interests were aspects of women's fundamental natures. Above-par social graces and domestic skills were highly valued. The ability to provide delightful entertainment at dinner parties by reading aloud with proper elocution was considered a charming accomplishment. Mary was a known charmer in the personal sense. Whether she painted or played a musical instrument, or had specialized knowledge of plants and wildlife, is not.

Mary's vivacity quickly led to developing a circle of friends in Sacramento, and she became an avid patron of the Tehama Theater. Impresario and talented tragedian James Stark offered a full schedule of Shakespeare and other works to appreciative audiences at this venue, often appearing in roles opposite his equally talented future wife Sarah Kirby. The company's repertoire was a large one—the playbill changed every three or four days—with two performances per night, usually a drama followed by a farce. Between March and June, Mr. Stark produced and starred in *The Honeymoon, Illustrious Stranger, The Lady of Lyons, Richard III, Macbeth, The Merchant of Venice, Pizarro, Hamlet, The Iron Chest,* and others. Between performances he found time to give "intellectual readings" of essays and poems to the Mercantile Library Association and the church where Mary Zabriskie was a member. Reviews in the *Sacramento Daily Union,* always highly complimentary, took care to note that "the fair admirers of poetry and beauty" were regular attendants who, on at least one occasion, outnumbered the gentlemen despite rainy weather and muddy streets.

Mr. Stark was venerated more than once by Sacramentans for his "surpassing merit." As his tour drew to a close a group of ladies publicly requested the privilege of giving him a testimonial in the form of a complimentary benefit. The flowery-phrased letter in the June 12, 1851, *Daily Union* is signed by seventeen women, including the names of Miss M. Zabriskie and Miss E. [Lizzie] Zabriskie. The actor, of course, gratefully accepted this distinguished honor. James Stark and Sarah Kirby returned in two years to again grace the city's stages.

Mary joined a highly regarded, well attended church, probably soon after arriving in town. One of the first things Colonel Zabriskie did in Sacramento was to become a founding member, in 1849, of Reverend Joseph Benton's deliberately non-denominational First Church of Christ Congregational. Reverend Benton was a charismatic man of the Gospel, respected by townspeople and transient miners alike for his character and the natural moral influence he exerted with a quiet, practical tolerance and forgiveness of sinners, if not the sins themselves: gambling, drinking, forsaking the Bible, and general debauchery. He often sponsored musical concerts and informational Sunday afternoon lectures on secular topics after the morning religious services as well as public fund-raising events to augment his church's coffers.

One such event the Zabriskie women helped to coordinate was the Ladies' Fair in mid-April 1851 at Lee's Exchange (a theater) on J Street. As the *Daily Union* reported on April 18, the fair's president Mrs. White, and Mrs. James Zabriskie had charge of the quality, quantity and sale of refreshments while Mary and Lizzie managed and sold tickets to assorted entertainments and exhibits. Articles were auctioned, and the ladies cajoled a soda fountain owner to sell his product onsite and donate half of his receipts to the cause.

The successful Ladies' Fair was but one small slice of her overall happiness. Mary was betrothed and planning her upcoming marriage to John Neely Johnson, the young attorney who had chaired the Statehood Celebratory Committee the previous October when Sacramentans were awakened to the news of statehood from the cannon-booming steamship *New World.*

Almost certainly she met John through her father, who might even have mentored the affable, courteous young man who was only four years older than James' eldest son William, and whose legal career in Sacramento began in a manner that paralleled the establishment of his own law practice.

John Johnson, known publicly and professionally as J. Neely Johnson, was born in Gibson County, Indiana, on August 2, 1825, the son of Thomas and Juliet Neely Johnson and grandson of General John Neely, Adjutant-General of Indiana. His parents moved to Illinois, where John grew up and "read" law as a teenager, completing his studies in Iowa. He was admitted to the Bar before he was twenty-one. Lured overland by the California Gold Rush, Johnson arrived in Sacramento in early July 1849 exhausted and "flat broke," as he later told newsmen. Finding no opening in his profession, he hired on as a mule team driver between Sacramento and Stockton. Taking his pay of fifty dollars ($2500 at present values), Johnson mined at Cook's Bar on the Cosumnes River. He returned to Sacramento after three months, audaciously opening his own law office in a tent on J Street between Fifth and Sixth, equipped with only a pine chest, a copy of *Blackstone's Commentaries,* and a sign nailed to an oak tree. He soon became a favorite around town, especially after July 1850, when as a state's agent he led a relief expedition with supplies to emigrants still out on the Plains, where, it is said, he gave his boots, coat, and stockings to a needy family.

Early in 1850, while California was still officially a U.S. Territory, President Fillmore appointed John Neely Johnson as a special agent to take the would-be state's census. When he submitted his report in April 1851, Johnson admitted his count of 117,000-plus white individuals was imperfect due to the lack of adequate assistants—which led to the omission of several important counties—and the constant moving about of the typically remote mining population. A more accurate number, according to historian Theodore Hittell, was that the Euro-American population—even allowing for the fact that by mid-1850 outbound steamers carried away almost as many disappointed, home-bound gold miners as ships brought in new, cheering crowds of hopefuls—came closer to 150,000, with Sacramento County's share roughly 11,000 combined settled citizens and transients.

Before the end of 1850, John partnered with Ferris Forman. Johnson & Forman, Attorneys at Law on Third Street north of J, advertised their general services for both the Sacramento and San Francisco Districts in the May 1850 *PlacerTimes*. Johnson was elected as Sacramento City Attorney in 1850, before he met and courted Mary, and again in 1851.

James Zabriskie and J. Neely Johnson served together on various town council committees. They were both Democrats (although both later changed their political affiliations), knew the same people, and held similar views with regard to California's future and Sacramento's advancement. Johnson was a well-liked, up-and-coming lawyer-politico with enough ambition and industriousness to impress any young lady's father—and particularly a committed, forward-looking father like Colonel James Zabriskie, who certainly knew his charming, vibrant Mary was a prize.

They were married June 26, 1851 in Oak Cottage, the Zabriskie family home. The ceremony was performed by the Reverend Joseph Benton, the family's pastor and friend. The nuptials apparently occasioned quite a celebration with a reception following the service because Reverend Benton noted the affair in his journal under the page heading "1851 Sacramento City" as follows: "June 26. At 10 ½ A.M. married J. Neely Johnson to Miss Mary Bre. Zabriskie at the Ridge. Had a pretty fine time – back about 2."

There is no bridal portrait of Mary and her groom, nor is there any portrait of Mary extant at all. There is also no specific physical description of her or her hair and eye color, only the published praise that she was one of the most beautiful women in California. A sepia-toned photograph of her father, undated but probably taken when James was in his mid-sixties, is the only clue. The formal studio photo is of a gray-haired, light-eyed gentleman who might have been blond in his youth, and so, possibly, was Mary. A daguerreotype image of John (also undated) shows a clean-shaven, brown-haired, boyishly handsome man, solemn-faced for the photo as was the custom, and looking like he was a little afraid of the camera.

The couple may have lived for a time with her family or in another dwelling on the Zabriskies' acreage. Possibly they took up residence in Oak Cottage after the rest of the Zabriskie family built a larger home for themselves on The Ridge. This supposition is based on the fact that there is no evidence Johnson ever purchased any residential property in Sacramento (or that James sold a portion of The Ridge before the early 1860s), yet in the 1853-54 city directory, J. Neely Johnson lists his home as Oak Ridge, as does James Zabriskie. John Johnson did follow his father-in-law's lead by eventually buying downtown commercial properties.

Mary and John welcomed their firstborn on Sunday March 21, 1852. The exultant new father must have dashed down to the newspaper's offices first thing the following morning to have this announcement in the Monday, March 22 issue of the *Daily Union*: "Births. On Sunday the 21st inst; the lady of J. Neely Johnson

Esq. of a son."

According to the special 1852 California Census, they named him Wm. M. N. Johnson, almost certainly William Mann Neely Johnson in honor of Mary's brother William Mann Zabriskie and John's brother William Neely Johnson. The same source (somehow the Johnsons were recorded twice on different dates) reveals the family called the boy "Willie," and that Mary's sister Lizzie was living in the Johnson household instead of her parents' home, to help care for the new mother and infant.

Around this time Mary's husband became more active in statewide politics. In the November 1852 general election he won a seat in the California State Assembly on the Whig ticket, for the 1853-54 sessions to meet at the state capital in Benecia. But before he could take office—that same election night, in fact—a disaster literally swept Sacramento.

The alarm sounded ten minutes past 11:00 o'clock the night of November 2, 1852, when someone spotted smoke billowing from Madame Lanos' millinery shop on the north side of J Street near Fourth. From there, gale-wind-whipped flames quickly exploded into an uncontrollable wall of fire as it fed on a town filled with ramshackle wood buildings, canvas structures, candles, and gas lamps. Before it at last burned out, the fire destroyed nearly ninety percent of the city. The soaring, roaring, leaping flames, allegedly seen from a hundred miles away, destroyed a hospital, several churches, hotels, warehouses, the printing office of the *State Journal* (a portion of the *Daily Union* offices were saved), the Market House (a meat market) in the center of M and Second Streets, and hundreds of dwellings.

The Johnsons' home in Oak Ridge a good distance beyond the range of the inferno was unaffected, but thousands of people were left homeless and devastated. Before the ashes cooled, Assemblyman-elect Johnson was hosting Relief Committee meetings each day at 9:00 a.m. and again at 7:00 p.m. in his law office at the

Bruces Building on Second Street, which had, miraculously, been spared from total destruction although damages sustained were reported as $2,000. Unstated was whether the losses were just for personal property, or included damage to the office suite itself. In any case, a loss of $2,000[2] was equal to the whole of Johnson's annual salary as Sacramento City Attorney. The duties of this Relief Committee, as spelled out in the *Daily Union* of November 5, 1852, were to "receive and disburse all monies, provisions, etc. contributed for the relief of needy sufferers of the late fire," which proved to be a herculean, wrenching task. Ladies' relief committees sprang into existence too, as appreciatively noted by the *Union's* editors, who did not print the ladies' names. Mary Johnson could certainly have led or taken part in one of those committees and, given her husband's involvement and the civic-minded family atmosphere in which she was raised, probably did.

Sacramentans rebuilt, this time mainly in brick with iron shutters over windows to prevent fanning by flame-driven winds. Another improvement to city life followed. Telegraph service was inaugurated in October 1853, allowing "instant communication" to dash between Sacramento, Marysville, San Francisco, San Jose, and Stockton.

Sometime in 1854 Mary, John, and their toddler Willie moved to a home on F Street between Ninth and Tenth. They were living there, again beyond range of the flames, when the second major fire struck on July 13, 1854, destroying several downtown blocks. The thirty-one months-old courthouse, a two-story building replete with four giant pillars and a lovely cupola, was leveled to ash. Sacramento, not yet the legal state capital, was determined to remain host to the legislature. Right away plans were drawn for a newer, even more impressive and capacious building tailored to the needs of state government. The new Ionic-style structure at the same location was higher, wider, and longer than the first courthouse. Fronted by a portico supported by ten massive pillars, and containing chambers for the Senate, Assembly, and constitutional officers, it was completed in just over three months.

The heady, rough-and-tumble days of the Gold Rush were giving way to more settled communities throughout the state. Sacramento was rapidly evolving into a major supply and distribution center, with freight and passenger ships plying the Sacramento River at all hours. The wonder of boiler-stoked steamboat speed, so important just six years earlier to impatient gold miners wanting to reach the Mother Lode in a hurry, was not only expected—but for some less than responsible ship captains, an amusing contest. Such a contest developed when the steamship *Pearl's* captain bet cigars with his crew that he could out-run the *Enterprise* coming alongside them on the Sacramento River as both ships were returning from Marysville. Mary Johnson could hear the flaming explosion of the *Pearl's* over-wrought boiler from her home at shortly past noon on January 27, 1855, as the sound reverberated from just south of the mouth of the American River, where the explosion occurred, to thirteen blocks away. Boatmen trolled the river for days, finally recovering seventy bodies that were laid out in a public building in hopes of being recognized. Few were claimed. Meanwhile the city ordered a public funeral on January 29 for the upwards of forty victims already recovered. Inasmuch as three thousand people, including seven hundred Chinese mourning their eighteen dead, attended the solemn ceremony, and that her husband was part of a committee to assist the funeral procession's Chief Marshal, it is quite probable Mary was present at the services.

J. Neely Johnson's political star continued to rise. In the Assembly, he gained a reputation for his active opposition to controversial bills favoring private companies as monopolies and for his equally outspoken, successful lobbying for Sacramento as the permanent state capital while Vallejo, Sacramento, and Benicia all took turns as California's capital city. By 1855 John was a prominent man in legal and political circles—and had changed political parties. The Whigs were in a state of disintegration, the Democrats were ideologically split into two warring wings, and the Republican Party was yet in its infancy. Into this breech stepped the American Party, known derisively as the "Know-Nothings" for their collective refusal to publicly discuss the substance of their meetings. The Know-Nothings opposed the spread of slavery, but their major platform was opposition to non-Americans having the right to occupy public office. The Party nominated ex-Assemblyman J. Neely Johnson as their candidate for governor of California. Johnson was described as "the most startled man in the State" when the electorate gave him the governorship in September 1855, by a comfortable margin.

Mary Zabriskie Johnson, the daughter of a lawyer who was heavily involved in politics (albeit mostly behind the scenes), must have been thrilled for her husband's success, and it was a happy year on a personal level too. Now aged twenty-eight, she celebrated the arrival of another half-sister during the months she was expecting a second baby of her own. Her father's wife gave birth in 1855 to a daughter christened Emily but called Lulu by the family. Right before Christmas John and Mary greeted their second child, a girl. The *Daily Union's* announcement appeared December 19, 1855: "Births. In Sacramento, Dec. 17th, the wife of Hon. J. Neely Johnson, of a daughter." They named the baby Elizabeth Douglas Johnson and called her Bessie.

Mary likely would not have attended Reverend Joseph Benton's Ladies' Society's Festival held on the Thursday evening three days after her daughter's birth, a benefit held to finance the introduction of gas light into the church. That month the Sacramento Gas Works' "gasometer tank" facility on Front Street was completed and citizens were excitedly lining up to apply for service. Nor, most likely, did she appear at the lavish First Annual New Year's Ball thrown by the Knickerbocker Fire Engine

Company, promised to be "the Ball of the season" with a superior band and a supper provided by the best caterer, even though her husband's name appears among a long list of the Knickerbocker Ball's committee members.

J. Neely Johnson was inaugurated as California's fourth governor on January 9, 1856, aged thirty when he raised his hand to take the oath. He was, and still is, the youngest California governor ever to take office. The rain-swept night before the swearing-in ceremony, Governor-elect Johnson was feted at California's very first Inaugural Ball, held at Sacramento's newest jewel: the elegant, opulent Edwin Forrest Theatre. Only the night before the Forrest had featured benefit performances of *As You Like It* and *Poor Pillicoddy*. However, as the *Daily Union* gushed on January 8, 1856, the theatre was about to be transformed by the presence of bright-eyed celebrants, beautiful gowns, enlivening music and the blaze of gas lamps, into the scene of a "*fete . . . never before approached in point of brilliance in this city,*" with the ball itself the feature of the season. Written invitations went out to Sacramento's elite. Ordinary citizens could purchase Inaugural Ball tickets at two local book stores, one music store, or the city's premier Orleans Hotel. The same newspaper's story the day after reported:

> The immense stage and parquette had been . . . tastefully arranged as a dancing floor, and from the first hour . . . was festooned with chequered groups mingling in the mazes of the merry dance. The dress circle throughout the evening was crowded with an array of loveliness and manliness seldom seen congregated on similar occasions.

As the mother of a three-week-old nursing infant, Mary may or may not have been there at all. If she stood next to her husband in the formal reception line at the start of the evening, she was

Forrest Theatre

7. Edwin Forrest Theater after Conversion to a Gym.
Site of the 1856 Governor's Inaugural Ball.

Courtesy California History Room, California State Library, Sacramento

probably whisked home in a hired carriage before the sumptuous supper was served after midnight. Several tables upstairs were "laden with viands of every description," and decorated with much-admired pyramids of confectionery. She and Bessie could have been asleep when the last of the ball guests departed for home as dawn was filtering through the windows. San Francisco and Sacramento newspapers, alike, reported a "large number of ladies and gentlemen present," without mentioning specific names, male or female.

The first Inaugural Ball in California was a successful affair meant to herald a successful gubernatorial term. Yet by strange coincidence, on the very same day it reported this gala event, San Francisco's *Daily California Chronicle* of January 10, 1856, also ran a story that would have ominous consequences for the new governor. Printed on the same page as the headlined "The Inauguration Ball at Sacramento" article, was a two-and-a-half column piece titled: "The Cora Case—Testimony Continued," a play-by-play account of the murder trial, in San Francisco, of the infamous Charles Cora. Before too long Cora's sensational situation would become enmeshed in a lawless fray that would shatter the personal confidence and political viability of Governor J. Neely Johnson, and affect his family.

Just before John took office, the Johnsons and their two children moved into another house at the corner of F and Eleventh Streets (nineteenth century California governors lived in their own homes, not a state-supplied residence). On the morning of his formal inauguration held behind the closed-door chambers of the Legislature, the sound of tromping boots and gunfire suddenly erupted in the quiet residential street. Mary must have quieted her startled babies, then sped to the upstairs porch window to watch and listen to the impromptu saluting guns and parade of several military companies, including Sacramento's own Sutter Rifles, as her surprised (and amused) husband stood on their home's front steps awaiting his carriage.

Now known as the Alkali Flat neighborhood, the area then, as today, was shaded by old oaks and sycamores. The Johnsons' still-standing dwelling is a two-story, brick and masonry construction, built circa 1853–1856, most likely by California's first governor Peter Burnett, who owned the land. The architectural style is Greek Revival, a style then common in Tennessee where Burnett was born. The home's gray-white exterior features a gable roof and two front porches, fashioned of wood, both supported by stylized Doric columns. Records of the interior in 1856 have not survived; if typical of its period there was a two-story high entrance hall with a staircase to one side or at the rear leading to the second floor. Interior design preference for an entrance hall in this period was French wallpaper, printed and installed in numbered squares, rather than rolls, with mural-like scenes of ancient Greece or Rome or then-current European vistas. Glass-bowled, overhead entry-hall chandeliers and wall sconces throughout the house were lit by wax candles before gas light became available city-wide in 1856. The kitchen would have been in the rear behind the dining room, unless it was a separate building of its own attached to the main house by a roofed breezeway. Full-sized cast-iron wood-burning stoves were widely available, eliminating the need—as had been the norm for safety's sake in decades past—for a separate room where cooking and baking were done over a massive open hearth. Floor plans varied somewhat, but one important downstairs room was the formal guest parlor. Often there was a first floor library, the master bedroom, and a morning room used by the lady of the house. More bedrooms and private family sitting-rooms occupied the second floor. A privy stood in the rear yard, connected to the back porch by a worn path. When Mary lived there gardens and hedges graced the home's exterior.

California's new governor had the perfect wife for a man of his position. Mary Zabriskie Johnson was a well-bred, educated, charming woman of more than ordinary intellectual gifts who was raised from a young age to understand diplomatic protocol and the proper deportment of a lady in the presence of important men. Then as now, governor's wives had their duties, although in that era Mary's were less defined. She had no official role, no office space, and no staff. Certainly she was expected to be seen as supportive of her husband's concerns for his constituents and to be a gracious hostess in her own home for private political gatherings and informal receptions. By the time her husband became governor Mary was able to set her dining table with the finest tablecloths, silver cutlery, serving dishes, and crystal glassware being imported from all over the world through the now very important port of San Francisco. Rococo Revival furniture—mahogany or rosewood elaborately carved with flowers, fruit, leaves, and scrolls, with seats, back, and armrests upholstered in rich brocades—was very popular.

Since no diary (if she kept one) or social calendar of Mary's has survived, we cannot know her feelings and opinions, or even her exact activities. Women would not win the right to vote for decades to come—yet news editors of the period report the presence of women as interested, informed bystanders at political rallies. Women like Mary read newspapers, formed their own opinions, and were quite capable of intelligently discussing the often turbulent events in California. It would be incorrect to imagine that Mary Johnson was unaware of or unaffected by her husband's political issues and problems, or that she was not an active, behind-the-scenes sounding board for him.

Modern political wives lend their names and support to various civic and charitable organizations, and grant interviews to further their chosen causes. In Mary's day, newspaper articles seldom printed women's names in connection with these efforts, and the ladies' committees she might have chaired as a recognized social leader would have met in her own parlor. There were many benevolent causes in 1850s Sacramento; there is no reason to think that "Mrs. Governor Johnson" as she would have been formally addressed, did not meet her public obligations. Mary was a well-liked young woman who enjoyed a large circle of friends, living in a city still small enough that many men and women of both similar and disparate social and political persuasions could know her personally. Privately she was a daughter, sister, wife, and mother. Like other high-status women of her time Mary was expected to efficiently run a well-appointed household and devote time to charitable causes. Census records from 1860 show that she had a live-in domestic, a common practice in both middle and upper class households.

The first weeks of her husband's regime marked another high-excitement celebration: the official opening of the Sacramento Valley Railroad on February 22, 1856. The line was finally completed, at the then astonishing cost of $1,380,000,[3] some seven months after the first rail had been laid. The Grand Railroad Fete was advertised days ahead in the *Daily Union*, with more than sixty committee members—Governor Johnson's name listed first—promising to make the event "the most delightful ever given in California." Gentlemen were implored to inform the reception committee of the names of the ladies accompanying them, as arrangements had been made to convey said ladies from their homes to the depot. The request indicates that Mary, her then twenty-four year old sister Lizzie, and her step-mother Mrs. Colonel Zabriskie were present. Price of the tickets was ten dollars—to include carriages and railroad cars and the Grand Inauguration Ball at Folsom City.

The original plan was for the railroad to run from Sacramento through Folsom and hence north to Marysville. Financial setbacks that ultimately limited the line from Sacramento to a terminus in Folsom twenty-two miles east dampened no one's enthusiasm. It was, after all, the first commercial railroad west of the Mississippi!

As the *Union* reported three days later, about one thousand ladies and gents crowded the platforms for the first free excursion. Tables were piled high with a cold buffet, and champagne flowed. The fact that a mishap on the rails prevented the three o'clock train from leaving as scheduled didn't mar anyone's festive spirit. The *Union's* editor noted the presence of "his Excellency Governor Johnson" and several more dignitaries who were all, as the reporter groused, apparently unprepared to address the gathering until Colonel Zabriskie, who had been involved with the project for some time, responded with a few appropriate remarks after being loudly called for. At last Captain William T. Sherman (later General Sherman in the Civil War), vice president of the railroad company, delivered a short address declaring that the object of the excursion was not to make speeches but to show the people what was possible. The first train at last left the Third Street depot at 7:30 p.m., arriving in Folsom at 9:00 p.m. where a gala ball in the brightly lit Meredith Hotel began an hour later and lasted into the night. Reportedly the dance floor was alive with flying couples clad in every variety of dress from the rough canvas and calicoes of the miners and shop girls to the swallow-tailed coats and low-necked muslins of the "beaus" and "belles." Presumably present— if not at the ball, then at the depot—was Theodore Judah, a listed member of the Grand Railroad Fete Committee and the line's Chief Engineer. Like Sherman, Judah had a larger role to play in history: he was the brilliant visionary who later engineered the western half of the first transcontinental railroad.

The iron horse had usurped the old mule pack trains—one more step toward the civilization already enjoyed in the far-off Atlantic Coast. Not so civilized was the trouble escalating in the Pacific Coast City by the Bay that would, by its strange aftermath, precipitate discord in the life of Mary Zabriskie Johnson.

For years a number of San Franciscans had been distrustful and disdainful of their city officials, charging them with corruption and ineffectiveness at maintaining law and order. A Vigilance Committee dormant for five years sprang back to life as a much larger, even more defiant organization in May 1856. The catalyst of their renewed rancor was the shooting death of James King of William, editor of the *San Francisco Bulletin* and very outspoken critic of corrupt officials, by James Casey, a purportedly corrupt city politician. The resurrected Vigilance Committee members were outraged at the authorities' perceived failure to mete out swift justice to Casey as well as to the villain Charles Cora, who was still languishing in custody after drawing a hung jury in his first trial.

Cora was a tall-dark-and-handsome, dandily dressed, suave-mannered, well-known professional gambler. The woman who loved him called herself Belle Cora, although they weren't married. Belle was a beautiful, high-class madam whose business made her very wealthy. Weeks after their arrival by ship in late 1849, they were in Sacramento for some high-stakes gambling before moving on to the smaller mining towns. Together the couple enjoyed the pleasures and amusements of the burgeoning Gold Rush cities, blatantly (as the morally offended charged) showing themselves openly. In 1855 they were living in San Francisco where Belle owned a sumptuously-appointed house of prostitution known to be patronized by high-ranking gentlemen. One night the couple attended the American Theatre, where a respectable lady was offended by the presence of a silk-clad, bejeweled prostitute sitting within eyesight. The lady's husband William Richardson, who happened to be a U. S. Marshall, made clear his wife's feelings that the Coras should leave. They refused. Hot words ensued. Two days later Cora shot and killed Marshall Richardson, claiming self-defense. Belle used her illicitly-earned gold to buy her beloved the best defense lawyer to be found, and the result was a deadlocked jury. Unfortunately for Charles Cora, the murder of James King of William sealed his fate.

The Vigilance Committee rallied sympathizers to their cause, erecting a barricade around their headquarters to repel city police from removing their presence. Thousands strong and formidably armed, the vigilante mob overpowered jail guards to grab Casey and Cora. Utterly unable to cope, city officials frantically appealed to Governor Johnson for assistance, begging him to intervene with military force. J. Neely Johnson reacted quickly, going to San Francisco for an angry face-to-face confrontation with the ringleaders who declared themselves the city's rightful law enforcement. Johnson's authority was completely disregarded; James Casey and Charles Cora were hanged by the Committee on May 22, 1856. Belle begged permission to remain with her lover that day, and an hour or so before the noose slipped around Cora's neck Belle got her wedding ring. She and Charles were married in a jail-cell ceremony conducted by a Catholic priest.

Governor Johnson returned home to Sacramento, by many accounts reeling from his inability to stop the lynchings. The whole affair was scandalous and unsavory, not least from the perspective of respectable ladies. What Mary Johnson thought of Belle Cora is unknown. She might have pitied a fallen woman's personal tragedy or despised the harlot whose devotion to a gambler inadvertently contributed to a volatile situation that had such cost to her own husband. However, she must have been heartsick and filled with anxiety on John's behalf because the matter did not end there. The Vigilance Committee continued its activities by investigating other offenses and making arrests. Governor Johnson had recently appointed retired Army officer William T. Sherman, now head of a prestigious San Francisco banking house, as Major-General of the State Militia. In early June the governor summoned him to lead forces against the vigilante insurgents. Sherman was willing to take command but had no weapons for his troops. Johnson issued a proclamation declaring San Francisco to be in a state of insurrection and requested the needed arms from General Wool at the United States Arsenal in Benecia. Wool denied this request on the basis that no one except the President of the United States had the authority to requisition federal arms. Sherman resigned his appointment, and was replaced. The vigilantes remained the de facto law in San Francisco and continued to make headlines.

Mary likely read those headlines and articles with her morning coffee and might have heard angry, raised men's voices emanating from behind closed doors in her own home. She was an intelligent woman who had plenty of valid concerns. Adding to Mary's distress was the public perception as later outlined in the memoirs of United States Senator Cornelius Cole, a Sacramento lawyer during the vigilante crisis, charging that her husband was listening to men of bad judgment and that he was vacillating and incompetent. Other prominent men, William T. Sherman among them, felt J. Neely Johnson was a young man of high personal character and pure principles who was deserted by old friends when the storm burst, and left to rely on men who were considered extremists. Johnson's supporters opined that the debacle wasn't his fault, citing the same failure of his predecessor Governor John McDougal five years earlier, also attributed to enforcement problems, to quell a disturbance fomented by the first San Francisco Vigilance Committee uprising. (Sacramento, too, had a locally organized Vigilance Committee while McDougal was governor. Lacking the cohesion and authority of its Bay Area brethren, it soon fell from favor.)

Negotiations between legal authorities and the revitalized San Francisco Vigilance Committee continued throughout the summer of 1856. These efforts would backfire in unforeseen ways and have a devastating effect on the Johnson-Zabriskie families.

One mediator Governor Johnson dispatched in June to reason with the Committee ringleaders was fiery-tempered Judge David S. Terry, a sitting Justice on the California Supreme Court. By 1856 the very early gold miners' personal codes of honor and peaceable attitudes carried from their eastern homes had disintegrated. Now the prevalent mentality was one where might was right, where certain self-righteous, self-important men had no qualms at delivering bare-knuckled violence. Such men thought the rules didn't actually apply to them, and Judge Terry was a man imbued with that hubris. He was, among other things, an outspoken agitator for the extension of slavery into California, flagrantly disregarding the fact that California was admitted to the Union as a free state. On June 21, 1856, Judge Terry's "law-and-order" contingent was in a meeting in San Francisco when Sterling Hopkins of the Vigilance Committee Police came to arrest one of their members. The details are somewhat convoluted; the upshot is that Judge Terry stabbed Sterling Hopkins in the neck with a Bowie knife. Within an hour four thousand armed Vigilance Committee members swarmed the streets; within three hours a mob took Judge Terry prisoner. Another potentially explosive situation threatened. Hopkins had not yet died of his wound (he eventually recovered) but it was certain that Judge Terry, an acknowledged advisor to the young governor, would be hanged if he did.

Faced with this latest disaster-in-the-making Governor J. Neely Johnson turned to one man he knew he could trust, a man eminently qualified because of his solid character, extensive legal knowledge and experience, his connections and influence, and his reputation as a man of reason and oratorical skills. Governor Johnson recruited his own father-in-law, Colonel James C. Zabriskie, and another Sacramento lawyer named James Allen.

The two governor's agents sped to San Francisco on July 2, 1856, to meet with the Committee and secure Judge Terry's release under certain conditions. The Committee was to surrender to state authorities the arms they stole from the Naval Armory and disband. Judge Terry would be tried in a public court of law and would resign the bench if found guilty. In exchange, Governor Johnson would instruct San Francisco authorities not to prosecute anyone who had acted for or on behalf of the Vigilance Committee. Or at least, these were the authorized instructions both Zabriskie and Allen agreed they had received from Governor Johnson. Fifteen days later, an angry and frustrated James Zabriskie provided a San Francisco newspaper with each and every news article and personal letter thus far published or exchanged along with Allen's corroborating statement. Zabriskie said he felt compelled "by a sacred regard to truth, justice and my reputation, which is all I have to bequeath my children" to explain the facts. He thus effectively made the press his jury, in keeping with his son-in-law's indirect communication through the *Marysville Express,* which denied that Governor J. Neely Johnson had granted any such official authority. Titled "To the People of California" Colonel Zabriskie's side of the story was published in the *Daily Alta* July 17, 1856.

The story was long and contentious. James claimed that Johnson had fled to Marysville to avoid a face-to-face meeting upon James' return from San Francisco with news of a hoped-for favorable outcome in the negotiations. The governor, who remained in Marysville, sent a personal letter "respectfully" asking his agents to publicly repudiate, via the Sacramento press, their claims of having been given executive powers. Exactly what his objections were isn't clear from the transcripts. Mid-month Zabriskie and Allen demanded a stop to the circulation of dirty innuendoes against them which they felt were sanctioned by the governor himself. Neither side mentioned whether Mary and the children were with John in Marysville. The *Alta* piece included James' disclaimer: "Under circumstances involving questions of ordinary interest I would have remained silent; content to suffer a wrong myself, rather than inflict a wound upon the reputation of Governor Johnson, which must necessarily reach a portion of my own family."

No further explanation was necessary. Everyone knew Colonel Zabriskie's eldest daughter Mary was the governor's wife.

Mary's feelings and reactions over this very public row between her father and her husband aren't known, but the strain and unhappiness she and the rest of her family assuredly felt can be imagined. Enmity between the two men may have bitterly continued, or else John's successful court action against his wife's father a year later was merely a matter of form. The 1857 lawsuit was for damages of $737 plus interest accumulated from 1853, and might have arisen from an earlier, rather complicated transaction of commercial real estate transferred from Colonel James and Dr. Christian Zabriskie to J. Neely Johnson.

The Vigilance Committee gradually dispersed in August, a week or so after they released Judge David Terry, who was never tried and didn't resign. In early November 1856, Governor Johnson revoked his proclamation of insurrection.

Family life went on. Later that same month they celebrated the marriage, in Sacramento, of Mary's sister Lizzie to Richard Sinton of San Francisco. The Reverend Joseph Benton again performed the wedding service as he had done five years before for Mary and John.

In the second year of J. Neely Johnson's administration, an advertisement in the January 12, 1857 *Sacramento Daily Union* affords a brief insight into Mary's activities. The large ad touted The Union Academy for the Education of Young Ladies, to open the following Monday at J and Nineteenth Streets, in a building surrounded by a large garden where pupils "might take healthful exercise." The Academy's curriculum offered courses in bookkeeping, mathematics, foreign languages, the natural sciences, drawing or embroidery, and music. Three references were listed at the bottom, all socially prominent women identified by their husband's names. The last was "Mrs. Johnson, wife of Gov. Johnson."

Mary's daughter Bessie was just over a year old then, too young to attend school at all. Mary may have been looking at her daughter's future schooling, or perhaps her support was more of an official First Lady endorsement of educational betterment for Sacramento's girls. Either way it seems likely she met with the school's founders, possibly several times, and granted permission to use her name in print. Eleven months later, Mary could have been among the numerous ladies and gentlemen reported present as spectators for the annual scholarly examinations at her half-sister Annie Zabriskie's grammar school. Annie won an award for arithmetic.

Bad news received in late 1857 bowed family heads in sorrow. Mary's youngest brother Alexander had removed to Honolulu some months earlier in hopes of restoring his poor health. He died there October 28, 1857 aged twenty-three, of pulmonary consumption, known today as tuberculosis. A notice in the *Daily Union* dated November 28 advised readers that his remains had arrived from Hawaii by ship and the funeral would take place the next day from the home of Colonel James Zabriskie on The Ridge. Alex Zabriskie is buried in the Sacramento City Cemetery.

During his term, J. Neely Johnson cut government expenditures to reduce a growing state debt, in the process slashing his own annual salary from $10,000 to $6,000.[4] This salary reduction might explain the Johnson's move, in his second year of office, from the house on F Street known today as the J. Neely Johnson House, to a dwelling on N between Sixth and Seventh Streets. Another major accomplishment of Governor Johnson was his approval of funds for the future State Capitol building in Sacramento. Nevertheless the Vigilance Committee strife soured his political influence and he lost his party's nomination for governor in the 1857 general election. In December 1857, the beautiful Forrest Theatre, the site of Governor-elect Johnson's gala Inaugural Ball, was sold to a party who transformed the building into the Sacramento Gymnasium. His two-year term ended in January 1858; however, Mary's tenure as a politician's wife was not over.

John soon became politically active in the newly-created Nevada Territory, where his efforts contributed to Nevada's admission as a state in 1864. He first went to Carson City around 1860 to administer the fantastic Bowers Silver Mine, although Mary and the children may not have moved at the same time. From 1860 to 1862, the Johnsons were reported as living with her family, perhaps preparatory to their permanent relocation. Both the Johnson and Zabriskie families appear on the 1860 Sacramento Census record residing near each other.

In 1867, when Mary's children were teenagers, J. Neely Johnson was appointed to fill a vacancy in the Nevada Supreme Court; afterwards he was elected to the post for a full term. The family lived in Carson City. Although undocumented, Mary almost certainly traveled to California in May 1870 to be with her parents after the sudden death of her forty-nine year old brother William Mann Zabriskie, for years a highly esteemed, well-liked San Francisco attorney. When John's term on the Nevada high court expired in 1871 he resumed his law practice, but by then his health was declining. It's not clear whether the family moved to Salt Lake City or if John went there alone for business or other reasons. He died of sunstroke (alternatively known as heatstroke) in Salt Lake City on August 31, 1872, at the age of forty-seven. His obituary does not list the names or residence location of his surviving family, merely that he left a wife, a son aged twenty, and a daughter aged seventeen. Son Willie is not listed with his family in the 1870 Federal Census in Nevada (the year he was eighteen), and may have been away at school.

Mary Brevoort Zabriskie Johnson married again. Her second

husband was Colonel Sylvester H. (Harry) Day, Assistant Adjutant General of the Nevada National Guard and Carson City's first Postmaster.

Eleven years after Mary buried her first husband, she and her surviving siblings gathered at the bedside of their dying father at his home in San Francisco. Colonel James C. Zabriskie died July 10, 1883, leaving his widow, four daughters, several grandchildren and one remaining son—Mary's youngest brother James Albert Zabriskie, then United States Attorney for Arizona. Several months before his death, the *San Francisco Post* published a short biographical sketch of the Colonel mentioning that the New Jersey Zabriskies were reputed to be descended from deposed Polish kings. The article opined that the entire family was remarkable for their talents, learning, industry, elegance of manner, and physical attractiveness.

Four short years after her father's demise, Mary succumbed to heart disease on November 23, 1887 in Carson City, her residence of nearly twenty-seven years. Her obituary in Nevada's *Morning Appeal* headlined "Death of Mrs. Harry Day" recognizes her daughter Mrs. Guy Thorpe (Bessie) and a married niece. There is no mention of Mary's siblings or her granddaughter, Bessie's six-year-old daughter Marie. Mary's obituary is also oddly silent as to her son William Johnson, who would have been about thirty-five if he were still alive in the year of his mother's death. William Mann Neely Johnson's last known whereabouts comes from the 1880 Census. Twenty-eight at the time, he was unmarried and apparently living alone in Virginia City, Nevada, where he worked as a postal clerk.

The *Morning Appeal* obituary goes on say that Mary's death would cause sincere regret among her large circle of acquaintances, complimenting her as a woman of "high breeding and more than ordinary intellectual gifts." Her death announcement appeared in the *Daily Alta California*, headlined

"Death of a Well-known Lady," copied by the *Sacramento Union*. It is only here—in these obituaries—that Mary's charm, vivacity, beauty, intelligence, and role as a social leader were praised in print.

Mary Brevoort Zabriskie Johnson was the first California governor's wife to live in Sacramento the entire time of her husband's gubernatorial term. Her gift was the measure of refinement she brought to a male-dominated, rough-edged city that needed women's gentling influences.

End Notes, Mary Zabriskie Johnson

[1]Colonel Zabriskie paid $500 apiece for two lots southeast of town in a largely undeveloped area, when most of the population preferred to reside west of Twelfth Street. His exact address was not shown in city directories, only the designation "Oak Ridge," and later as a tongue-in-cheek "Poverty Hill." Current assessed values between U and V, Twenty-first and Twenty-second Streets, for land only, range between $135,000 and $376,000 per parcel.

[2]Using the gold ratio formula, $2,000 x 50 = $100,000. According to a recently published City of Sacramento salary schedule, Sacramento's City Attorney's salary is currently budgeted between $157,800 and $236,600 annually.

[3]Current rail road construction costs are impossible to pinpoint without a detailed engineering study, but officials at the California State Railroad Museum estimate between $1 million and $2 million *per mile* to build the Sacramento Valley Rail Road today.

[4]From $500,000 to $300,000. Twenty-first century California governors, whose compensation is presently determined by the California Citizens Compensation Commission on an annual basis, receive far less. In 2010 the governor's salary was $173,987, reduced 18 per cent from $212,179 in 2009.

Housewife and Church Founder: Margaret Frink

Margaret Frink's diary, written in 1850 as she and her husband journeyed from Indiana to California in their covered wagon, is one of the most articulate, informative, delightful accounts of American history to survive the intervening decades. The personalities of the pair are discernable on every page. Margaret was clearly a warm, self-confident, capable, observant, down-to-earth woman with an irrepressible sparkle. Her husband Ledyard (always referred to in the diary as "Mr. Frink") surfaces as a personable, compassionate, highly competent man of integrity, with natural leadership skills.

They were educated: he in his native state of New York and she at her family's home in Virginia. No misspellings or grammatical lapses are found here, unlike in other trail diaries. As was typical of pioneer women who were too busy to continue their observations once they settled, Margaret's daily jottings dwindled to condensed highlights within a year after their arrival in Sacramento.

They weren't people who had to "start over" anywhere. In her early entries Margaret unabashedly admits, with an unmistakable thrill of excitement infusing her words, that their purpose in moving to California was to find gold. They had lived in Martinsville, Indiana, for six years, where they had, she says, a very pleasant home. Her husband, in partnership with Margaret's younger brother Azariah Alsip (who usually identified himself as just A. B. Alsip), was a successful merchant. The Frinks were financially secure. Yet the childless couple was restless, Margaret explains, and

8. Mrs. Margaret A. Frink.

Courtesy California History Room, California State Library, Sacramento

the exciting reports coming back from the Far West gold fields filled them with the same fervor it had likewise instilled in thousands before them.

Still, the Frinks were not a couple to whom things just happened. They planned together for the outcome they wanted, and they systematically prepared for the journey. Ledyard ordered the construction of a good, light weight covered wagon with built-in storage compartments in the floor. Family wagons headed west were regular farm wagons, often customized as the Frinks did, not the heavy Conestoga conveyances such as the ones used to haul freight between St. Louis and Santa Fe and drawn by twelve yoke of oxen. Like most emigrants they affixed a surprisingly accurate cog-driven odometer to their wagon wheel, carried a compass, and took hand-held instruments to roughly determine latitude and longitude in unfamiliar territory.

Margaret hired a seamstress to stitch suitable clothing. Garments for her would include a face-protecting sunbonnet, muslin aprons, and wool-fabric dresses (cottons and linens were not recommended because they didn't protect against the sun) with the hems raised several inches above the norm for easier maneuvering. Lead shot was sewn into the hems to keep the full skirts from lifting in the prairie winds. Clothing for Ledyard consisted of flannel shirts, thick pants reinforced where they came in contact with a saddle, stout, knee-high boots large enough at the top to tuck the pant legs inside, and a broad-brimmed hat. In addition to the clothes, pioneers were advised to pack bar soap for laundering, large needles, buttons, good linen thread, a paper of pins, and a thimble.

One important item the Frinks shrewdly planned for was their future house in the West, although there is no indication they decided where they wanted to live before setting out for California's mining towns. Like everyone else, they knew about

9. Ledyard Frink.

Courtesy California History Room, California State Library, Sacramento

John Sutter's Sacramento Valley fortress as a safe bastion where they could gather more information. Learning (or believing) that the price of lumber in California was an exorbitant $400 per thousand feet compared to three dollars per thousand feet in Indiana, they decided to have a pre-cut cottage shipped ahead. Lumber of all necessary sizes was measured, cut, and fashioned ready to assemble. Ledyard arranged for these materials to be floated on a raft down the White River to the Wabash, the Ohio, and the Mississippi Rivers to New Orleans. From there the stack was shipped around Cape Horn to Sacramento.

Margaret and Ledyard were married eleven years and had no children of their own, but they were providing a home for an orphan named Robert Parker, and after four years of this arrangement all three were mutually attached. The Frinks secured consent from the eleven-year-old boy's legal guardian to take him along. When their preparations were complete, they tied a small sheet-iron cooking stove to the hind end of their wagon and were ready to depart. The plan was that Margaret's brother A. P. Alsip and his family would remain behind in Martinsville to close the mercantile business before emigrating themselves, and so the couple and their ward bade farewell to friends and family on March 30, 1850. At almost the last minute Aaron Rose, a young clerk in the store, decided to accompany them. This little group of four planned to travel much of the way alone—as Margaret put it—meaning they weren't part of an organized company. Only fools embarked on a journey of that magnitude over poorly mapped territory *alone*. For their own safety, the Frinks joined larger groups as they came upon them, and were never far from sight of the great canvas-topped wagon trains caravanning over the prairies.

Margaret was thirty-three and her husband thirty-nine when they set out from Indiana in the spring of 1850. They were several years older, possibly wiser, and perhaps more aware of—or financially better able to provide for—preventable pitfalls experienced by many Argonauts (another name for gold-seeker, taken from the Greek fable of Jason's search for the Golden Fleece). Although they had some unpleasant experiences on the trail, their foresight and good common sense allowed them to avert disasters that befell many others. Ledyard refused to drive his draft animals too hard or too fast, knowing it would result in the deterioration or death of creatures they depended on for transport. Fresh fruits and vegetables were scarce at best during the multi-month trek. Because foodstuffs that were nonperishable or cheaper to purchase didn't contain ascorbic acid, thousands of overland emigrants succumbed to the spongy gums and debilitating limb weakness of scurvy. To prevent this, the Frinks wisely packed crocks of sour pickles and casks of vinegar. These cautions and other measures they practiced allowed their party, wagons, personal possessions, and animals to arrive in California basically whole and healthy.

At around noon on September 7, 1850, they came to Sutter's Fort, two miles east of Sacramento City proper. Margaret was riding sidesaddle on her horse, as she had done for most of the 2,418 miles their odometer told them they had traveled from Indiana. There wasn't much left to see of this famous, once self-sustaining bastion in the wilderness whose genial, helpful host had since removed to his farm on the Feather River. The outbuildings were gone, razed for their lumber. Vandals, thieves, and squatters had stolen, ransacked, or stripped Captain Sutter's livestock, corrals, tack, tools, fruit orchards, and loose adobe bricks. They had trampled his wheat fields and vegetable gardens. The adobe walls of the main building were beginning to crumble although the fort was owned by someone new and was semi-occupied.

The Frink party rode on three or four miles southwest, skirting the town, through scattered groves of trees. Thousands of acres still contained undisturbed wild grapes and other natural vegetation where coyotes, rabbits, and quails occupied the undergrowth. South of the business district they passed a fair amount of outlying tents, shacks, and lean-to shelters. The little band of travelers reached Sutterville, the settlement John Sutter himself proudly laid out before the gold discovery. Margaret, Ledyard, and young Robert set up camp. Aaron Rose, the clerk from Ledyard's Martinsville mercantile, said goodbye and set off for the gold mines on the Yuba River with a friend they met on the trail, buoyantly optimistic that he would soon strike it rich.

The Frinks, who had withstood freezing storms, crossed blazing deserts, forded swift-moving icy rivers, endured blinding dust clouds, suffered fatigue and hunger—all for an admitted, consuming gold fever—wished him well and stayed put.

Instead of rushing off to the rough-and-tumble hinterlands of the gold fields, they looked for familiar signposts of civilization. On the following Saturday, September 14, the couple forayed into Sacramento City to inquire about the Baptist Church. They were directed to the home of Judge E. J. Willis, known to be entertaining the visiting Reverend Osgood C. Wheeler, who came to California from New York in 1849 to organize the faithful and had already established Baptist churches in San Francisco and San Jose.

The Frinks met that day with Judge Willis, Reverend Osgood, and Reverend John W. Capen, who would become their first pastor. There was as yet no church, just the intent to form a congregation. Then and there, Margaret gave the clergymen the customary, formal letter declaring her baptism and prior church membership. Margaret Ann Frink appears on the record, along with four other women and eleven men, as a founding member of Sacramento's First Baptist Church. The next day, Sunday, the Frinks attended worship services led by Reverend Osgood at a privately owned building on J Street instead of the church's make-do meeting place in the Court Room, where the courts themselves were in temporary, rented quarters.

Listed under Churches in the 1851 Sacramento City Directory is: "First Baptist Church, Rev. John W. Capen, Pastor, meeting at the Court House, corner of 5th and I Streets; worship every Sunday 10 ½ AM and 3 o'clock PM." On that first Sunday, at least, Margaret attended both sessions, but not the special evening service held that night. Several months later the Baptists formed regular Friday night gatherings as well. Margaret remained active in the First Baptist Church all her time in Sacramento, her home for seventeen years. A Ladies Social Circle soon developed, and although Baptist ladies' names were never mentioned in the church's newspaper announcements, it is almost certain Margaret cooked or served at the several Social Circle-sponsored fund-raising events or charitable public suppers over the years.

A scant two weeks after their arrival, Margaret and Ledyard sold their wagons and draft animals, likely at the busy Horse Market on Sixth and K, and moved into town. They rented an unfurnished, poorly-constructed, former retail store on K Street, stuck a sign over the door lettered with "Frink's Hotel," and declared themselves in business. Margaret's kitchen was a tin stove in a tent erected behind the ramshackle building.

Town was a rowdy place, doubtless quite intriguing to observant, inquisitive Margaret. Arriving as they had in late 1850, the Frinks missed the 1849-1850 winter floods. Now in September the scorching summer sun baked the knee-deep mud holes into eddies of swirling dust wherever boots or hooves trod the streets, which was all day and most of the nights. With temperatures soaring above ninety degrees, Margaret's high-necked, long-sleeved day-dresses, worn over multiple petticoats, afforded little opportunity for river breezes to cool her skin. Music blared from saloons, untended cattle sometimes poked their heads through open windows, and gold dust was often left carelessly on counter tops.

Stages, freight wagons, and pack-laden mule trains constantly clattered noisily in and out of town.

With no shortage of customers, Margaret and Ledyard did well from the beginning. Neither they nor their hotel business were listed in the 1851 Sacramento City Directory (issued with information gathered in late 1850), although they were there and operating in time for the publication deadline. The 1850 Census, dated October 21, lists Ledyard's occupation as "boarding house." The report also lists Margaret, Robert, and the names of their boarders, two single men and a married couple. From Margaret's diary notes it appears that theirs was a public boarding house, open to all coming-and-going miners and other sojourners, as opposed to so-called private boarding houses, which generally rented to bachelors with steady city jobs.

The Frinks' new success, as well as the town's, was about to suffer a downturn. The day before the census taker called, an unidentified immigrant was found on the levee, dying of cholera or, as people then called it, The Pestilence. The dying immigrant, at least in the public eye, marked the beginning of a virulent epidemic in which, Margaret's diary reports, one thousand people died. Her claim is probably close, but an exact count was never tallied; people were dying too fast and the community was too highly charged with confusion and fear. The population was about 7,000 citizens, with an estimated additional 3,000 passing through on their way to and from the gold mines or other points in California, camped out in tents and lean-tos or bunked at the many hotels and boarding houses in gold-boom Sacramento.

Many of the dead couldn't even be identified. Margaret herself gives one chilling example of a young stranger who boarded with them one evening, asked for a doctor in the morning, and was dead by midnight. Panic spread until an estimated eighty percent of the population fled. The epidemic lasted about twenty days, during which time future governor John Bigler valiantly administered to the sick and destitute himself, holding a lump of gum camphor to his nose. He was lucky—for the camphor's only value was in blocking odors. When it was over, seventeen devoted doctors were buried along with their patients.

The Frinks didn't leave the city during the epidemic. They sickened, but survived. It is not clear that they contracted cholera or some other prevalent, similar-symptom malady like dysentery. It was *possible* to survive cholera, but not probable. Along with their hopes of finding a fortune many ill-fed, exhausted immigrants brought diseases acquired overland or in crowded ships, adding to the contamination of the city's air and water. Unless the issue was an emergency, settlers and miners self-medicated with known, tried and true, home-spun remedies. Cayenne pepper induced sweat to relieve joint stiffness and pains; dandelion root teas acted as natural diuretics and laxatives; dandelion juice dabbed on the skin of feet and fingers healed blisters. Charcoal powders and peppermint stopped dysentery. Mustard plasters were applied for respiratory complaints. The easily purchased, quite legal laudanum (tincture of opiate) was swallowed for everything painful from toothache to broken bones, and as a treatment for cholera.

After they recovered the Frinks moved their hotel business to another rented house on J Street between Sixth and Seventh. A month later Ledyard bought three milk cows. Many townspeople kept livestock on their residential property, and the Frink's bovines likely lived behind the boarding house or were pastured on surrounding vacant lots. Little is known of Ledyard Frink's growing-up years or his father's occupation, except that he was born and raised in Genesee, New York, a rich agricultural region of vegetable and wheat crops and dairy farms. Perhaps this is where the successful Indiana merchant developed the animal husbandry skills he displayed both on the overland trails and afterward in Sacramento. Margaret served the milk from these first three cows free to their boarders, and this proved to be such an attraction that they bought more milk cows until they owned thirteen. For a few more months the Frinks continued to operate their J Street hotel, selling the excess milk in the city for a handsome profit. Their success at this new enterprise showed them that full-scale dairying was an attractive opportunity they needed more space for, because the city's urban character was upgrading.

Plans were already afoot before the Frinks settled on J Street to plank it from the levee out to Ninth Street. This proposed public improvement to combat winter's mud-pocked roads—estimated cost $57,612—was widely supported by the *Sacramento Transcript*.[1] "It seems to us," one editorial opined, "that the businessmen on J Street will have no hesitation in paying the expense for constructing so important a work." The Frinks were certainly J Street businessmen, though not land owners, and yet Margaret's journal says nothing of the necessarily raised rents to tenants as the street planking progressed along J to other major downtown streets. In addition, proposed levee enhancement remained a hot issue. An earnest editorial in the November 16, 1850 *Sacramento Transcript*, the very day it announced the end of the cholera epidemic, exhorted taxpayers to raise $10,000[2] to pay the levee contractors the sum owed them by contract or else let the work stop just as the rainy season was about to start. The Frinks must have wondered what sort of expensively calamitous area this was in which they had settled. The levee work was finished but followed by a winter too mild to test its strength.

The couple was still living on J Street In February 1851, when the *Sacramento Transcript* noted the Baptist Society's growth to a "quite respectable number of members." The paper publicized the congregation's efforts to raise money for a building of its own, praising County Judge E. J. Willis as the "very gentlemen to take the lead in this matter." Judge Willis was so successful at collecting members' subscriptions that a week later, the *Transcript* reported that a 28- by 40-foot wooden church building, to be topped with a twenty-four-foot-high spire, was already under construction at the northeast corner of Seventh and L Streets. More commendation followed the day before its dedication on March 9 when the finishing touches were viewed by the press: the handsome wallpaper representing columns with finished cornices and caps, and the magnificent six hundred pound bell enclosed within the spire. According to one source dated many years after the event, the cost of construction was $4,000.[3] The timelier estimate, published in the March 3, 1851, *Sacramento Transcript,* pegged the cost as "slightly higher" than $2,500, also remarking that Judge Willis had raised slightly *less* than that amount. One of the church's first public functions was a temperance meeting on March 24, 1851. A month later, founding clergyman Reverend Capen left for another church in the territory of Nevada and was replaced by Reverend Benjamin Brierly from San Jose, whose first sermon was entitled "The Duties of a Good Citizen." As a wife and helpmate, Margaret's duties revolved around domestic concerns.

Between cooking and baking and serving, house cleaning, laundering clothing and bedding on corrugated metal washboards, and hefting coal-heated flatirons over sheets for her family and the Frinks Hotel's paying guests, Margaret had precious little free time. Like most, if not all Sacramento and San Francisco residents, Margaret must have wielded broom and rake in a near daily battle against the rats that sneaked aboard ships in East Coast America and foreign ports to prodigiously multiply on the seas and spill into Far West towns. "Nothing more or less than the death of all rats in Sacramento City," was the rally cry of the *Sacramento Daily Union* in mid-April 1851, proclaiming that every mercantile firm in the city had signed a declaration of warfare against the odious rodents. Successful extermination came only after better buildings provided more secure grain storage, and more systematic efforts kept rubbish heaps cleared. If Margaret had domestic help, they were day-servants, not live-ins; no servants appear on their census entries. Eureka Flour Mills, situated at the junction of the Sacramento and American Rivers, supplied the trade with the freshly ground flour, corn meal, and barley Margaret needed in her hotel kitchen. Five more mills opened the following year. Local gardeners offered watermelons, lettuce, beets, and other produce in season. A farmer named Armistead Runyon realized $9,000 (approximately $450,000 today) in one year from just six acres of vegetables.

Just before the church building was dedicated, the Frink's pre-cut house—always afterward referred to by the family as the "White River Cottage" for its beginning transport point in Indiana—finally reached Sacramento from around Cape Horn. There was a delay of several months, though, between the house's arrival and its erection, which could have been due to ordinary business distractions or the prevailing confusion surrounding available property. Sacramento land titles were in appalling disarray. Foreclosures against landowners who could no longer afford their high mortgages or property taxes sent real estate values plummeting, which meant losses for some and opportunity for others. With cash in hand, the Frinks turned the situation to their advantage. Over the next two years they purchased no less than twelve lots, tracts, or parcels in and around town, paying absurdly low prices even by the standards of the time. Several, including their dairy, were acquired by payment of delinquent taxes. Margaret's name is absent all of the deeds conveying ownership to Ledyard Frink, despite the fact that California's Constitution gave women the right to own property.

Margaret's diary states that they purchased an established dairy for $2,250. There is no record of a Frink land deed for that price. The amount paid was just for livestock, equipment, supplies, and tools. Records at the Sacramento County Recorder's Office do confirm that in August 1851, the Frinks acquired portions of downtown business-area parcels, plus two large lots bordered by X and Y, Eighth and Ninth Streets at a duly posted Sheriff's sale for delinquent real estate taxes—all of it for $89 dollars.[4] The land at X and Y became their new dairy lands. In October they purchased two lots between M and N, and Seventh and Eighth Streets, each measuring 80- by 160-feet, from a private seller, for just $175.[5] This is where they put up the pre-cut cottage. Title to this parcel must not have been entirely clear, because five months later another deed records purchase of the same property, from yet a different private party, for an additional $250. The Frinks' real estate experience was shared by others, who were understandably outraged to discover that unscrupulous parties had sometimes sold the same lots two or three times to different buyers during the heyday of land speculation.

The White River cottage was assembled within a week of the October 1851 land purchase. Its weatherboarding lumber was of yellow Indiana poplar. The joists, sills, studding rafters, and flooring were fashioned from long-lasting ash. Finish work for the exterior and interiors could be hired from local tradesmen; there was at least one of each expert at lathe-and-plastering, house painting, cabinet making, paper-hanging, and window-installing. The city directory and the *Sacramento Union* carried ads from dealers in stoves and hardware, plus merchants happy to provide made-to-order mattresses and pillows. Dishes, glassware, other household accouterments, and "fancy goods" were available at various stores. They planted a Mission fig on the south side of their M Street residence, a picturesque tree that would grow and spread, provide fruit and shade, and eventually outlive them.

In the midst of those real estate transactions that hot, dusty summer and fall, they sold their boarding house business, relieving Margaret of the myriad daily maintenance chores for paying guests. In her spare hours she loved to ride her pony, sitting on the same sidesaddle she used to cross three-quarters of a continent. She rode out to their dairy and made occasional inspections about the ruins of Captain John Sutter's once-vital New Helvetia fortress. Their former Indiana store clerk and plains-crossing companion Aaron Rose returned from the gold mines, having achieved moderate success but certainly not the exorbitant riches of every miner's dreams. In this he was typical of thousands of others, a fact that hardly mitigated his probable feelings of disappointment. What advice and consolation the Frinks offered him isn't known, but they did hire him to sell their milk. Within two years Aaron Rose succumbed to homesickness and returned to Indiana with his $3,000 gold pile.[6]

Meanwhile Robert Parker was of an age to be attending school several hours a day, but educational opportunities were limited when the Frinks arrived in Sacramento, and nothing is known of Robert's early schooling. In 1851 Reverend James Rogers operated a private school in rooms provided by the Methodist Church, and two more private academies appeared in 1852 and 1853. In 1852 local bookstores offered texts in grammar, arithmetic, geography, and history for those pupils, and parents who were willing and able to instruct their children at home. The first tax-funded public school didn't open until February, 1854, when Robert was fifteen.

In early 1852 they acquired an adjoining tract to the X and Y properties, this one bordered by W and X and Tenth and Eleventh Streets—a second dairy, or expansion of their original one. The deed includes the transfer of ownership of various "appurtenances." This transaction must be what Margaret referred to when she said they bought a second dairy that, combined with the first, gave them a total of twenty-five cows, two horses, a wagon, chickens, turkeys, milk cans, and other implements. Their dairy business flourished. In a town filled with doctors, lawyers, general and specialty merchants, livery stables, saddle and harness makers, wagon makers, milliners, brewers, blacksmiths, flour mills, apothecaries, hotels, restaurants, saloons, butchers, tinsmiths, jewelers, booksellers, and at least one clothes cleaner, theirs appears to be the only local dairy that furnished the city with milk, butter, and cheese.

That spring two members of Margaret's family migrated west to join them, her mother Mary Du Beau Alsip Thompson and her eighteen-year-old sister Laura C. Alsip, who traveled together by steamer from New York via Nicaragua. The travel itinerary may have caused Margaret some moments of anxiety. The rush to the gold fields was still strong; in their headlong push for speed, the steamers' wood-fueled boilers were known to sometimes explode. These accidents became so common the newspapers didn't detail the particulars of all of them; however, two major disasters were known about by most. The previous year the *Fawn* had burst her boilers just four miles north of Sacramento, killing two and injuring several others, and before the *Fawn* disaster, the *Sagamore's* explosion at the San Francisco wharf killed outright or severely injured up to one hundred passengers. At the time Margaret's mother and sister were aboard ship, the *Pearl*'s explosion on the Sacramento River was still three years in the future.

To the family's relief, the female relatives crossed the ocean safely. It is not clear if this was the same year, or two years later, that Margaret's brother finally closed the Martinsville, Indiana, mercantile store and headed overland to Sacramento with his wife and eight-year-old son Edwin K. Alsip, driving a fine herd of American cattle. Azariah Alsip persevered to Sacramento with most of the livestock, and Ledyard resumed his partnership with his brother-in-law, this time in the cattle and dairy business.

In the space of about two years Margaret and Ledyard had transformed themselves from successful eastern merchants to real estate investors and successful western farmers. With this new focus, they surely attended the Great Agricultural Fair organized by Boston-born horticulturist James L.L.F. Warren in September 1852, at his New England Seed Store on J Street. Earlier that year, in February, Warren had introduced the camellia to Sacramento—as live plants he imported from Japan—the start of Sacramento's eventual designation as Camellia Capital of the World. His establishment was a frame building with the lettering "Agricultural Hall" prominent across the face of its second story, trading in fruit trees, seeds, agricultural implements, and general provisions. Warren's Great Agricultural Fair offered trophy cups and medals as awards for outstanding entries from farms and nurseries, plus mineral displays and lectures on various subjects. The event was such a success that he sponsored a larger show in San Francisco the following year. Recognizing the growth and importance of California's agriculture, the state legislature created the State Agricultural Society in May 1854, which organized the first Agricultural and Horticultural Fair in San Francisco that October. This agency and its successors sponsored the annual exhibition, which in time became the California State Fair and Exposition, held in various cities until it returned to Sacramento in 1859, where it was housed in a specially built, magnificent pavilion.

The second annual Agricultural and Horticultural Fair in September 1855 took place in Sacramento. According to the *California Farmer and Journal of Useful Sciences* newspaper, Ledyard was a judge in the Dairy Category. Throngs of people attended. With the exhibition in her own town and her husband an active participant, it is safe to assume Margaret went to the Fair, too, where there were displays of silverware, pottery, tin-work, hats and capes, floral designs, embroidery, and water-color paintings in addition to livestock and farm implements. Information supplied by their family asserts that Margaret and Ledyard were frequent State Fair prize winners for their cheese and butter. This could only be confirmed for the year 1863, when the *Transactions of the California State Agricultural Society* cited their dairy as being awarded a commemorative book for second best butter, and spoons worth $10 ($500 today) for best cheese. It is not known if Margaret had a personal hand in the manufacture of these products, but she did find satisfaction in other, more social pursuits.

Her Ladies Social Circle put on a public dinner in the District Court Room to raise funds for the enlargement of the Baptists' wooden church on July 3, 1852. The *Union* approvingly reported that "the ladies vied with each other to render their guests comfortable," and that the music, speeches and toasts were kept up to a late hour. Reverend Osgood C. Wheeler returned to Sacramento as pastor of the First Baptist Church in time to deliver an appropriate sermon on the completion of the church's new addition at the end of the month. In August his sermon on duelling drew a crowd too large for the building, new addition notwithstanding.

The population was indeed growing and more were expected, raising fears of new health issues. The City Council approved an Ordinance for the Prevention of Disease in September, decreeing that no stagnant water or garbage was allowed on city lots. Further, citizens were mandated to fill their privys with lime "in sufficient quantities" to prevent unwholesome stench. Business activity expanded. More livery stables, stage lines, flour mills, and grocers made their appearance. Wells Fargo, a New York firm, opened a Sacramento branch office for its express services. A fish market opened on Front Street, entrepreneurs began importing ice to a grateful populace, and a new hat and cap factory supplied men's headgear. Jacob Knauth laid out the afterwards famous Sutter Floral Gardens at J and Twenty-ninth Streets, and started Sacramento's first pottery with a kiln capable of turning out 3,000 flower pots at one burning. An enterprising farmer started a small pickle factory, thereby offering an alternative to homemade goods to housewives like Margaret. Two photographers opened

Sacramento's first daguerreotype studio and gallery on Front Street, entreating ladies and gentlemen to sit for their "faces divine" using the latest and best improvements in the art. News editors waxed rhapsodic at the lately-completed brick hotel and substantial brick stores replacing the old shanties of 1849 in the business district. These, they opined, were ornaments to the street as well as being "perfectly secure against fire."

They were mistaken.

Bells began frantically ringing ten minutes past eleven o'clock the night of November 2, 1852, when fires broke out in a drought-parched town mostly filled with ramshackle wood buildings for tinder. A gale wind had already risen that night, instantly fanning flames fueled by boards, shingles, canvas, gunny-sacked grains, barrels of liquor, kerosene lamps, and tallow candles. Firefighters rushed in. Some were members of the original, volunteer Mutual Hook and Ladder Company crew—organized in 1850 after a fire burned eight downtown buildings. All were helpless to control the wall of flame. The inferno crackled and roared across forty square city blocks from the north side of J Street at Front, south along Front to M Street, east to L and Ninth Streets and sporadically south across town, claiming lives, devouring most structures yet bypassing others. Parts of the Frinks' investment properties on I, J, K and L Streets were damaged or destroyed, while others north of town nearer the American River were untouched.

The eastern-most, southeast-spreading section of the conflagration stopped, or rather wore out, right across the road from the Frink's home on M Street.

The family was safe, and very fortunate. Hundreds of people were left with no shelter and no possessions save the clothes they were wearing. While the fire storm whipped to and fro Margaret must have been beside herself with fear for the lives of her family and their livestock. Luckily, the fire never reached as far south as the dairy on X Street, but it did reduce the frame-and-board First

Baptist Church downtown to rubble, along with a few of the new brick stores supposedly impervious to flames. Reverend Wheeler saved less than a fourth of the church's furniture before flames rushing through the floor drove him back and turned the sanctuary to a pile of smoldering ashes. The marvelous six hundred pound church bell lay melted amid the ruins. Within a month, 761 structures were re-built, many of them in brick; many installed with iron shutters to help retard fire-wind fanning. In December 1852, Margaret's Ladies Social Circle arranged a post-fire Holiday Fair as a church benefit.

More tribulation followed. The ashes of the great fire had barely been swept away before the rivers again overflowed their banks the following January, churning floodwaters even higher and farther out than the major flood of 1850. Frantically applied dirt and grain-filled bags failed to seal a break in the levee and the bridge across Third Street at China Slough (also called Sutter's Lake) was swept away. Downtown was submerged, with water reaching nine miles to the east, effectively cutting off transit to the mountain mining camps. It was estimated that a thousand people, plus animals, mercantile houses, and supplies, retreated to higher ground at a temporary town named Hoboken, located near today's Sacramento State University campus. Although the dairy location at X and Y was on somewhat higher ground than the core city, Ledyard and his brother-in-law may have moved their herds to Hoboken—or to the levee at Front Street.

The Frinks' home, as well, lay on ground sufficiently elevated to provide better flood protection, making it desirable property for this very reason. Still, water lapped at Margaret's porch. She impulsively rescued some uprooted grape vines that were floating past her window and gave them to a Mr. Pardee. Ten years later, that gentleman and his friend James L. L. F. Warren, now editor of the *California Farmer*, happily determined that Mr. Pardee's flourishing San Francisco vines had their genesis from Warren's gardens at Third and K which the 1853 flood destroyed—except for Margaret's intervention. The waters surged again in March and then receded, reportedly causing less damage than the 1850 inundation. Once again the river levees were ambitiously repaired and raised, not for the last time.

Dry ground brought renewed activity. A new broom factory produced 7,000 units from ten acres of corn, the first shop for curing bacon and hams opened, and brickyards sprang up. Brick buildings in Sacramento grew numerous and the filling and planking of city streets resumed. Taxes remained high. Emigration over the plains contained larger proportions of families coming to settle.

Margaret's family set aside daily considerations in early July 1853 to celebrate the marriage of her sister Laura to Elisha C. Winchell, a lawyer and Justice of the Peace for Sacramento City. The nuptials took place in the White River Cottage, with the Baptist Church's Reverend Osgood Wheeler officiating. Unless Margaret tended to this detail herself, the couple sent a portion of sugar-coated cake to the *Daily Union's* staff, who then published a longer, more personal wedding announcement than was ordinary. Margaret and Ledyard built and moved into a new two-story brick home on the M Street double lot, relinquishing the cottage to the newlyweds. Laura's son Lilbourne Winchell was born in the White River Cottage in October 1855. The Winchells lived there until they moved to Fresno County shortly after the birth of a second son, christened Ledyard, four years later. Margaret's brother A. P. Alsip and his family were the cottage's next occupants. The extended families remained close despite the distance; Lilbourne's later letters and published articles tell of several visits, and his unending fascination at hearing the stories his aunt and uncle told of their overland covered wagon adventures.

~~~~

After the great fire the Baptist congregation returned to the courthouse for its services while it raised funds for another building. A Grand Concert in August 1853 at the Sacramento Theatre, featuring world renowned violinist Miska Hauser, drew a large audience. All proceeds from the concert went toward a new house of worship. The new structure on the west side of Fourth Street between K and L, three blocks from the one that had burned, was dedicated June 18, 1854. Said to be the finest church edifice in the state, the main building measured 38- by 65-feet with a parsonage in the rear. The roof height measured thirty-three feet, topped by a twenty-five-foot cupola. The interior held seventy pews. Construction and furnishing costs were at least twice the amount of the first church building, and despite many months of concentrated fund raising, the Baptist Society was obliged to assume some debt. The structure was saved from destruction by the strenuous efforts of its congregants during the city's second major fire in July 1854.

Margaret's devotion to her faith was supported by her husband, who took an active part in church affairs as a trustee. Ledyard Frink, by many accounts a man of high integrity who was liked and respected by all, was elected a City Alderman for the 1855-56 term, serving on the Ways and Means Committee. This role as a public servant must have widened the couple's contacts and social obligations, a development Margaret doubtless enjoyed because one's impression of her, from her overland diary, is that she was gregarious. The Frinks knew many of the Sacramento pioneers, several of whom were neighbors with children who played with their nephews. Among them were the Edwin and Charles Crocker families, Leland and Mrs. Stanford, and Sacramento's Harbormaster John Requa and his family.

Maintaining a home and a livestock-based business required considerable time and physical energy, but there were amusements too. The Frinks attended weddings and church concerts and

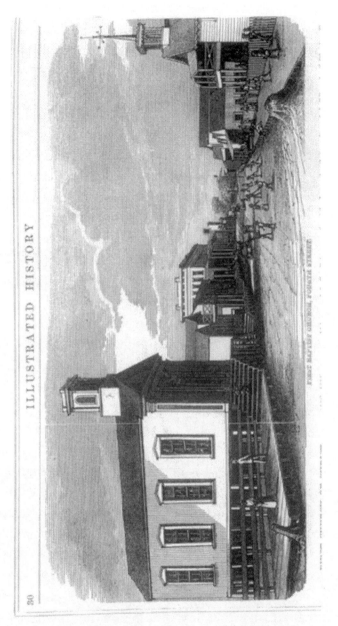

10. First Baptist Church on Fourth Street, 1854.

Courtesy California History Room, California State Library, Sacramento

exchanged visits with friends. Sacramento had many theatres, and by 1855, its own philharmonic orchestra. Libraries expanded their collections. The Baptist Choir and its accomplished female singers were mentioned again and again in newspaper articles. Margaret probably borrowed library books; whether she had any vocal or other musical talent is unknown. Surely she participated in the church's Thanksgiving supper at the Dawson Hotel in 1854, an activity organized to hopefully raise enough to liquidate the Baptist Society's debt. Net receipts fell short of the goal although the turnout was gratifying: four hundred ladies and gentlemen crowded the hotel.

New city improvements and other labor-saving conveniences appeared. In 1854 the city fathers passed an ordinance mandating twelve-to-fourteen-foot wooden sidewalks in the business sections, which was effective, and another to tag dogs in the hope of eliminating the throngs of strays—which wasn't. The city's Water Works, initially funded from a voter-approved tax increase and the sale of $284,495[7] in bonds, was completed in 1854. The Water Works piped water to individual customers for two dollars per month, via 2.25 miles of underground waterlines from its site on Front Street. This system, though, was handicapped from the start. The gravity-driven mechanism meant that, beyond five blocks at the most, there was a significant drop in water pressure. Margaret and Ledyard may have continued to buy their water the old way, in barrels delivered by horse-drawn wagons. Indoor gas lighting slowly began replacing camphene lamps and candles in late 1855. Labor saving sewing machines, which were lighter, less expensive, treadle-operated, and simpler than the elaborately configured machines invented in 1836 for garment factory production lines, were available to the ordinary Sacramento housewife by the late 1850s.

Margaret loved native Californian shrubs and wildflowers and enjoyed the increasing luxuriance in her yard's landscape.

city ordinances passed in May and September of 1851, and again in 1854, that forced them to "buy" back their own properties for "unpaid" taxes, publicly posted as such at the courthouse and in newspapers. The amounts ranged from $11.94 to $59, depending on the property assessment, not so paltry a sum at a time when a full-course, restaurant steak dinner cost less than a dollar. Their last two Sacramento purchases, in 1854 and 1856, were additional land around the dairy which included improvements, appurtenances, and half of a standing crop; plus four lots bounded by Tenth and Eleventh and H Streets, also with appurtenances, tenements, rents, and profits. Yet even then the Frinks were looking at other opportunities elsewhere. The mid-1850s is about the time when Margaret's husband and brother acquired a large tract of ranch land in Solano County, on the Sacramento River 2.5 miles below Rio Vista, which were originally part of the 17,724 acre Los Ulpinos Land Grant deeded to John Sutter's clerk John Bidwell in 1844 by the Mexican government. Nothing is known of Margaret's involvement during the years the brothers-in-law would necessarily have built or improved suitable barns and some type of temporary housing for themselves and laborers, while the family's home remained in Sacramento. In March 1860 Frink & Alsip advertised, in the *Daily Union*, 100 head of stall-fed steers for sale at the Solano ranch.

Undeniably, though, these were busy years for Margaret, even exciting ones as the Frinks' diversification, responsibilities, and prosperity increased. Other excitement not of their making came to the West at the beginning of the new decade.

At 2:00 a.m. on April 4, 1860, a young, superb horseman named Sam Hamilton picked up mail shipped upriver from San Francisco aboard the steamer *Antelope*, added thirteen more onion-skin-thin Sacramento letters, and galloped east down night-darkened J Street on a fast horse. He was the first east-bound Pony Express rider; his west-bound counterpart left St. Joseph, Missouri, the day before. Sam rode for sixty miles then handed his mailbag over to Warren Upson, who took it—in a blizzard—over the Sierra Nevada. Ten days later, Sam retrieved the westbound rider's mail pouch from Sportsman's Hall, twelve miles east of Placerville, and brought it back to Sacramento, riding hard. There, at 5:30 in the afternoon, he was greeted by cheering, ecstatic crowds who lined J Street amid banners, ribbons, and flags. Hats and ladies' handkerchiefs waved in the air; church bells rang, and a cannon salute boomed. Margaret was not the sort to miss being part of this triumphal celebration for anything. She probably waved a pennant until her shoulder ached and screamed until her throat was dry like the rest of the euphoric, bedazzled mob.

The Pony Express only lasted eighteen months. Its promoters were swamped by the expense of its relay stations, high-quality horseflesh, special saddles, and fearless riders. Danger was ever-present but actual losses were few. In one instance, a courier riding across Nevada in 1860 vanished, but his pouch was recovered, intact, two years later. The glorious thundering mounts racing between Sacramento and St. Joseph, covering nearly two thousand miles in ten days each way, were finally bested by a government-funded mail stagecoach line and the transcontinental telegraph.

A somewhat less exciting development than the romantic dash of the Pony, although more enduring, was commencement of construction of the long-awaited Capitol Building in the middle of M Street between Tenth and Twelfth, almost directly east of the Frink's backyard. Court appointed commissioners reported $65,615[8] in compensation due to the owners of land condemned for the building site; accordingly, a tax was levied on Sacramento citizens for that amount. Excavation of ground for the foundation began September 24, 1860. The cornerstone was laid on May 15, 1861 with impressive Masonic ceremonies before a large crowd. Progress would prove to be long and tedious, beset by legislative squabbles and nature's furious onslaught against a town grown

155

complacent.

Another flood—the worst one yet for its length and breadth and damage—inundated the city from December 1861 through January 1862 as the rain-swollen Sacramento and American Rivers surged over their levees in several places. A northeast levee broke, followed by another at Burns Slough (present day McKinley Park). The steamer *Gem* was hurled through an American River levee break near Twenty-Eighth Street, landing a thousand feet from the river. To relieve and hopefully drain rising water levels, city workers cut the levee at R and Fifth Streets, causing several houses to be swept away in the current. On January 9, 1862, a wall of water from the Sacramento River surged up M Street, rushing over porches and doorsteps to swiftly and completely flood everyone's lower floors, inundating some homes up to the second floor landing. Margaret's two houses at the southern corners of Seventh and M had their ground floors awash in filthy river water. Getting about town meant using a raft or rowboat, accessed through a second-story window. The Frinks doubtless stayed upstairs for the flood's duration, as many Sacramentans were forced to do, cooking, eating, sleeping, and living in bedrooms while they worried about the damages below.

People and animals took refuge wherever they could. Temporary shelters included the second floor of the Read's Building in the business district, the high ground at so-called Poverty Ridge, and the two-year-old State Agricultural Pavilion at Sixth and M. This Romanesque-styled edifice, with its projecting wings, arched doors and windows, and a main hall touted as the largest public room in the United States, was the pride and joy of the city. Best of all for the flood refugees, a flight of twenty-three broad steps separated its main floor from the ground.

Gradually the flood receded, leaving Sacramento's merchants and housewives to clean up the resultant ooze, muck, and mold, order new carpets and drapes, and salvage wood furniture.

Property losses were enormous. Nearly nine years free from inundation had lulled Sacramentans' concerns about their levee system and the bottom-land location of the city. Two years after the flood the city fathers, yielding to mounting pressure, passed an order to raise the level of the core-city streets and buildings above high-water mark. The project would not affect the Frinks' residential or dairy properties. However, it must have made milk and butter deliveries to downtown hotels and restaurants during the next ten years more challenging as streets, sidewalks, and buildings were lifted in an erratic sequence that followed no master plan.

Among the many who suffered severe losses in the flood were the contractors who had been working on the Capitol; they quit January 1, 1862. Members of the Senate and Assembly met in Sacramento that month for the thirteenth session of the Legislature but quickly adjourned to San Francisco. The impetus for Sacramento's elevation was further strengthened by post-flood, renewed circulation of nay-saying public commentary, doubts raised by mostly out-of-town special interest groups, and general controversy that Sacramento was unfit to remain the California State capital city because it was much too vulnerable to fire and flood. In early March 1862, Senator Perkins introduced a bill to suspend construction on the State Capitol building, claiming his San Francisco constituents wanted the capital located there instead. Local newspaper editorials advocating for Sacramento pointed out that the state had already accepted costly property from Sacramentans for the contracted purpose of building a state house and continuing the city as the state capital. Waxing eloquent, the *Union* opined that Sacramentans' already demonstrated indomitable spirit in the wake of natural calamities would prove superior to future misfortunes.

Work on the building re-commenced in June 1863. Foundation walls were raised six feet higher lest floods strike again. The Civil

War then in progress made materials hard to obtain and the legislature cautious about advancing funds. Construction proceeded slowly until the brick and granite Capitol Building was finally completed in 1874. As the dome began grandly rising over the landscape, Governor Haight and the Secretary of State moved into their quarters in 1869, with scaffolds and ladders still in place. Most of the exterior work, including entrance porches, steps and porticos, the rotunda and parts of the dome structure were still unfinished. Throughout construction, Margaret and Ledyard could see each addition and finishing touch to the massive walls from their yard, or observe up-close during an evening stroll two blocks east.

Another construction was underway in other quarters of the city. Margaret's nephew Lilbourne later wrote about the groundbreaking ceremony for the Central Pacific Rail Road he attended with his family when he was eight. That day in January 1863 was clear and unseasonably warm, although the streets were still fouled by mud from several previous days of heavy rains. Bales of hay were scattered along K Street for spectator seats, but most people preferred wagon beds or horseback seats to witness the speeches and ceremonial dirt-shoveling. Governor Leland Stanford used a silver-bladed shovel to scoop a few pounds of earth from a cart onto the levee, as did railroad construction superintendant Charles Crocker. The band played "Wait for the Wagon and We'll All Take a Ride."

Lilbourne didn't say if Robert Parker, the young boy the Frinks brought overland with them from Indiana, was at that ceremony. Robert, who moved away from Sacramento sometime before his twenty-first birthday, is shown in the 1860 Census as residing in Montezuma Township, Solano County, where he owned a butcher shop. At age twenty-four, Robert Parker was elected Assessor of Solano County in 1863 and served until 1864, with duties that only involved part-time work. Montezuma

Township was in the general area where the Frinks owned their cattle ranch. It is unknown whether Robert initially moved there to help keep an eye on things until the family took up permanent residence there themselves.

Margaret was forty-nine in 1867 when she, Ledyard, her mother, her brother Azariah Alsip, and his wife permanently relocated to the ranch near Rio Vista after completion of a slow, years-long transfer of their dairy and cattle business. Some of the last functions Margaret might have taken part in with her beloved First Baptist Church were the outdoor Christmas 1864 Festival and an 1866 Christmas Tree Pageant complete with fruit-decorated evergreen branches above beautifully wrapped packages for the city's children. At her new home Margaret roamed about on horseback from time to time, still using her sidesaddle. The Frink and Alsip families manufactured butter and cheeses there for several years until their interest turned to wheat farming.

The two families were listed in the 1868 Sacramento City Directory as farmers in Solano County with Sacramento residences at 210 and 218 M Street. Azariah's son (and Margaret's nephew) Edwin K. Alsip, now aged twenty-four, remained in Sacramento where he was a clerk employed by real estate and insurance agent A.C. Sweetser. Twenty years later, Edwin K. Alsip developed the new community of Oak Park.

Robert Parker returned to Sacramento at some unknown time. By 1879 he was partnered with a Mr. C. E. Ranlett in a grocery and butcher market located at 1700 M Street, just blocks away from the White River Cottage where Robert grew up. He was still engaged in the grocery business when he was appointed Superintendent of the Sacramento City Cemetery in 1889. From the early 1990s until his death in 1919, he was self-employed as a cement contractor. Margaret and Ledyard loved Robert Parker and raised him well. When he married Mary Ellen Chisholm and had his own children, he honored his foster parents by naming one of

159

his sons Edward Frink Parker.

During their years in Rio Vista both Margaret and Ledyard were members of the California State Grange, an organization of individuals actively engaged in agricultural pursuits that not only welcomed, but encouraged women's participation. According to her descendants Margaret labeled herself a Republican, an expression in name only of her political views, since during her lifetime women were denied voting rights. In 1875, when Margaret was fifty-seven, she and Ledyard retired from active farming and moved to a fine home they built in Oakland.

Margaret's last known written words, undated but penned in Oakland as an appendage to her trail journal, declared she had no regrets about leaving Indiana despite the hardships of wagon-train travel or the fires and floods she endured in Sacramento. Instead she had warm memories of her shrubbery-filled yard on M Street and the fig tree's welcome summer shade. She died in Oakland on January 17, 1893. After her death Ledyard received requests from their many friends for a copy of Margaret's overland journal, jotted down in a different world now forty-three years past. He appended some paragraphs of his own, printed fifty copies, and gave them as gifts to fellow pioneers and newer companions. Ledyard lived until March 6, 1900. Both the White River Cottage and the two-story brick house were still standing well into the 1890s, until they were moved to make way for a large apartment house. The section of M Street between the river and Thirty-first was renamed Capitol Avenue in 1940.

End Notes, Margaret Frink

[1]This estimate was based on lumber, both plank and timber, at $100 per thousand feet, labor at five cents per foot for 189,920 feet, and 80 kegs of spikes at $6 each. Lot owners along the proposed route were encouraged to subscribe $250 each, thus raising $67,000 and leaving a surplus for contingencies. At the current ratio of gold, $67,000 x 50 = $3,350,000. Today we use other materials for road construction, and road crew wages are calculated in hours, a factor not considered in 1850.

[2]$10,000 x 50 = $500,000

[3]As of 2008, estimated construction costs for church buildings in Sacramento ranged from $139 to $172 per square foot, resulting in $155,680 to $192,640 to replicate the 1,120 square foot, 1851 First Baptist Church. However, these modern estimates assume concrete block, a building material that was only available to Sacramentans at very high cost in the 1850s. The First Baptist Church edifice was made of wood.

[4]Payment was for delinquent taxes, not the actual land market value. The Frinks acquired all of these parcels for $4,450 in modern money.

[5]Today the Frinks' former residence is the site of government buildings. As an exempt parcel, no property information is publicly available. A nearby parcel of the same square footage as the Frink's two lots is assessed at $480,000 for land only.

[6]Using the gold-ratio formula, $150,000.

[7]$14,224,750 in modern money.

[8]The source does not specify the exact properties acquired by right of eminent domain. Therefore without taking into account current assessments for these unknown parcels: $65,615 x 50 = $3,280,750 today at minimum.

Midwife, Physician and Fiery Suffragette: Lavinia Waterhouse

L avinia Gertrude Goodyear Waterhouse was a talented, resilient, resolute, amazing woman who recovered from personal adversity with renewed strength, commanded respect as a successful business owner when women's mandated "place" was in the home, and tirelessly crusaded for women's rights.

She was schooled in hardship from a young age. Born November 14, 1809, in Genoa, New York to John Goodyear and Julia Bradley Goodyear, she was just sixteen when both parents died, leaving Lavinia and her seventeen-year-old sister Hannah to raise themselves and nine younger siblings. At twenty-one, she wed Charles Claghorn Waterhouse on November 24, 1830, a man five years older than she, who had a son, John, from a previous marriage. Together the couple shared the grief of burying ten of their own thirteen infants. Cornelia, born nine years into the marriage on November 18, 1839, was their oldest surviving child. They called her Nellie. Their son Addison arrived in March 1842, followed by Franklin in January 1850.

In 1852 Lavinia, her husband of twenty-two years, and their three children left their home in Brooklyn, New York to seek a new life on the Pacific Coast. Apart from the exciting discovery of gold, the new State of California offered, or so it seemed, the promise of independence and a chance to better one's condition in a healthful environment. Theirs was not an impulsive decision, although it appeared to be exactly that to their daughter Nellie. Her adolescent diary penned some four years after their relocation still questioned the "suddenness" of the cross-continent move, while also acknowledging that her father's health had been poor for many years. Probably unknown to young Nellie, Charles Waterhouse confessed in a July 1851 letter to his brother-in-law John Goodyear that he had sold his lumber yard with the intention of emigrating to "somewhere" in the West. Profit-minded promoters touted not only the balmy climate, but the myth of a disease-free paradise to be found in California. It became their destination.

Their date of departure or mode of transport from Brooklyn isn't known; a combination of rail and steamboat routes was available from New York to the three main "jumping off" points along the Missouri River: Independence or St. Joseph, Missouri, and Kanesville, Iowa. Or, they might have opted for overland travel from home.

Records do confirm they were part of a company that left Kanesville, Iowa (today's Council Bluffs) in June 1852, westbound for the Great Salt Lake. The wagon train, captained by Mormon Elder James McGaw, was a good-sized one consisting of seventy-five men, sixty-eight women and ninety-six children, fifty-four wagons, 248 oxen, ninety cows, nineteen horses, four mules, and 24,435 pounds of provisions plus guns and ammunition. Charles and Lavinia Waterhouse owned three wagons driven by three hired teamsters to transport themselves and their household goods. The Waterhouses were not members of the Mormon faith. It was simply prudent to winter in the Great Salt Lake Valley settlements—which were already swelling to 20,000 inhabitants— because it was impossible, in animal-drawn conveyances, to traverse the continent from the Atlantic States to the Pacific Coast in one travel season's safe months of April through September.

Their children were young. Nellie was twelve, Addison ten, and baby Franklin was just two. No doubt it was a relief to

11. Lavinia Waterhouse and Children.

Courtesy California History Room, California State Library, Sacramento

Lavinia—who had to cope with the daily camp-style meals and sleeping discomforts plus the specific needs of a toddler—when McGaw's Eleventh Company arrived in Salt Lake City on September 20, 1852.

The family left Utah Territory sometime in the spring of 1853, but there is no record of their journey westward from the Mormon settlement. Newspaper articles from Oregon to Sacramento reported severe hardships among some wagon trains in the 1853 emigration season but relative ease with others, all noting an increase in the numbers of women and children.

When they arrived in the Sacramento area, several months had passed since the young city had suffered its second devastating flood in the winter of 1852-53, and the inhabitants were once again in the process of energetically raising their river levees against future inundation. Downtown streets, planked that year with wide, thick boards of Oregon fir and California pine in a jagged pattern through the major business district, were no longer as dusty in summer or as muddy in winter as they had been just a year earlier. Gold mining in the eastern mountains and foothills was still paying well and the season's gold yield was expected to be high. Fresh produce was abundant at low prices compared with former years: potatoes, cabbages, beets, and onions were available for pennies apiece instead of dollars; barley and beans were reduced to six cents per pound. Local newspapers extolled the city's attributes, claiming that "Here the pure breezes of heaven are tempered by healthful and invigorating influences, which impart to the body strength and to the cheek a freshness like the bloom of the rose . . . such a thing as sickness is hardly known . . . " and so on, hyperbole that lightly skimmed over certain facts. Despite ordinances passed three years previously mandating all owners or occupants of property to remove filth and rubbish in streets and private yards, the city's environment was not ideal for sufferers of diseased lungs, the affliction that beset Charles Waterhouse. Indeed, a doctor's report of internments and causes of death published the following year counted more deaths in Sacramento from diseased lungs in 1853 than in 1852. Whether this mortality increase could be blamed on truly unhealthful conditions or the influx of too many consumptives (tuberculosis patients) who hoped California's fresh air would cure them isn't known.

Health issues aside, the Waterhouses destination all along may have been a friend's ranch at an unspecified location in a rural area outside the city, because there are hints in Nellie's diary that they already knew this ranch owner. The children enjoyed watermelons and summer evenings on the porch, but the family didn't remain there very long. Nellie recalled August 2, 1853, as the date they first came into the city, but it's unclear if this was the month they arrived from Utah, or the actual date of their move to a rented house in Sacramento on the west side of Fifth Street opposite the fire department's Number 4 Engine House.

Fifth Street was a typical, mixed-use neighborhood. Surrounding their new home were two saloons, a shoe store, a carpenter shop, a gunsmith, the Hibernia and St. Louis Hotels, a furniture store, sewing machine shop, and eight other private dwellings. Further down on Fifth Street and along nearby I Street, stood a dozen or more crudely built wood frame structures known as "Little China," the homes and businesses of Chinese immigrants who originally came to mine gold. Lavinia—there was no listing for Charles in the 1854-55 city directory—was shown as Mrs. L. G. Waterhouse, Hydropathic Physician, on Fifth between J & K.

Most likely this move was for reasons of economic necessity as Lavinia watched her husband's health further decline. If she needed to support the family, then Sacramento City's twelve thousand-plus population of combined residents and transient gold-miners had the potential for a wider customer base than rural ranchlands could provide. Lavinia named her business The

Sacramento Water Cure and placed her first advertisement in the *Sacramento Daily Union* in April 1854.

A hydropathic practitioner administered the popular "water cure" accomplished by various means, including warm or cold baths (as the individual practitioner preferred), wrapping or packing the patient from neck to toes in wet sheets, and the patient's consumption of mineral waters. Hydrotherapy, or hydropathy as it was then called, had quickly gained popularity and practitioners since two devoted patients of its Austrian founder immigrated to New York in the 1840s. The 1850 Census at Brooklyn reported no occupation next to Lavinia's name; however, it is almost certain she practiced both the water cure and midwifery there. Her first advertisements in the *Sacramento Daily Union* (and recurring regularly thereafter) inform the public of her "long experience and marked success" as both a water cure practitioner and *Accoucheuse* (a French word meaning "a woman who assists during childbirth").

Establishing herself as this type of care-giver was not difficult, and no code existed to prevent her from practicing or advertising. As a result of Jacksonian political and social ideals, the decades from the 1830s to the 1860s were eras of largely unregulated medical practice, when even medical schools—open only to men—conferred degrees with about two years of formal classes followed by three years of apprenticeship. For those who wished to educate themselves there were texts, pamphlets, broadsheets, manuals—hundreds of them, some illustrated—and lectures in the specialties of midwifery as well as the homeopathic, botanical, and hydropathic systems of treatments and cures.

Lavinia may have been the first water cure specialist in Sacramento (others soon followed), but she immediately competed as a midwife from at least one other provider: Madame Del Banco, Midwife, in the alley between Fourth and Fifth and L and M Streets as advertised in the May 18, 1854, *Sacramento Daily*

Union. She faced competition from an abundance of certified physicians and surgeons as well: Sacramento had two hospitals by 1853 and no fewer than fifty doctors. Nevertheless it appears that Lavinia's dual businesses flourished from the start, because by mid-1857, her newspaper advertisements boasted "The liberal patronage received is the best proof that the public appreciate [sic] the advantages of the [hydropathic] system." Within four years the city directory carried a full-page ad for another competitor, Dr. Barlow J. Smith's Water Cure and Motorpathic Institution on Seventh Street, purporting to cure fevers, rheumatisms, and diseases of the spine.

Running a business was just one responsibility. Lavinia was also a mother concerned with her children's welfare. From February 1854, both public and private schools were open to educate them (free common schools were supported by a tax of one-fourth of one percent on all property, real and personal) but this opportunity appears to have benefited only her sons. Lavinia's daughter completed her formal education at age thirteen, suggesting that Nellie attended school while wintering in Salt Lake City but abandoned formal studies afterward, perhaps because her help was needed at home. Lavinia probably continued to home-school this child whose personal diary, written in a clearly educated manner, not only confesses Nellie's love of books and poetry but also contains some of her own insightful poems.

Disaster struck just as life was stabilizing for the Waterhouse family. At one o'clock in the afternoon of July 13, 1854—as Sacramento citizens were already sweltering in one hundred degree weather—a spirit lamp (also known as a camphene lamp, containing a mixture of alcohol and turpentine) toppled in a small frame building behind Newcomb's furniture warehouse in the block bounded by Third, Fourth, J and K Streets. The lamp exploded, engulfing the boards in flames that quickly leapt to the rear kitchen of the K Street-fronting Sacramento Hotel, simultaneously igniting the frame buildings on the same block. An instant later, the Crescent City Hotel on J Street was ablaze. Firefighters sprang into action, and this time, as opposed to the horrible conflagration of 1852, the prevailing breeze was minimal and there was an abundance of water due to the brand new Water Works and strategically placed cisterns. The fire, though—once alive—had its own will, flaring again in places thought to be under control, forcing its way down the city blocks to Fifth Street.

Panic prevailed. The firefighters were forced to work on densely crowded streets as people tried to save what they could. Black smoke made lungs gasp for breath and blinded watering eyes. Between the effects of the July weather and the intense heat of the fire, hundreds of people sank into exhaustion and had to be revived, rescued, or treated for injuries. Several firemen collapsed with heat prostration and were carried to places where fresh air and water could be found. It was nearing three o'clock before the roaring inferno reached Fifth and I Streets, where, in minutes, it reduced all of the Chinese frame buildings to ashes. Amid this chaos and terror, the Waterhouse family had precious minutes to save themselves and whatever they could grab of food, clothing, household goods or family mementos. One piece they managed to save was Charles Waterhouse's wooden rocking chair.

All told, the fire burned the better portion of twelve city blocks, destroying the Congregational Church, the Court House (although all the legal documents and papers were rescued), four brick buildings, the Oriental and Crescent City hotels, and two hundred frame homes and business. Engine House No. 4, across the street from Lavinia's home on Fifth, burned too. The *Union* editors estimated losses at $350,000[1] but also reported that at five o'clock that same afternoon at least one property owner was already busily re-erecting a dwelling on Fifth Street between J and K. Lavinia's name wasn't mentioned in this newspaper account, possibly because she was a renter, not an owner. It is unclear whether her residence was restored or the family moved into another rental on the same street. Nellie's later diary alludes to living in the "same old house since they were burned out in 1854." Lavinia Waterhouse appeared at the same general address, Fifth between J and K Streets, in the following year's city directory.

Before, during, and after the fire's devastation, Lavinia was charged with caring for an ailing husband who, it can be assumed, she treated according to her hydropathic beliefs, which disdained conventional medicine. Followers of hydropathy were committed to health-enhancing diets, fresh air, and exercise as disease preventatives, and baths or packs as remedies. At some unknown point between 1853 and the end of 1855, the couple went to the coast seeking its renowned healing climate, possibly during reconstruction after the 1854 fire, when Lavinia might have felt compelled to remove her ailing husband from the soot, debris, dust, and noise in Sacramento. According to a great-grand-daughter, both were so taken with the wholesome, quiet, pristine beauty of Pacific Grove that Charles asked to be buried there among the few graves already lovingly nestled among the pines near the sand dunes.

Charles Waterhouse died from consumption on January 4, 1856, in Sacramento. His death notice in the *Daily Union* invited friends to attend funeral services at the family's Fifth Street residence. He was buried in Sacramento City Cemetery without—as his daughter Cornelia grievously lamented—a headstone. Evidently this first gravesite was intended to be temporary, because on March 28, 1857, his body was removed to another lot in the same cemetery. The early pioneer burial sites Charles saw in Pacific Grove were formalized as El Carmelo Cemetery in the 1880s, and his remains were re-interred there at some unspecified date.

No record remains of the manner in which Lavinia expressed her grief upon her husband's death—Victorian mourning customs decreed that household mirrors be covered with black crepe—or her emotional reaction to the certainty that she alone was now responsible for her children's care. The surviving spouse was to wear black clothing for the requisite one year period of deep mourning, during which time church attendance was the only permissible social activity for a widow. Mourning etiquette for children of the deceased was less strict, and Nellie's diary tells that she and a friend went to the Ladies Festival that December. The event was a social occasion with a noble purpose: a fundraiser sponsored by the ladies of Reverend Benton's Congregational Church, where the Waterhouse family worshiped, to pay off the church's debt. The festival raised $1,000[2]; Nellie did not stay for the dancing. She made no mention of the family attending the Christmas Tree Festival held at their church the week after Christmas, a children's party where songs were sung and gifts given to Sabbath School children, which possibly included Lavinia's six-year-old-son Frank.

Lavinia herself left no personal diary. What does remain is her account book for the years 1857–59, a 4- by 12-inch ledger sub-divided into A to Z sections, where she recorded the services she rendered and the prices she charged.

Many of the hand-written entries are very faded, yet it can still be discerned that Lavinia received and sometimes lodged patients at her home and care facility (as she advertised) and also made house calls to other towns where distances often necessitated extended visits. She regularly recorded trips to Putah Creek, a community near today's Winters approximately thirty-two miles west via ferry across the Sacramento River; to Colusa, fifty-two miles north by stagecoach; and twenty-two miles east to Granite Township, a settlement that changed its name to Folsom as the Sacramento Valley Railroad neared completion. From late February 1856 forward, Lavinia could board a train that departed twice daily for Folsom, for two dollars each way.

Although not all of the entries below were dated the same year, a sampling of Lavinia's Account Book reveals the focus and extent of her practice:

> Sept. 3: "She came for packs"
> Oct. 4: "She came in the afternoon for packs—took packs one week"
> Oct. 10: "Was called to Mrs. Brown and children on Putah Creek Sunday returned Monday with her and children"
> Nov. 10: "Was called to Mrs. Spaulding at Mrs. Emersons—called every day until Nov. 19"
> Feb. 6: "Coffin baby sick, called twice"
> Feb. 6 (1859): "Mrs. Bright was confined of a son before I got there Thursday . . . was there and I came one hours [sic] after and bathed her and left"

Some of her patients became friends. Among them was Margaret Crocker, whose lawyer husband Edwin was the brother of Sacramento merchant and future railroad baron Charles Crocker. In early November 1857, Lavinia as midwife delivered Margaret Crocker's third child, a daughter named Nellie Margaret, for her standard fee of $25.[2]

Even more interesting than the jottings for her livelihood are the newspaper and magazine clippings Lavinia (or someone else) pressed between the pages of her 1857-1859 account book. These mostly undated items are poems and short articles, food for thought or affirmations of her beliefs in Spiritualism, equality for women, and self-improvement. The composition "Victory at Last," by W. Wylley (almost certainly a sister suffragette), speaks to women's battle for equality. J. N. Wilson's "What I do not believe" is poetry for the spiritual-minded, and an article titled "An Inquiring Mind" explored the subject of previous lives and human responsibilities. The clipping titled "Tobacco and Lunacy" evidently validated her own feelings, which were doubtless affronted each time she passed any one of Sacramento's dozens of cigar sellers.

In 1857 Lavinia's older sister Hannah Goodyear, who had earlier written that she "was thinking of coming west," surprised the family on April 15 by appearing on their doorstep at two o'clock in the morning. The reunion was exciting and joyful for both Lavinia and her three children, but Hannah didn't stay more than a few days at her sister's home because there was no spare room for her to settle in. Lavinia housed a changing assortment of private boarders to augment the family's income, as well as having rooms set aside for her water cure practice. From Nellie's diary entries, the-longer-term boarders appear to be young bachelors who worked in town. The shorter-term guests were Lavinia's patients. Hannah moved into her own home and acquired her own boarders.

Lavinia must have felt the stress of many obligations. She had growing children to raise, educate, and support. Certainly her livelihood demanded many hours, quite a few of them away from home overnight. Daughter Nellie complained about her mother's absences and "total engrossment in her business" in the pages of a diary beginning November 18, 1856—Nellie's seventeenth birthday—and ending October 3, 1858. The diary is filled with teenage angst and anxiety: Nellie felt shy, often lonely, frequently melancholy, and despairing because she was not beautiful. She felt that no one understood her (especially her mother), and she was concerned that she would never find someone to marry. She sorely missed her late father, whom she eulogized as "holy and good." Many entries recorded religious thoughts interspersed with her daily activities, which included plenty of chores.

Nellie swept carpets, ironed clothes, and cleaned the upstairs rooms. She learned several aspects of her mother's vocation, too; more than once she administered packs and other elements of the water cure to her mother when Lavinia wasn't feeling well. For one so avowedly shy, Nellie also reported a fairly active social life, while sourly protesting her mother's disapproval of some of her friends and beaux.

Excitement of a disturbing nature beset the Waterhouse's and their nearby neighbors when a brick building under construction on J Street between Fourth and Fifth suddenly collapsed on its faulty foundation the morning of March 27, 1857, resulting in one death. Four months later at four o'clock in the morning on July 19, 1857, fire erupted on the southwest corner of J and Fifth Streets, destroying most of the one-story frame buildings in the area known as Tukey's Block. Engine House No. 4, directly across the street from Lavinia's home, would have checked the flames sooner except, as the *Union* reporter noted, for the rotten condition of their fire hoses. Luckily, well directed firefighting efforts succeeded in stopping the fire at a paint shop in the middle of Fifth Street just after the cloth ceiling of an adjacent building was reduced to ash.

The use of camphene and other highly combustible lantern fuels began to decline as gas light gradually became available to buildings pipe-fitted for this new luxury. Sacramento Gas Works' "gasometer tank" facility on Front Street was completed in 1855. The *Sacramento Daily Union* proudly announced itself the pioneer of this enterprise, informing its readers on November 22, 1855, that the first gas meter in town was placed in its offices. The Sacramento Gas Company commenced general operations July 1, 1856 with service to homes, shops, and offices. By the end of that year they had 113 customers, mostly businesses. One prominent customer was the city itself. In December 1856 the Council contracted to install thirty gas lights on the corner of each block in the downtown district, illumination that was installed at the intersection near Lavinia's home. The street lamps on J and K were lit just before Christmas, prompting the *Union* to exuberant prose in praise of dispelling the thick darkness. Yet scarcely were they aglow before complaints began that merchants' awnings and signs were impeding the light, a theme the newspaper expounded on by calling attention to the careless driver of two-mule team who knocked a gas post sideways. The Council directed the Marshall to remove the obstructions. The paucity of funds, always an issue in Sacramento City, proved a greater impediment. The following April the City Council economized by mandating that the street lamps would remain dark so long as star light and moon light were visible, for which they were immediately vilified in the press as the "Dark Lantern City Fathers."

By late summer of 1857 Lavinia was prosperous enough to afford a newer, larger, eastern-styled two-story, multi-windowed brick house with a fine front porch on the corner of Eighth and I Streets, surrounded by shade trees. An artist's drawing of this combination home and business establishment, embellished with the sign "Sacramento Water Cure" emblazoned across the roofline in the graphic, appears as a full page advertisement in the 1859-60 city directory. Nellie dreaded the preparations for moving day and probably so did Lavinia. A hired car man transported the furniture, carpets, and multiple boxes of books on August 5. Nellie herself saw to the relocation of her potted rose bushes, caged canaries (one named Nellie Bly), her pet Old Pussy and the cat's two young kittens. Afterward she confided to her diary that the move was a "dreadful undertaking" but within two weeks admitted the new home was a very pleasant one: among other amenities, it boasted a large parlor and a cozy sitting room with a stove. Lavinia may not have been an early subscriber to the Sacramento Gas Company service, or else found—as others complained—that the light glowing from sconces and chandeliers was not very strong, because Nellie continued to use candles to read by and light herself through the rooms after dark.

Lavinia was able to hire a servant girl at the new house, freeing a large portion of Nellie's time to sew some new-fashioned hoop skirts, spend time at ice cream parlors with friends, and learn to drive Lavinia's new horse and carriage. Soon after settling in the new house, Nellie began pestering her mother for a piano. Lavinia countered by claiming that her taxes and other expenses were too enormous to afford one. More pleading and argument ensued until Lavinia, undeniably exasperated, finally snapped at Nellie that she should marry a good man who might buy her one. Since this statement was contrary to Lavinia's previous adamant pronouncements that her daughter would not be allowed to marry until she was twenty, it engendered yet more feelings of hurt and bewilderment in Nellie. Somewhat petulantly, she informed her diary that her mother was a very forceful lady of high spirits who had sensibilities quite different from her own.

Occasional discord between a strong-minded, disciplinarian mother and a teenage daughter longing for romantic love and independence were inevitable, yet most of the time they enjoyed each others' company and Nellie admitted she was often lonely when Lavinia was away from home on business. Together they attended morning worship services and afternoon church lectures, and shopped the mercantile establishments on J Street. Mother and daughter went to hear phrenology Professor Pinkham's lecture on Spiritualism and discussed it afterward. (Phrenologists studied the human skull in the belief that shapes and protuberances revealed character and mental capacity.) They went to weddings and funerals and paid social calls on friends together.

Other outings were made as a family. On Election Day evening in September of 1857—an election that, like all others before it, excluded women from voting and so likely raised Lavinia's ire—the Waterhouse family and friends sat on The Dawson House Hotel balcony to watch the impressive, torch-lit Procession of the Settlers Parade. They witnessed the afternoon inauguration ceremonies of California's fifth governor, John Weller, the following January. Lavinia had a patient among the widely renowned Smith family and paid house calls there, but occasionally she, Nellie, and young Frank took a pleasure ride in their carriage east along the American River to A. P. Smith's Pomological Gardens and Nursery, a favorite pleasure resort and showplace. The ninety-acre grounds, located near today's northwest section of the River Park residential area, contained hundreds of shade trees, fruit orchards, vineyards, lavish flower gardens, and beautiful lawns around the family house, all showcased amidst elegantly paved foot paths and driveways. Smith's produce was of the highest quality and his strawberries and raspberries sold for a premium price of $1.50[3] per pound. The great 1862 flood destroyed much of the Pomological Gardens, despite its owner's efforts to restore it, and nine years later the flood of 1871 reduced the once-fabulous Gardens to a mere landmark.

There was much visiting and church-going with Aunt Hannah, too, but it was a relationship that ended abruptly and tragically in mid-July 1859 when the death of Hannah Goodyear, then about 52 and never married, was ruled a suicide by hanging. Lavinia buried her sister in Sacramento City Cemetery and then, as either she or her sons did for her husband Charles, later removed Hannah's remains to Pacific Grove's El Carmelo Cemetery.

During this terrible family time, Lavinia's business enjoyed a growing clientele and rising income; she began advertising herself as a medical doctor and hired more employees. When the *Daily Bee* (soon thereafter the *Sacramento Bee*) published its first issue in February 1857, Lavinia abandoned the *Daily Union* to place her advertisements in a newspaper more editorially in line with her own thinking—as she told the *Bee's* editors. She ran this large ad in the *Daily Bee* on June 3, 1859:

SACRAMENTO WATERCURE
Corner 8th and I Streets
IS IN SUCCESSFUL OPERATION
Introduced in this Valley years ago by
MRS. WATERHOUSE, M.D. has
the BEST accommodations in California for the sick;
has a large, commodious brick house;
fine bathing rooms, hot and cold water.

Also, a GYMNASIUM and the
appliances of the best EASTERN CURES.
In Obstetrics she has never lost a mother.
She has the best male and female nurses in the State
Board, room and treatment from $10 to $25 a week
Patients attended at their homes
Obstetric cases attended to for $25
The Galvanic Battery for the use of patients.

Galvanic batteries were used by Spiritualists and others to cure diseases with a flow of electricity sufficient to produce a proper beneficial proportion of electricity in the blood. A year after this advertisement, the federal census of July 1860 recorded Lavinia and her children sharing their home with a thirty-year-old lumber miller, another board and room renter. Eighteen-year-old Addison was looking forward to his future education in the law, meanwhile likely tinkering with some experiments; in later years he would become a locally renowned inventor. Ten-year-old Frank was still in grade school, and Nellie was twenty, going on twenty-one.

Two months earlier, Abraham Lincoln had been nominated as the Republican candidate for the Presidency against the Democrats' northern-wing candidate Stephen A. Douglas. The hotly divided national political system broke down as the southern wing of the Democratic Party nominated John C. Breckenridge of Kentucky, and a newly-formed Constitutional Union party nominated John Bell of Tennessee. Their campaigns brought the decades-long, bitter North-South sectional turmoil over the expansion of slavery and its related economic and social issues to a crisis. Mr. Lincoln was victorious in November, despite being outpolled by his combined opposition. Before he was sworn in on March 4, 1861, seven Southern states had declared their secession from the Union. Hostilities erupted April 12, 1861, when Confederate forces attacked a United States military installation at Fort Sumter in South Carolina. The Civil War would rage until 1865, with Sacramentans, in the main pro-Union, as passionate, and

However, most of her daily life can only be surmised. She must have swept floors, baked pastries, prepared meals, tended a home vegetable garden, made jam, washed windows, chatted with her relatives while shelling a bowl of fresh garden peas, and beat rugs like every other Sacramento housewife in the 1850s and 1860s. By 1860, if not sooner, she had help from Anna Gaffney, a live-in servant from Ireland. Margaret's household was full that year. Her foster son Robert Parker was on his own, but her mother and other unrelated individuals shared their home: a couple and their toddler, a young schoolteacher named Jennie Kercheval, a ten year old orphan named Kate Bowers, and three dairy employees. Margaret would have participated in family entertainments like card and board games, outdoor lawn games, and picnics in the country. As was the custom, she would have paid and received weekly formal social calls from other ladies.

Margaret was enthusiastic, energetic and resourceful. It could have been she who proposed (or organized) the Baptist Ladies' ice cream and floral festival in 1855 and another festival in 1856, both to raise money to finish paying the church's debts. The ladies' successes, extolled in the press, apparently weren't quite sufficient. A public notice in the July 27, 1857, *Sacramento Daily Union* headlined "Sheriff's Sale" in bold type proclaimed a court order for a public sale of the First Baptist Church of Sacramento City to satisfy the $1,500 debt still owed to its contractor. Members of the congregation dug into their pockets for part of the money or made some kind of appeasement arrangement with the contractor because the building remained theirs. Margaret's Ladies Social Circle presented a general music concert in 1858 to raise the unpublicized balance due on the new church and the recent gas fittings.

The Baptists were by no means the only target of court-sanctioned creditors. Like everyone who owned real estate in Sacramento, the Frinks were plagued through 1856 by retroactive

153

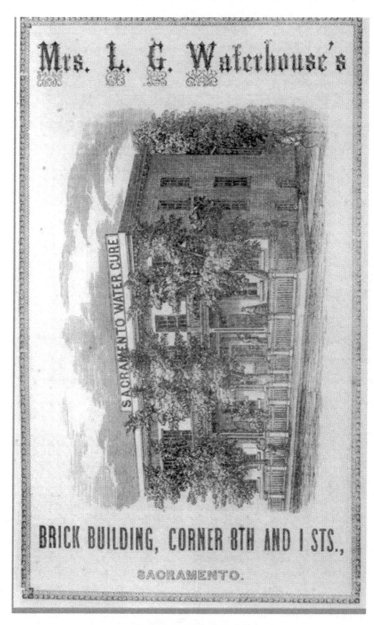

**12. Sacramento Water Cure
Advertisement in 1860 City Directory.**

Courtesy California History Room, California State Library, Sacramento

divided, in their opinions as the rest of the nation. Lavinia, for one, made no secret of the fact that she loathed the entire conflict.

Shortly after the war began, Nellie Waterhouse married Edwin Councilman, described as a Nevada resident in the *Sacramento Daily Union's* announcement, on June 27, 1861. The wedding ceremony was performed by the Reverend J. D. Blain, Pastor of the Methodist Episcopal Church, and likely took place in the parlor of the family home as was customary at the time. No reason for the Waterhouses change in church membership, if such was the case, is known.

Sacramento newspapers had no ladies' social pages featuring descriptions of bridal finery. Bridal fashions of the time ranged from hoop-skirted gowns of beribboned white silk crepe with long-sleeved, high-cut bodices and a veil, to pastel silk taffeta with a profusion of lace trim beneath a plumed hat. Nellie's outfit was as fashionable as her mother's purse and war shortages of eastern-manufactured goods allowed; Nellie was an avid devotee of the colored fashion plates, stories and articles in the *Godey's Ladies Book* magazine. Edwin Councilman was not mentioned in Nellie's girlhood diary (which ended on the eve of her nineteenth birthday), so presumably she met him after 1858—the husband she longed for in page after page of those diary entries—a man she could love who also had the steadfast character and worldly discernment to win her mother's approval for the match.

Soon after their marriage the young couple moved to Edwin's established residence in Humboldt County, in the Territory of Nevada, where the discovery of rich silver ore deposits was drawing men from all over the world to seek their fortune. They built an adobe house in newly-established Star City (later part of Pershing County). The Councilmans returned to California for Edwin to enter a Napa health sanitarium while Nellie stayed with her mother in Sacramento. The exact dates of this visit are unclear; it's possible Nellie was residing with her mother during the latter part of 1861 and early 1862 when everyone's plans and routines were interrupted by the disastrous flood that inundated the entire town.

It rained hard in December of 1861, a deluge of 8.64 inches, followed in January 1862 by another 15.04 inches of rainfall. Miles of levees surrounded the city—starting from south of today's Broadway north up the Sacramento River and east to high ground along the American River—constructed in the 1850s and rebuilt and improved since the 1852-53 flood with tremendous outlays of money and labor. The levees proved not high enough, nor strong enough, to contain the rain-swollen rivers. Water from the American River crashed through its own and the Sacramento River levees, rushing through the city streets. On January 22, 1862, the levee at China Slough, near Seventh and I Streets, fell. When this happened, if not before, there was no chance that Lavinia's home and furnishings on Fifth were spared the ravages of the cold, swirling waters. Local newspapers ran columns of flood information side-by-side with dispatches from the Civil War front. The *Sacramento Daily Bee*, located on Third between J and K, published a special edition "flood sheet" for distribution while its own building was underwater.

The disaster was finally enough for city officials and citizens alike to agree upon the need for drastic change. Most agreed that the core city, which had been laid out as a grid fourteen years earlier with little thought to land elevation relative to the two rivers converging around it, needed to be raised. Indeed, various civic groups had argued in favor of this for years. As early as 1853, laborers with wheelbarrows and wagons and jack screws had graded and raised sections of downtown by about four feet. This early effort was abandoned when assessments for raising store fronts up to the higher street levels became a hardship on the merchants. The arguments went on, though. Some favored raising the streets and buildings only another few feet or so. Those advocating a high-grade effort of eight feet or more prevailed.

By mid summer of 1863 a street grading program was under way, a project that ultimately impacted Lavinia's property at Eighth and I. Property owners were required to provide brick bulkheads to contain the fill, raise the fourteen-foot-wide sidewalks, and raise or modify their own buildings. There were many problems. Tons of fill materials had to be brought in and then left for months to settle. Incomplete sections were difficult to navigate by foot, horseback, or wagon. Pedestrians risked their limbs on sidewalks which were sometimes raised before one store but remained at the old level at the next, necessitating crude ramps or stairways to get from one level to another. Four blocks west of Lavinia's home and business establishment, the Saint George Hotel at the corner of Fourth and J Streets, weighing 1,900 tons, was lifted eight feet by dozens of men using 250 jack screws.

The entire city-raising process was a mammoth undertaking, completed around ten years later with the streets, sidewalks, and buildings in the core city area elevated twelve to fifteen feet. Between raising the city and constructing the new state house during the decade of the 1860s into the 1870s, the added din and dust and inconvenience doubtless occasionally wore thin the patience of townspeople. In addition, for most of these years the city's sewer system also required constant updating. The first primitive sewer system put in place in 1853 was designed only to handle excess rain water. Human waste and bath and laundry water were dumped into outdoor privies or China Slough; water closets inside hotels, public buildings, and ordinary private homes would not make their Sacramento appearance until 1870. According to her 1859 advertisement, Lavinia at least had hot and cold running water, if not indoor flushing toilets.

A few weeks after the 1862 flood catastrophe, Lavinia's daughter and son-in-law returned to the Nevada mines. In July of 1862, Nellie wrote to her mother revealing, in circumspect phrases, that she might be pregnant. Either her symptoms indicated another condition or she miscarried, because Nellie gave birth to her first child, a son named Charley on October 30, 1863. She died five days later of childbed fever, three weeks shy of her twenty-fourth birthday.

A stunned and grieving Lavinia, an experienced midwife, demanded an explanation of her daughter's death from the attending physician. His answering letter explained that Nellie had given birth on a cold and snowy morning in a damp room with only a mud floor, adding that he had done everything possible "despite his patient's general bad health."

Health of both the writer and his or her family was a subject often mentioned in nineteenth-century correspondence. Various fevers and influenzas often referred to collectively as "ague," abounded and were of common concern. The need for sterilization was unknown, the practice of medicine was in its formative years, and childbearing often led to lethal infections. Dentistry was not much more advanced either, yet advertisements were proudly placed in directories and newspapers offering Allen's Gum Dental Work (dentures) formed of a silicious compound fused on platinum plate. Nellie Waterhouse Councilman, whose girlhood diary recorded many days of toothache over a two-year period, was wearing artificial teeth by the time of her death.

Twenty months before her daughter's death, Lavinia married William Muldrow on Sunday, March 2, 1862 when she was fifty-three and widowed for six years. Possibly Nellie and Edwin, who had not yet returned to Nevada, and her two sons Addison and Frank, were present at the ceremony. What they thought of their new stepfather isn't known. Others might not have held him in high regard.

A man named William Muldrow, a California pioneer during the Gold Rush who lived in Sacramento off and on, became quite infamous for his Muldrow Claims. In 1860, he filed an unsuccessful suit claiming ownership of a generous portion of Humboldt County, California, for territory that included Bodega Bay and Fort Ross. Other pioneers in the area called his suits phony and the man himself a swindler.

The 1868 city directory cited a William Muldrow residing a block away from Lavinia on Eighth Street between H and I. Presumably this listing was for the litigious Mr. Muldrow who, in mid-April 1868, filed seventeen suits in one day against various Sacramento parties for recovery of lots and blocks he claimed title to, properties that amounted to nearly the entire city from Front Street east to Thirty-First and from G south to U streets, with additional lands along the American River thrown in for good measure. This effort was no more successful than Muldrow's earlier lawsuits in Humboldt County. He returned to his native Missouri at some unknown date and died there in March of 1873.

It is uncertain whether this William Muldrow, the infamous proprietor of the "Muldrow Titles," or another same-named gentleman was Lavinia's husband, and it is equally uncertain if she ever lived with the man she wed that April Sunday. In any case, it was a union she must have soon regretted, as the back-and-forth correspondence exchanged with her son-in-law after Nellie's death gives evidence. A November 29, 1863 letter from Edwin contains a somewhat stiff and bewildered apology, in response to Lavinia's letter to him dated November 13, for addressing her as Mrs. Muldrow, protesting that he didn't know of her name change (evidently, from Muldrow back to Waterhouse). Also in this letter, an anguished and heartbroken Edwin further apologizes for not knowing enough about the water treatment to risk it in such cold weather to save his beloved wife. With the letter, he enclosed a lock of Nellie's hair and some of her lace collars as sorrowful mementos that were perhaps lovingly stroked by Lavinia's fingers as she dutifully composed the black-bordered notes that began "It is my painful duty to inform you . . . ."

Even before Nellie's death, women's health and well-being was a cause Lavinia had actively promoted for years, both as a hydropathic practitioner and as a midwife. Now the effort intensified. In addition to advising her patients in private, she sponsored lectures to inform a wider range of Sacramento ladies. A December 1865 issue of the *Sacramento Bee* printed this notice: "Those interested are informed that Mrs. Gore will give readings of character and examination for disease during this month at the residence of Mrs. Waterhouse, corner of 8th and I Streets." In the wake of her daughter's demise Lavinia became active in, and at one time was vice president of, the Sacramento Spiritualist Society.

Mid-nineteenth century America was a bubbling cauldron of energetic religious change, characterized by "new" styles of beliefs and methods of worship that shifted away from Calvinist orientation. Adherents of Spiritualism believed in the continuous existence of the human soul and that it was not only possible, but beneficial, to commune with the departed—a belief that offered solace at a time when too many children failed to survive childhood. However, Spiritualism was discredited by established clergy and various newspapermen as delusional and fanatical, even as the philosophical religion continued to grow and attract new members. What might have angered Lavinia was the content of another undated newsprint piece she kept, a short article deriding spiritualists as an "irresponsible source" during the investigation of the deaths of two Sacramento men. Spiritualism's principles also stressed personal responsibility for one's own soul, a duty toward others, and the fellowship of man with each other and God. More, the spiritualists' principles treated women equally, recognizing equal opportunities and authority for women, when the Victorian Era prescribed that women and children were legal chattels of fathers and husbands. The religious philosophy of Spiritualism empowered women to be independent, in turn helping to fuel the rising women's rights movement launched by Elizabeth Cady Stanton and Lucretia Mott at Seneca Falls, New York, in 1848.

Starting in the mid-1850s, Santa Cruz resident Eliza Farnham, a writer, avowed Spiritualist, proponent of the water cure, and firm advocate for women's equality, began a series of lectures in northern California. Several were held in Sacramento, attended by large audiences. Whether or not Lavinia Waterhouse knew Mrs. Farnham personally at that time, the themes she discussed certainly meshed with Lavinia's strong personality and independent spirit. Eliza Farnham died in 1865, but other California ladies took up her cause, including Lavinia, who became an active suffragette.

According to newspaper accounts and woman suffrage historians, Lavinia Waterhouse was a pioneer in the steadily rising movement for women's rights. The California Suffragists organized in San Francisco in 1869, and Lavinia was recorded in their files as a member of the Sacramento County Woman Suffrage Association as of February 1870. She was noted as a regular participant at suffragette conventions in San Francisco from 1872 through 1874, and she was a member of an "indignation meeting" called in Sacramento when the 1879 state Constitutional Convention failed to pass a woman suffrage amendment. Lavinia was chosen to head the group's committee on finance. Two years later, she became a member of the San Francisco Board of Directors for the California State Woman Suffrage Educational Association.

The women's rights movement had their own newspapers such as *The Revolution,* edited by Elizabeth Cady Stanton, and later the *Woman's Journal,* both of them national publications of great influence. In Sacramento, a suffragist journal *The Winning Way* was edited and published more or less weekly until March of 1874 from offices in the St. George Building at Fourth and J Streets.

Lavinia's own letters to Sacramento newspapers were missives of local impact. One example is an undated clipping—

from its content, probably written in 1871—signed "Mrs. L.G. Waterhouse" and addressed to the editors of the *Sacramento Bee,* found stuffed between the pages of her 1857–1859 account book.

The headline was "Concerning Woman—Her Rights and Her Wrongs." In the letter, Lavinia asserted that she should have the same rights to vote as any man because she had paid taxes for eighteen years in Sacramento, took an informed interest in America's affairs, and raised and educated two sons. (The 1868 city directory cited Addison Waterhouse as an attorney and Frank as a clerk—when clerking was a job description of educated, middle-management employees—in the office of insurance and real estate agent William Coleman. Both sons were residing with their mother.)

She reviled the Civil War, calling war revolting and "a relic of barbarism," and vowed to use all her influence for those who favored woman suffrage. Found with this twelve-inch clipping was another, shorter piece titled "About Dress"—most probably a continuation of her women's rights theme and published with it—objecting that women's cumbersome, restrictive fashion code forced many ladies at Governor Booth's Inaugural Ball to wear long trains and a worried look lest they or someone else step on their gowns. Hooped skirts had been replaced by tighter, more closely fitted skirts that often made walking difficult, and formal wear dictated ultra-long trains of delicate fabrics. Presumably, Lavinia was attired more sensibly, because she continued with: "I was surprised to see some of our good, substantial women of Sacramento dragging yards of velvet and beautiful silk and lace after them. What a waste in this time of distress," she wrote, adding, "Surely, these may be classed as woman's wrongs."

Precisely when Lavinia began painting and writing poetry isn't known, although some of her work was dated in the early 1870s. Two of her poems, "My View of San Francisco Bay" and

"The Sacramento," were published posthumously in the *Overland Monthly*, both accredited to L. Gertrude Waterhouse. Another, "The Mountain Brook," appeared in *Californian* magazine. During the time she was an active suffragist she painted an 11- by 13-foot allegorical canvas using Yosemite Valley as a background, depicting the politically unaware woman as "The Sleeping Giantess," the painting's title. A much-reduced print of this painting, with explanations of the symbolic figures "The Goddess of Liberty," "Drowning Women," "Mrs. Opposition," and twenty-one other iconic depictions, along with four of her poems, was published in a twenty-three page, compact 4- by 6-inch pamphlet. The title poem, also named "The Sleeping Giantess," filled seven pages and expressed Lavinia's frustration, utter incredulousness, and despair that so many women—collectively, The Giantess—were either ignorant or apathetic about their gender's political oppression. The eighth stanza, however, expresses hope and determination:

> Above are women, with rolls in their hands,
> The Constitution, which gives them the plans;
> The Fourteenth and Fifteenth Amendments will stand
> To cause woman to be equal with man.

The "Sleeping Giantess" pamphlet was dated 1873; it may have been distributed at the San Francisco suffrage convention Lavinia attended that year. Included in this little booklet is another multi-paged, rhyming verse titled "A Woman's Right to Propose"—marriage. This piece, originally written to introduce the idea as a subject of discussion at the December 9, 1871, private session of the Woman's Suffrage Council in Sacramento, when Lavinia was president of the Sacramento County Woman's Association, was read aloud after initial greetings opened the meeting. The two-day public forum of the Woman's Suffrage Council, held at the Congregational Church, had ended successfully with nationally known speakers Susan B. Anthony and Laura De Force Gordon, as advertised, in attendance. "A Woman's Right to Propose" outlined Lavinia's reasons why a woman had a right to not only choose her own mate and companion but be empowered to put forth the crucial question if the man didn't speak up. Whether she was inspired by a romantic situation of her own is impossible to tell; she did not marry again.

In 1879, the year Lavinia turned seventy, Thomas Edison's electric light innovation was the talk of every town across America, but he was not the only person working in this field, nor the only one attempting to improve on his original experiments at producing "arc light," the general term for lamps that produced light by a voltaic arc. Lavinia's lawyer-turned-inventor son Addison Waterhouse ranked among the names of various experimenters known as "Edison's Rivals." A news story published January 9, 1880, by the *Sacramento Daily Record-Union* lauded Addison and his partner Dr. Brewer for their inventions and improvements, claiming these Sacramento inventors were the first to bring the electric light into practical, everyday use. Seven months later, the same newspaper reported Addison and his partners' success at "producing the most perfect and practical light" (incandescent light) with their "improved engine, generator and lamp" at an exhibition held in Cooke & Sons' Pioneer Box Factory on Front and M Streets.

Addison's demonstration occurred almost a year after another spectacular exhibition. During the 1879 State Fair week, Weinstock & Lubins Mechanics' Store, in cooperation with the *Record-Union,* co-sponsored a display of arc lighting using a steam-driven mechanism which "produced an output equal to 4,000 candles," and further, the "brilliant illumination reduced the gaslights on K Street to a sickly flicker . . . of a pale yellow dog."

Yet despite these crowd-wowing effects, gas proved a tough competitor for electricity. The necessary infrastructure for gas already existed, whereas new-fangled electric light required wires strung from generating plants. In addition, gas could be used for heating and cooking as well as light. The first pole for the Waterhouse system, thirty feet long and made of redwood, was erected in front of the D. O. Mills bank building four years after Addison's Box Factory demonstration, and in another four years Lavinia's son was praised in newspapers from California to Chicago for his advanced incandescent light invention. Ongoing improvements during the 1880s brought full electricity into gradual acceptance as a main source of power. In July 1895, a booming 100-gun salute announced a major technological change as a small dam and powerhouse on the American River near the town of Folsom began generating electricity in the longest electrical transmission in the world—twenty-two miles downstream to Sacramento.

Lavinia may have extended her visit to Sacramento to observe Addison's electric light demonstration at the Pioneer Box Factory in November 1880. Although her name was not listed in the 1880 Sacramento City Directory, she appeared on the June 3, 1880, Sacramento Census, living in a hotel instead of a private home. Possibly soon after February 1879, when she took part in the meeting following the constitutional convention's failure to pass woman suffrage, Lavinia retired from active business life and relocated to a cottage built on land she had purchased earlier in Pacific Grove, a community in then sparsely-populated Monterey County, California. According to Monterey County archives, Lavinia donated eight of the more than fifty town lots she eventually acquired in Pacific Grove to the town for, as it was then called, "an old ladies home," a caring and generous bequest to provide for elderly homeless women who had no other options.

Lavinia Goodyear Waterhouse did not live to see the fruition of her campaign for women's rights; she died in Pacific Grove on April 1, 1890, at age eighty-one. Hers was a lavish funeral. According to Lucy Neely McLane's *A Piney Paradise,* a denizen of Pacific Grove proudly remarked that El Carmelo Cemetery's first body for burial was "imported" from Sacramento and that the funeral procession was half a mile long. Some confusion exists because the event was recounted by descendants of the eyewitnesses. The deceased in this story was referred to as "he," but the marker cited was "L. G. Waterhouse, 1890," above a mound wedged between tall pine trees. This would be Lavinia, not Charles, and surely it was Lavinia's funeral cortege that was so impressive, not her husband's. It is not known if Lavinia herself arranged the re-interment of her husband's and sister's remains or if this was done later by her sons. Frank Goodyear Waterhouse, who died in 1921, also rests in the family plot.

Lavinia devoted many years of her life to women's issues, but her most fervent and dedicated cause wasn't realized until twenty-one years after her death. In 1911, male voters in California—with strong support from both Sacramento's *Bee* and *Union* newspaper editors—granted women the right to vote in a statewide referendum. California was the sixth and largest state to approve woman suffrage; the rest of the country followed in 1920 with the passage of the Nineteenth Amendment.

Lavinia Waterhouse, who pioneered the movement, could rest in peace.

13. Lavinia Waterhouse Circa 1870s.

Courtesy California History Room, California State Library, Sacramento

End Notes, Lavinia Waterhouse

[1]Estimates were for both real estate improvements and personal property. The stated estimate translates to $17,500,000 in today's gold values. Given the higher cost of construction materials and wages as well as clothing, furniture, and household items today, the loss was much greater in modern money.

[2]The festival's intake approximates $50,000 and Lavinia's fees translate to $1,250.

[3]A. P. Smith's strawberries and raspberries, when there were few local growers, cost the current equivalent of $75 per pound. Today strawberries are available in season at fruit stands all over Sacramento for as little as $2.50 for a generous basket.

Benefactress to a Maturing City: Margaret Crocker

Margaret Eleanor Rhodes Crocker was a lady one liked immediately. Kind, warm-hearted, and cordial, she radiated a naturally happy disposition. These were her characteristics throughout her life, from her beginnings in near poverty through her later position as an esteemed community leader and great benefactress. Credit for her social prominence belongs to Margaret's own genial nature. Her largest charitable bequests, made possible by the immense wealth her husband secured for his family twenty-something years after their marriage, came from her compassionate awareness of those less fortunate.

As a young woman, Margaret had little hope of the gilded life she would begin to enjoy in her forties, nor any idea that her innate kindness would lead to public adulation.

Some years before she was born, Margaret's American-born German father and Irish mother left their home in Pennsylvania with their growing family to seek better opportunities on the nation's western frontier. They were among the first pioneers in northern Ohio, where they worked hard to establish their home and farm. Just when the farm was beginning to show a return on their labor, Margaret's father John Rhodes died from a rattlesnake bite. Mrs. Rhodes was left with twelve children—three girls and nine boys—and no other means to feed and clothe them except what they gained from the soil. With the help of her sons, Mrs. Rhodes worked the farm; several months after John Rhodes' death, Margaret Ellen (or Eleanor) was born on February 25, 1822. The little girl grew up accustomed to the hard-working toil and routine of frontier life. Nothing is known of her early schooling. The quality of her girlhood education and Margaret's scholastic aptitude can be inferred from her later letters, written in a fine, deliberate hand with immaculate diction.

Mrs. Rhodes died in 1848, when Margaret was twenty-six. The siblings separated after their mother's death, some moving to other parts of the country. Margaret lived with one or another for a time, finally moving to her married sister's home in South Bend, Indiana. This sister, Ann Rhodes Bender, was about four years older than Margaret and the mother of four children. Her husband was Jacob Bender, a tailor. Here, and probably in Ohio, Margaret earned money as a seamstress. According to the August 1850 Census, the Benders and Margaret lived in Portage Township, St. Joseph County, Indiana.

Living in the same township, according to the same census, was an attorney named Edwin Bryant Crocker, four years Margaret's senior. The facts surrounding their meeting are somewhat clouded, as there were different versions published in news articles several years apart. One story is that Edwin and his first wife Mary Norton Crocker became acquainted with Margaret Rhodes, who was a fine contralto vocalist, when all three were members of a local choral group, and the two women became close friends. The Crockers, both native New Yorkers before they met and married in Indiana in 1845, had a daughter, born in 1848, named Mary Norton after her mother. Mary senior became ill, and Margaret Rhodes attempted to nurse her friend back to health. Edwin's wife didn't survive, leaving him grief-stricken but increasingly more solaced, over time, by Margaret's gentle friend-ship. The date of Mary's death is unknown; it occurred sometime before August 1850, when Edwin appeared on the census rolls living in the household of merchant Henry Hine, without his wife and daughter.

14. Margaret (Mrs. Edwin) Crocker.

Courtesy California History Room, California State Library, Sacramento

The second story is a bit more romantic. In this version Edwin was already widowed when he ordered a suit of clothes from tailor Jacob Bender. Margaret helped her brother-in-law with the order, but in sewing the vest, put the inside pocket on the wrong side. The error wasn't noticed until Mr. Bender delivered the garments personally, offering explanations and apologies. To the tailor's relief, Edwin Crocker treated the error as a good joke and asked to meet the young woman who had spoiled his vest. After their introduction the two discovered their mutual love of singing and joined the same church choir. Margaret, remembered by her Indiana friends as "a stately, fine-looking girl, kindly always, a regular sweet, old-fashioned girl," must have made a good impression on Edwin—whichever story is true.

Edwin, who had originally moved to the South Bend area to study law after an unsatisfying year laboring on his father's nearby Marshall County farm, was a hard-working man. By August 1850 he had taken over the practice of his retired law partner and sent his young daughter to live with relatives. He worked long hours not only as a lawyer but also as an active opponent of slavery. Possibly, he was boarding with the Hines after disposing of his own property to prevent it from being confiscated by his pro-slavery opposition. Around this time Edwin defended a group of runaway slaves from Kentucky. He boldly told the slaves to leave the courtroom as free men before the jury had even deliberated, whereupon the outraged owners took their slaves and evicted Edwin from the building. Eventually, he was forced to pay damages. Still grieving for his late wife and with his legal career swamped in controversy, Edwin began looking about for other places to start anew.

California beckoned. His brothers Charles, Clark, and Henry lived there, having emigrated as gold-seekers in March 1850. By 1852, the brothers had abandoned their gold claims for the surer livelihood of merchants, with stores in the Sierra Nevada foothills settlements known as the Mother Lode region for its rich gold deposits, and another in Sacramento City. This, Edwin decided, was his destination—but not without the woman he had come to love, Margaret Rhodes.

He proposed and she accepted, but on their way to be married, they almost lost each other. The plan was for Margaret to visit relatives and friends in her home state of Ohio and then meet her fiancé in Canandaigua, New York so she could become acquainted with his little girl. Edwin arrived at the railroad station first. When he couldn't find Margaret, he thought she had changed her mind and unhappily booked passage on the evening train for a pressing business obligation in New York City. Margaret, delayed by lost luggage, was unable to find Edwin when she finally arrived at the station. Concluding that he had decided against the marriage, she sadly bought a ticket on another evening train bound homeward to South Bend. An hour before each was to depart they found each other at a local hotel dining room, to their great relief and joy. They were married July 8, 1852, by Congregationalist clergyman Reverend Henry Ward Beecher, the nationally known abolitionist and advocate for women's rights, in Reverend Beecher's Brooklyn home.

The newlyweds departed via steamship for California a few days later. Their itinerary took them across the Isthmus of Panama: treacherous, disease-ridden terrain though a steaming jungle. A year later Margaret's sister-in-law Mary Ann Deming Crocker traversed a comparatively easier, alternate route across Nicaragua with her bridegroom Charles Crocker, describing the journey in a letter to a friend. The scenery, she enthused, was beautiful and wondrous: trees with five kinds of leaves, calla lilies growing in wild profusion, orchids, and exotic fruits ripening. According to Mary Ann, riding a mule sidesaddle for twelve miles was an adventurous, laughter-inducing aspect of her journey. On the downside, the water was unfit to drink, and she and Charles were sick most of the time. On the whole, Mary Ann Crocker found her Nicaraguan crossing interesting. In 1852 Margaret and Edwin would have seen similar amazing sights on the Panamanian isthmus: beautiful flowers, birds with vibrant plumage, and chattering monkeys. Most likely they availed themselves of the under-construction railroad for part of the way, resorting to mules at the end of the tracks twelve miles from Panama City. Conditions tended to improve from one year to the next. Traveling earlier, the Edwin Crockers experienced the same or even worse dreary hardships than the Charles Crockers—but Margaret's impressions and opinions aren't known.

At Panama City Edwin and Margaret boarded the steamship *Northerner*, arriving in San Francisco at noon on August 26, 1852, after brief stops at Acapulco and San Diego. The *Northerner* had its own hazards; one passenger fell overboard and drowned and two others died on the voyage. Their stay in San Francisco was probably just long enough to recover from the typical bout of seasickness many travelers suffered on the sometimes turbulent voyage from Central America—and to savor a meal or two of longed-for fresh produce. Continuing on, they joined Edwin's brothers in Sacramento, where they moved into the upper rooms above the Crocker, Brother & Company dry goods store, a two story frame building at 246 J Street between Eighth and Ninth Streets.

They shared the upstairs rooms with Edwin's younger brothers Clark and Henry. Charles was just leaving, or had already left, for Indiana to wed his sweetheart. Edwin assisted with the mercantile operation in Charles's absence and Margaret set up housekeeping. She likely prepared many meals for the whole family, relieving her brothers-in-law from doing their own cooking or taking their meals at a continually changing choice of restaurants and hotel dining rooms. Given Margaret's space restrictions, she probably cooked and baked on small, portable tin appliances like the ones sold to miners for use in the outlying gold regions.

Margaret would have found her new home a very busy town. The city streets, shops, and saloons were constantly crowded as the daily influx of hundreds of new immigrants continued unabated. Diseases brought from the prairies and ships were still circulating although the severity had lessened somewhat. The need to sterilize polluted drinking water was unknown, and, until the Water Works was built in 1854 (which didn't filter or purify river water either), household water was siphoned directly from the rivers and sold door-to-door in barrels delivered by horse cart.

As a result many inhabitants contracted water-borne typhoid fever—as did Margaret. The night of the great fire on November 2, 1852, she was so ill her family feared for her life. She had to be carried on her mattress to a point of relative safety on G Street, upwind of the raging conflagration. The fire destroyed almost ninety percent of the city, although here and there a scorched California oak remained standing above the rubble. Lost were hundreds of homes, several churches, City Hall, the state hospital, and many hotels. Nine entire blocks of J Street were reduced to cinders, including the Crocker & Brothers frame building. The fire claimed fewer than twelve lives but left many more wounded.

Margaret recovered, and so did the devastated "City of the Plains." On the morning of November 4, hammers could be heard ringing out over the smoldering ruins. But like thousands of others, the Crockers were left homeless. With boards and materials costing fifty dollars[1] that he procured from somewhere in the burned-out town, Edwin threw up a crude one-room hut for their living quarters on the charred ground at the rear end of the lot where the store had been. The couple had hardly settled in when heavy rains in December swelled the rivers. An initial levee break was hastily repaired but the rivers rose again, sweeping away the bridge on J Street near Sutter's Fort. One morning Margaret and Edwin awoke to find their bedroom floor covered in several feet of water and much of the inside strewn with water-logged soda crackers that had been washed out from a box in the corner. Improvising quickly, they raised the little shed and their bed and stove on pegs and blocks, using a plank to walk the few feet from one side to the other. The flood ebbed and flowed; on New Year's Day 1853 the water stood six inches deep on their floor. Margaret sat on the bed to make bread and pies while Edwin baked them and prepared breakfast. Meals were walked back over the plank to the bed to be eaten.

The surrounding countryside had the appearance of one big lake with the carcasses of oxen and horses floating on the turbid waters. As had happened in the 1849-50 floods, citizens traversed the streets in boats. Hundreds fled to higher ground five miles east of town where a temporary settlement called Hoboken sprang into being with tent houses and lively places of business. The return of clear weather brought a decline in the waters and by the end of January stage lines resumed their routes to the mining areas. Hoboken disappeared as people returned to their homes in the city even though the ashes of the recent fire mingled with the soft earth made getting about fairly intolerable. City bonds were issued to raise funds for levee repair, and Sacramento's "New Levee" was completed the following January (1854) at a cost of $150,000. [2]

Edwin's brother Charles Crocker and his bride arrived from Indiana on a rainy day in March 1853, temporarily taking rooms in a hotel. After surveying the 761 new structures around town that had been erected since the fire, sixty-five of them in brick, he assessed the damage to his own property. Charles ordered an iron front from New York for his proposed construction of a new store in substantial brick, available and relatively inexpensive before the fire at $7 to $8 dollars per thousand,[3] but now in such demand that brickyards were taking orders. In the meantime he and his bride needed less expensive shelter than the $25 per week they were paying at their hotel. Charles and Mary Ann arrived on a Wednesday; on Thursday Charles bought lumber, exorbitantly high at $115 to $225 per thousand feet,[1] and built an addition to Margaret and Edwin's little one-room abode. This construction, finished in less than a week's time, became the bedroom for both couples partitioned only by a hanging length of fabric. The inside planks walls were decoratively covered floor-to-ceiling in cloth. In a letter to a friend, Mary Ann said she was quite content with her bedroom's washstand, small glass window, large looking glass, and pretty carpet. Each side of the partition had the same amenities; certainly there was precious little privacy. The original room Edwin built served as the family's common dining room, kitchen, parlor, and storage area.

With Charles' return, Edwin no longer felt the need to safeguard his brother's interests. No doubt happily handing back the reins, Edwin was admitted to practice law in California on May 7, 1853. On September 3, 1853, the *Daily Union's* "City Business Cards" column carried an advertisement for Crocker, McKune and Robinson, Attorneys and Counsellors at Law with offices in Read's Block on the corner of Third and J Streets.

The new Crocker & Brothers 25- by 60-foot, two story brick building at 246 J Street was ready for occupancy in mid-September 1853. As planned, the lower floor was used for the dry goods and clothing mercantile while the upper floor served as a dwelling for the two couples and Margaret's brother-in-law, Clark, who worked in the store. Henry Crocker had at some earlier time left the merchant business to become a printer at the State Journal Office and resided elsewhere, allowing more space for the other five adults to share.

Margaret and Edwin lived above the store for several months. It might have been during 1853 when they sent for Edwin's daughter Mary Norton to join them, but who escorted the little girl to California and exactly when she arrived is unknown. What is known is that Margaret welcomed her motherless step-daughter with open arms, possibly already expecting her own baby when Mary joined the household. On May 3, 1854, Margaret gave birth to a daughter they named Kate Eugenie.

That year the family moved into their own home, a modest wood-frame house at 83 Seventh Street between F and G, situated on two city lots in a thinly populated area north of the business district more habitats to quail, rabbits, and coyotes than humans. The Crockers had developed a keen interest in Sacramento's agricultural potential, and allowing for their house and some outbuildings, this location offered plenty of space to plant an orchard and vegetable garden.

First, though, the land had to be cleared; wild grape vines, masses of young trees, and a few sycamores crowded the arable portion. As Edwin later reported to the State Agricultural Society, "The expense of clearing the ground of stumps and roots was no small item" and, of course, neither was the cost of digging holes three feet across by four feet deep for the more than one hundred fruit and shade tree saplings they began planting in January 1855. Into the nurturing soil went several varieties of pear, apple, plum, peach, nectarine, cherry, apricot, quince, orange, pomegranate; two each of English walnut, fig, and olive trees. Several plots were raised for vegetables and masses of flowers. For shade they installed Pride of India, American elm, cottonwood, catalpa, and laburnum. Scattered about the house and yard were camellias, oleander, lemon-scented verbena, honeysuckle, and other shrubs.

All of this surrounded what Edwin described as "a small dwelling house." If similar in design to other ordinary 1850s Sacramento homes, it was likely a rectangular one- or two-story building constructed—in acknowledgement of the disastrous floods already experienced—upon a high-walled basement, with access to the front porch and door by a staircase stepping up from the ground. Guessing from subsequent census reports that listed only immediate family members, it was too small to accommodate live-in servants.

With the calamities of fire and flood behind them and their home garden established, Margaret and Edwin found time for other diverse outside interests: the arts and music, their church, their avid support of area-wide agricultural development, and, for Edwin, politics. Back home in Indiana, Edwin and his first wife had been members of the local Congregational Church; in Sacramento Edwin and Margaret joined Reverend Joseph Benton's established congregation of the same faith. Besides religious services the dynamic Reverend Benton offered frequent Sunday afternoon lectures on secular topics, charity "fairs" managed by the ladies, and occasional musical programs. In February 1853, the church opened its doors for a concert starring the "Swan of Erin," Catherine Hayes. Almost certainly the Crockers attended the first Grand Concert of the newly-formed Philharmonic Society held at the Congregational Church three years later on April 9, 1856. A follow-up story in the *Union* the next day reported that the spacious building was filled with a greater attendance than for any previous musical entertainment in the city. Selections for the varied program featured violin solos, arias, vocal solos, duets, and choruses—all, according to the press, "rapturously encored." Further, the *Union* opined, "the immense audience . . . evidence[s] an increasing desire . . . to foster and encourage the beautiful, refining art of music . . . ." The concert must have delighted the couple with not only the presentation but also the opportunity to make new friends among music enthusiasts like themselves. At these events and regular Sunday services, they met fellow church members who were already civic and business leaders, people who shared their views of the area's agricultural potential and the best approach to effectively promote cultural, economic, and political change.

Sacramento's population came to California from all over

America and the world, bringing with them their hometowns' cultures, beliefs, viewpoints, and prejudices. From its earliest days the citizens often hotly voiced dissenting opinions concerning squatters vs. landowners, Southern slave-owning interests vs. Northern abolitionists, and other issues. A new political party calling themselves Republicans emerged in 1854, organized by year end in all the northern states by groups who were concerned about the spread of slavery into the new territories petitioning for statehood. California was admitted as a free state in 1850, but this status did not at all deter the aggressiveness of pro-slavery sentiment within its boundaries. The Republican Party platform opposed slavery in the territories, favored a transcontinental railroad, and espoused national unity. Edwin Crocker, a committed abolitionist who had personally driven or guided runaway Southern slaves to freedom via the "underground railway" in Indiana, became a driving force behind the formation of the Republican Party in California, soon after his brother Charles was sworn in as a city Alderman in April 1855, for a one year term. Elected for the same term was Mark Hopkins, a hardware merchant on K Street, just one block away from Crocker's dry goods store. Charles Crocker and Mark Hopkins soon found that they had much in common, voting the same on education and anti-slavery issues. Charles introduced Edwin to Mark, and through him both met Hopkins' partner Collis Huntington.

Encouraged by his new friends, Edwin Crocker formed The Republican Club in early 1856 as a forum for discussion between like-minded men. The meetings were held in a room on the second floor of the Huntington & Hopkins hardware store and grew to include more than twenty-two members of diverse occupations. Leland Stanford, another K Street shopkeeper, joined the group later in the year. This is likely the time when Edwin, Charles, Hopkins, Huntington, and Stanford became well acquainted and

15. State Agricultural Pavilion on M Street Circa 1859.

Courtesy California History Room, California State Library, Sacramento

forged a sound bond that would lead to their joint efforts in civic improvements, political activity, and—eventually—a partnership to create the western end of a transcontinental railroad.

The environment in which the Republican Club members operated was frequently hostile, owing to their anti-slavery stance. In mid-May 1856, a handbill printed in large, conspicuous type was tacked up all over Sacramento accusing the group's members of traitorous agitation—and advocating the formation of a committee to hang its leaders. If she saw it, this "call to arms" by obviously hotheaded intimidators undoubtedly prompted chills of fear in Margaret's heart, perhaps soothed by her husband's watchful, fearless character and renowned common sense. Undaunted, the club held the first state Republican Convention later that month, drawing delegates from thirteen counties. The national caucus chose former California Senator John Charles Fremont as their nominee for President of the United States. Fremont lost to James Buchanan, but Edwin Crocker emerged as a more visible, prominent political force.

Since his admittance to the California Bar three years earlier, his growing reputation as an honest, capable attorney with an intuitive perception for the underlying principles of law, and his recognized expertise in common law, earned Edwin a large clientele and lucrative practice. Margaret would be publicly praised many years later for making charitable donations "as soon as she was able." Perhaps it was then, with family finances becoming more secure, that she began making quiet gifts to worthy causes and individuals when the ordinary amenities of life in a still fluctuating community weren't always available to those less fortunate.

Misfortune found them, too, in a different way. Margaret and her husband suffered their first family tragedy just as Edwin's fortunes and influence were rising. Their infant son Edwin Clark died of whooping cough September 21, 1856, only sixteen days after his birth.

Their next child was healthy. In mid-August 1857 the couple joyfully welcomed the arrival of Nellie Margaret. Their daughter Mary Norton was already attending school; now they had Kate and Nellie, who would, in a few short years, be old enough to enter the classroom. This reality may have led to a discussion of a way to aid their daughters' educations and benefit the community as well: the establishment of a public library. Interest in one had lagged for several years since the 1852 fire destroyed the Mercantile Library Association's holdings. In October 1857, prominent civic leaders Edwin and Charles Crocker, Mark Hopkins, Leland Stanford and twelve other leading merchants and lawyers raised $25,000[4] to found what eventually became the Sacramento Public Library. Some historians argue that this project was instigated by the gentlemen's wives.

By 1858 the Crocker's home garden was productive enough to garner awards at the State Agricultural Society's Annual Fair held that year in Marysville. Besides the fruit and nut trees, the garden boasted strawberry beds, currants, gooseberries, hops, asparagus, horse radish, potatoes, corn, tomatoes, cucumbers, and over a hundred grape vines. Margaret's entries won best exhibit for her dried pears, dried quinces, and canned fruits. The Crockers believed sun dried fruits were superior to oven dried—but either method was no small endeavor. The home garden harvest produced hundreds, if not thousands, of pieces that had to be hand-sorted for blemishes, washed, pitted or cored, and sliced uniformly to enable drying at an equal rate. Next the fruit was arranged in a single, spread-apart layer on wooden flats covered with cheesecloth or fine netting to discourage winged insects, and individually turned once a day for several days to promote equal drying. If Margaret didn't implement every detail with her own hands, she certainly supervised every step in the process. Edwin won a third-best award for a fresh pears exhibit and was elected to serve as the society's vice president for the year 1859.

The 1859 Agricultural Fair was held in Sacramento, its new permanent location after moving about between Marysville, Stockton, and San Jose. Margaret won a first premium for both dried and canned fruits, and second place for her raisins, homemade pickles and catsup. Mary Norton, only eleven, took second place for her sample of domestic wheat bread, winning a silver medal. Ladies' names were in evidence as committee members and judges, primarily in the categories of flowers, embroidery, and other handicrafts. Also exhibiting that year (and the prior year) was the artist Charles Nahl, who took a silver medal for best watercolor painting in 1858. For the 1859 competition, he submitted oils on canvas, India ink drawings, glass engravings, and a watercolor of two quails. The state fairs were likely where the Crockers, drifting from booth to booth of the exhibitors to share ideas and chat, became acquainted with the artist whose works they would later patronize.

The Crockers were appreciative, too, of the art and beauty found in nature. If the greenhouse Margaret eventually built and tended in the family's O Street mansion was any indication, she enjoyed cultivating flora and personally tending the more than thirty-seven varieties of climbing and bush roses, plus the geraniums, chrysanthemums, carnations, petunias, and bulb flowers in the Seventh Street home garden. The flower plots must have been spectacular and brought her joy and satisfaction when in bloom, with so many rose colors among the lilies and gladiolus and the white, lilac, yellow, red, purple, and maroon dahlias.

Margaret also derived genuine pleasure from helping others. It can only be imagined how many baskets of fresh produce and flowers from her garden found their way into the homes of the sick and destitute about town. Her flowers graced her own home and dining table too, for the sociable couple liked to entertain their growing circle of friends—simply at first in the modest Seventh Street home and more lavishly later on. The couple enjoyed the city's lively social scene: soirees, private house parties, social club gatherings and charitable fund-raising events. Sacramento's benevolent societies, several of them the recipients of the Crocker's financial support, expanded their facilities and good works through the end of the decade. The Sacramento Mutual Benevolent Association was organized in 1856, the Howard Benevolent Association in 1857, and the Protestant Orphan Asylum in 1858. The last two were especial interests of the Crockers.

Their own family was expanding and prospering as well. Daughter Jennie Louise was born in 1860.

By 1859 Edwin Crocker was practicing law as a sole proprietor after a period spent in partnership alone with Robinson. The 1859-60 city directory listed Edwin's former partners John McKune and Robert Robinson, respectively, as judges for the District and County Courts. Just as well he had no partnership obligations, for Edwin was increasingly drawn to a dynamic idea taking shape in the minds of men like his brother Charles and political associates Mark Hopkins, Collis Huntington, and Leland Stanford. A young, brilliant engineer named Theodore Judah had convinced them it was possible to lay steel tracks across the razorback spine of the Sierra Nevada to form the western leg of a transcontinental railroad. Many nights of discussion followed Judah's thought-provoking presentation to some thirty Sacramento businessmen and potential investors at the St. Frances Hotel the night of December 20, 1860. Several men at that meeting persuaded themselves and each other to finance a thorough survey of Judah's proposed route over the Sierras.

The project fell victim to the worst possible timing insofar as securing support from Congress for a transcontinental railroad.

During the latter part of the 1850s decade elected officials had their thoughts focused elsewhere as the nation was fast approaching a crisis over the question of slavery. Elected in November 1860, President Abraham Lincoln was sworn in March 4, 1861—but by then seven states had already seceded from the Union and war was imminent. Yet the Sacramento men who endorsed Judah's plan decided to go forward. The Central Pacific Rail Road of California was incorporated June 28, 1861, naming Leland Stanford president, Collis Huntington vice-president, Mark Hopkins treasurer, Sacramento jeweler James Bailey secretary, and Theodore Judah chief engineer. Charles Crocker was given a chair on the board of directors without formal office. Edwin Crocker drafted the articles of association and other necessary papers.

Just weeks earlier the Civil War had erupted on April 12, 1861, with the Confederacy's attack on Fort Sumter, North Carolina. Because troop transport to the warfront was so expensive, California's primary contribution was the money it raised for the Sanitary Fund (precursor to the Red Cross), begun in San Francisco in 1862. Edwin and Charles Crocker, along with Mark Hopkins and Leland Stanford, gave freely of their time to the Sacramento Valley Sanitary Association, while their wives formed a Women's Auxiliary to raise funds through concerts and picnics.

The women also carried the burden for the collection of lint (threads) from old linen, to be rolled into bandages and sent to the front lines. Leland Stanford's wife Jane chaired one of several Ladies Linting Associations about town, recruiting Frances Hopkins, Margaret and Mary Ann Crocker, and the wives of the other Central Pacific directors. In his memoirs Tim Nolan Hopkins, then the young ward of Mark and Frances Hopkins, recalled those women gathering together in their homes, and he remembered the poor lighting they endured while painstakingly picking apart squares of cloth. Sacramento's gas plant was operational, but their limited facilities afforded poor illumination.

Instead, Tim said, the general practice in private houses was to remove the curtains and shades from the windows, fit wooden laths across the sills and middle sashes, and fasten tallow candles on the laths with a cluster of nails. The lighted candles gave a surprisingly good result, but meant careful watchfulness lest the house catch on fire.

Margaret volunteered her time to the war effort early on. Mrs. E. B. Crocker and five other "Undersigned Ladies of Sacramento," as the headline read, made a public plea in the August 16, 1861 *Sacramento Daily Union* for patriotic men and women to meet at a local hall to assist in "furnishing clothing and other articles indispensible to the comfort of our soldiers [Sacramento's Washington Rifles] when far away from home." The differing circumstances of Margaret's co-volunteers in this appeal suggest the diversity of her wide circle of friends. One of the "undersigned ladies," Mrs. E. Baldwin, listed herself in city directories as a physician, a designation commonly used by water-cure practitioners; another was the wife of a steamboat captain.

In November 1861 the Republican Party succeeded in electing Leland Stanford as California's eighth governor on a staunchly pro-Union/anti-slavery ticket. Stanford's inauguration on January 10, 1862, was plagued with the worst recorded flood in Sacramento's history, forcing the Governor-elect and his wife to go to his inauguration in the only transport possible: a rowboat. The previous December a large wall of water had overflowed the American River levee at various points, flooding a large part of the countryside and most of the downtown city. The Crocker's house between F and G Streets—on somewhat higher ground than the city proper—quickly filled with three feet of water rapidly rolling over the roads from the northeast. In other parts of town the water stood six feet or more. Bridges collapsed; the Sacramento Valley Railroad lost sections of its tracks. After several days and desperate efforts by work crews the flood began to recede, but ultimately these measures were as ineffective as trying to bail out a sinking ferryboat with a tin cup.

Margaret and Edwin had scarcely begun evaluating their situation before incessant rains, coupled with melting snow in the mountains, again swelled the valley rivers and their tributaries. On January 11, 1862 the American River raged through a levee break east of Thirty-first Street, and by then nearly the entire Sacramento Valley was under several feet of water. As in the 1853 inundation, everything reeked of accumulated filth and the dead bodies of drowned animals when the water finally ebbed. For weeks afterward the only way of getting around was by wading through inches of mud. Walls, carpets, furniture, household goods and merchants' inventories were irrevocably damaged; even the underlying structures of homes and buildings had to be evaluated and, if necessary, repaired.

The Crocker's sizable, lovingly tended home garden required rescue and rehabilitation as well. No doubt portions of it were drowned past revival. Nevertheless, some of their produce was entered in the annual Agricultural Fair competition that October. The *Daily Alta California's* reporter opined on October 3, 1862, that the display at Sacramento's Pavilion "was rather limited in character," yet praised the variety of fruits. Edwin's name was listed as a contributor without giving details of his submissions. Continuing to the home productions category, the newsman claimed that the preserves, pickles, and jams department "was filled with the handiwork of Mrs. Crocker [and two other Sacramento ladies]."

During the flood clean-up good news came from a different quarter. President Lincoln signed the Pacific Railroad Bill in July 1862, granting government funding and land use, with certain caveats and restrictions, for a route through the heart of the country with two railroad companies building from opposite ends. The franchise for the western end was given to the Central Pacific. Additional support was expected to come from state subsidies. Theodore Judah, in Washington at the time of the bill's passage, wired his colleagues in Sacramento: "We have drawn the elephant, now let us see if we can harness him." Groundbreaking ceremonies were held at the foot of K Street on January 8, 1863, witnessed by a multitudinous and cheering crowd.

Five months later, in May 1863, President Lincoln appointed California Chief Justice Stephen J. Field to the United States Supreme Court. Sitting Justice Warner W. Cope succeeded Field as Chief, creating a vacancy in the high court of one chief and two associate justices then required by the California Constitution. Governor Leland Stanford appointed Edwin Bryant Crocker as Associate Justice to fill the unexpired term. The appointment was not well received in some quarters, particularly among those who feared conflict of interest because of Edwin's association with the railroad builders, and several local newspapers voiced their objections. Happily for Margaret and the children, Edwin's new duties didn't mean he had to leave hearth and home to serve. From late 1854 through the early 1870s, the California Supreme Court held their sessions in Sacramento's courthouse. Edwin served from May 1863 to January 1864, handing down a record number of decisions during his time on the bench. For the rest of his life he was known and addressed as Judge Crocker.

Throughout his tenure on the bench and possibly for years afterward, Margaret packed her husband's workday lunches (Judge Crocker was known for carrying a lunch pail to avoid wasting time away from his desk), warmed up suppers when he was invariably late for family meals, cared for their daughters, spent hours in the family's gardens, and gave time to church and charitable commitments. Like the other wives of successful Sacramento shopkeepers and professional men, Margaret probably used the services of a weekly laundress. Her merchant brother-in-law

Charles Crocker sold children's clothing as early as 1856, but given that Margaret earned her living as a seamstress in her single days, it is reasonable to suppose she might have found pleasure in stitching knee-length dresses and ruffle-trimmed pinafores for her little girls in the early years, before Edwin's income escalated. Gloves, ribbons, thread, gaiters, lace collars and parasols were also on the shelves at Charles Crocker & Company's fancy dry goods store to complete their wardrobes.

Meanwhile the Civil War raged on, and most northern California cities' sentiments were, in the main, pro-Union. In Sacramento, the almost simultaneous Union victories at Gettysburg and Vicksburg were the cause of a triumphant torchlight procession through the city streets in July 1863. Some one thousand citizens, on foot or in carriages, followed fire engine companies, militia units, and musical groups on a march that snaked along buildings festooned with American flags, culminating in fireworks in front of the preeminent Orleans Hotel. Margaret may or may not have participated in this celebration because on April 18, 1863 she gave birth to her fifth and last natural child, Amy Isabella, born when Margaret was forty-one.

Now the mother of four active girls while nursing an infant, Margaret somehow managed to find time for preserving their home garden's produce. She is noted as an "additional entrant" at the Tenth Annual Fair in 1863 where she entered nine varieties of dried fruit and five varieties of pickles.

When his term of office on the Supreme Court was completed in January 1864, Edwin was recruited as the Central Pacific Rail Road's chief counsel and general agent. It was a position to which he was well suited, not only for his mature expertise in common law but also for his education and experience when a younger man. Before taking up the law in 1842, he graduated from Van Rensselaer School (now Rensselaer Polytechnic Institute) in Troy, New York, class of 1833, with a concentration in scientific courses. For about three years after his graduation, until he relocated to his father's farm in Indiana, Edwin was employed as an apprentice civil engineer engaged in laying out several railway lines. Aided by Edwin's engineering knowledge and legal skills after Theodore Judah's premature death from yellow fever in 1863, the first eighteen miles of Central Pacific Rail Road track, from Sacramento to Junction (now Roseville), opened for passenger service April 26, 1864. Two months later, the tracks stretched to Newcastle.

Edwin took up permanent space in the railroad's offices on K Street above the Huntington & Hopkins hardware store and slowly began accumulating shares of railroad stock, both by purchase and as compensation for his services. By the 1870s he was listed as one of the company's largest private investors. A review of Margaret's later bequests to Sacramento suggests that the couple also must have begun modestly investing in local real estate at this time.

While Edwin immersed himself in earlier-established workaholic habits, Margaret enjoyed her private endeavors, although neither confined themselves to narrow breadwinner-homemaker roles. Both, it appears, had boundless energy. (When she was sixty Margaret was still noted for her firm step, upright posture, and ability to tire out her younger companions while traveling or exercising.) The couple was known in Sacramento for their cordial hospitality—and Margaret, personally, for her continued efforts to seek out the poor and provide aid. Together they sponsored church programs, served on civic improvement committees, and spent much time and effort in their garden. Undoubtedly they hired help for the harder labor, yet winning State Fair prizes required a good deal of personal care, attention, and planning. Quickly, as evidenced by Edwin's report to the Agricultural Society, they became knowledgeable about growing seasons and the various harvest times of their fruits and vegetables—from peaches in late June to grapes in July, August, and September. Margaret knew their asparagus was ready to eat and savor in March.

By the spring of 1865, the CPRR was open thirty-six miles east from the city terminus, resolutely headed toward a 2,400 foot elevation in the upper Sierra foothills at Colfax. The Associates, as the railroad directors called themselves, were closing in on the requisite forty miles of laid track before they could receive federal funding.

And in the South, General Lee surrendered. Sacramento's joyous, days-long celebration of the war's nominal end was barely over before telegrams from Washington—received on the morning of Saturday, April 15—communicated the shocking news that President Abraham Lincoln had been assassinated. Nearly every door and window in town was draped in black cloth, as were the Central Pacific's locomotives. By common agreement among the city's clergymen, the usual Sunday evening programs were cancelled in favor of public gatherings where, the *Daily Union* announced, "citizens might express the deep and profound feelings pervading the community." Before a large assembly at the First Congregational Church, following Reverend Dwinell's Scripture reading and relinquishment of his pulpit to "this meeting of citizens," Edwin Crocker was the first speaker, delivering a long and patriotic eulogy.

Sometime in the spring of 1867, the foundations for the railroad's Sacramento shops were in place for work areas that would encompass a machine shop, car shop, roundhouse, foundry, paint shop, two storehouses, and other necessary quarters that would initially employ five hundred men. In the early summer of that year the Central Pacific's offices moved into expanded quarters, which Edwin dressed up with maps, pictures, and portraits (of himself and Charles), cajoling the others—without success—to have their own portraits or daguerreotypes made to complete his "art" display, one of his first public displays among associates who surely already knew of his growing interest.

In 1868 Central Pacific's tracks cleared the Sierra Nevada summit: elevation, 7,042 feet.

The year the railroad surmounted the mountains, Edwin was fifty, Margaret forty-six, and their girls aged five to twenty. Since 1854 the family had lived and flourished, entertained friends, refurbished after floods, and celebrated the marriage of their daughter Mary Norton Crocker to Charles Scudder, at their little house in today's Alkali Flat neighborhood. By this time they were not without means; perhaps they had been waiting for just the right property to come on the market. They found such a property in January 1868, when they purchased the home of pioneer banker Benjamin Hastings, including some furnishings, outbuildings, and three adjoining lots at the corner of Third and O Streets.

The Hastings home, built in 1852 or 1853, was a handsome Georgian-style, elaborate structure with broad verandas. Judge Crocker's new personal project became the renovation of the home and grounds, a project he expected to happily occupy his few leisure hours away from a heavy work schedule. He chose the same architect his brother Charles had earlier employed, the eminent Seth Babson. The historical record gives him the credit for the home's renovation, although surely Margaret's input, desires, and ideas were just as crucial and welcomed by her husband. When finished the home was a dignified residence, standing on a terrace several feet above the street. A formal porch stretched across the front; pilastered columns joined by arches supported the flat roof of an open porch for the second story. A veranda on the south side was converted into a conservatory where Margaret raised exotic plants. The interior featured two parlors, a dining room, and Judge and Mrs. Crocker's bedrooms downstairs with more bedrooms and sitting rooms on the second floor. The basement contained servants' quarters and the kitchen, connected with the dining room by a dumbwaiter. Walls of the public rooms were decorated with gold-leafed, frescoed panels separated by long mirrors. The servants' quarters in the basement were luxuriously tiled and furnished. Stables and out-buildings for the family's horses and carriages occupied one of the lots.

The ambitious home-renovation project hadn't even begun when Edwin suffered his first stroke in April 1868. Weakened but iron-willed and unwilling to disappoint his associates, he returned to work two weeks later—undoubtedly over Margaret's objections—but the weight of his responsibilities in an already immense business was crushing. On doctor's orders to get fresh air and more exercise, Edwin began spending more time on out-of-office excursions to inspect the railroad's progress and taking pleasure jaunts to San Francisco, where Margaret probably accompanied him.

The five men who were the railroad's key investors and the ones most heavily involved in building it—Mark Hopkins, Leland Stanford, Collis Huntington, and the two Crocker brothers—all suffered from enormous stress. Their hours were long and their problems were many: shortages of iron, delays in receiving supplies, spiraling costs, delays caused by weather and the need to build twenty-three miles of snow sheds to protect the track, the inherent dangers to life and equipment in blasting fifteen miles of tunnels through solid granite, labor issues, controversy and litigation against the company, a sometimes hostile press (particularly the *Sacramento Daily Union*), and recurring financial quagmires. Charles Crocker, already a moderately wealthy merchant before undertaking the job as railroad construction supervisor, had, by 1859, moved his family into a stately home surrounded by wide lawns on Eighth Street between F and G. Designed and built by Seth Babson, it was an elegant, mansard-roofed, three-story residence the size of a private hotel. Charles claimed he spent no more than three nights in it during the six years of railroad construction.

To Edwin fell certain administrative tasks: negotiations to absorb smaller lines, a host of legal issues, voluminous correspondence, and a good amount of time spent in public relations. He applied himself with vigor, often rallying his partners forward, to a monumental effort that called upon his engineering education and experience, legal expertise, political connections, and personal charm.

The great endeavor hurtled forward. Even before the east-west tracks joined in Utah, the Central Pacific Railroad was among Sacramento's leading employers. The shops produced wheels, cars, machine parts, and eventually locomotives in the growing complex of buildings. A herculean push in April 1869 laid ten miles of track across the desert in one day, and on May 10 the celebrated Golden Spike, made of eighteen carat gold alloyed with copper, was ceremoniously pounded into the ties between facing locomotives to unite the Central Pacific and Union Pacific lines at Promontory, Utah, witnessed by a number of dignitaries and countless spectators. The event was a major milestone for America; coast to coast travel was now possible in days instead of weeks.

In Sacramento, bonfires lit the night skies and hundreds flocked into the city to witness the splendorous parade of banner-festooned carriages, wagons, marching bands, and fire engines. These were followed by hundreds on horseback, all underscored by canon fire and a fifteen-minute chorus from the steam horns of twenty-one locomotives. The two Crocker brothers, Mark Hopkins, and the company's clerks and engineers were feted at the official ceremony and post-parade programs all day. Margaret and the other directors' wives were not mentioned in news stories of the celebration. The ladies, whose homes were lighted with colored lanterns from basement to roof throughout the festivities, watched the spectacle from a second story balcony of the Hopkins-Huntington building.

A month afterward Edwin Crocker was in San Francisco on business when he collapsed on the steps of the elegant Lick House Hotel, victim to another stroke that left his right side partially paralyzed. It is not known if Margaret was with him on that trip, only that he was transported home as soon as possible. He never fully recovered, although he did improve: two weeks later he was able to get around inside his own home without the aid of a crutch. His speech and mobility were affected but apparently not his mind, innate graciousness, or interest in life, although he was forced to retire from business. Shortly thereafter Edwin and his brother Charles, who also decided he wanted to leave the company, began negotiations to sell their railroad interests to the other directors. The settlement, when finalized (although neither brother sold their CPRR stock), was a reported $1.8 million[5] each.

Margaret, it is said, gave up all her other commitments to care for her husband. On Monday, August 9, 1869—as the *Sacramento Daily Union* reported—Judge and Mrs. Crocker and their younger daughters left Sacramento by rail for a recuperative sojourn in Europe, leaving their home renovation and planned connecting art gallery building in the capable hands of their architect. Daughter Mary Norton and her husband Charles remained in Sacramento, living some of the time in the newly remodeled mansion.

The family's primary destination was Germany for its spas and museums. While they were abroad, Napoleon III's declared war on Prussia motivated many nervous art dealers and artisans to sell their inventories at reduced prices. The couple returned home nearly two years later on May 5, 1871, bringing back four railroad cars filled with paintings, drawings, and unusual pieces of Bohemian glass. Katie, seventeen that year and a talented budding artist who must have been thrilled and inspired by the grand paintings she saw in Europe, came home a month later while the other girls remained with family and friends in the East. That summer Margaret and Edwin broke ground for their gallery annex at the southeast corner of Second and O Streets.

In November they celebrated the birth of their first grandchild, Mary and Charles' daughter Kate Norton Scudder. The following February, they were among seven hundred guests at Leland Stanford's dazzling housewarming party to celebrate his spectacularly renovated mansion—by architect Seth Babson—at 800 N Street. For the occasion Margaret wore a maroon velvet gown embellished with satin folds and a pompadour corsage, a departure from her usual elegantly simple, unadorned attire. In May 1872, Margaret and Edwin traveled east to rejoin their three younger daughters.

They returned home in late September 1872, to find their gallery complex, which was more than just exhibition space for artwork, almost completed. The structure included a ballroom, a library with elaborately carved bookcases handcrafted by master cabinetmakers, a skating rink, bowling alley, and billiards room on the ground floor. Once the Italian-villa style building with its deep red frescos, Corinthian columns and rich woodwork throughout was finished, the carloads of paintings from Europe were installed Victorian-style, almost floor to ceiling, with their frames nearly touching. A skylight and artfully placed gas lights afforded good light to the pictures both day and evening. Starting near the northeast corner, a wing extended from the gallery, permitting access to the Crocker's private residence.

It is reported that Margaret was keenly interested in the art gallery's construction. Aside from the niches and cabinets on the south wall of the ballroom that held her own collection of art objects of exquisite glass work, it is not known which of the other finishing details or decor were her personal choices. Curious Sacramento newsmen, who couldn't help noticing the teams of men working about the grounds for months on end, noted progress from time to time. The entire project—residence, gallery, grounds—was completed circa 1873. Judge and Mrs. Crocker invited a number of local orphans to visit the gallery and have some carefree fun on the ground floor skating rink. Pipes found years later in the basement suggest the Crockers installed the newest, most wondrous convenience of the decade: an indoor toilet.

Exactly when Edwin and Margaret developed an avid interest in collecting art is unknown. Edwin might have begun to appreciate art in his student days in New York in the 1830s; certainly railroad business in the 1860s took him to San Francisco, where there were numerous public galleries and private studios owned by individual artists. Both, perhaps, became enraptured with the beauty of works displayed at the Agricultural Fairs they took part in. There is no doubt that cultural enrichment—art, music, literature and education—was important to both of them. At the couple's home, their personal library held a number of books on art dating back to the 1840s, which they might have read and discussed together.

Edwin acquired and cherished the collection of images taken by the CPRR's official photographer documenting the construction of the western half of the transcontinental railroad. The Crockers purchased artworks from local artists before their trip to Europe and bought dozens more afterward in 1872 and 1873. Two of the hundreds of works they ultimately acquired were purchased in the mid-to-late 1860s, before the O Street mansion and gallery were built. These were Thomas Hill's 40- by 54-inch *Sugar Loaf Hill* and Charles Nahl's *Race for the Bride,* although it's not known if they hung these pieces on the walls of their Seventh Street home or left them on display in San Francisco galleries while they were formulating plans to erect their own. Edwin and Margaret developed a personal relationship with the talented, acclaimed Nahl, commissioning several works—most notably Nahl's monumental, six- by ten-foot oil on canvas *Sunday Morning at the Mines*. In the early 1870s, the Crockers hired Nahl as an art tutor for their daughter Kate, who was talented enough to have her paintings shown at the San Francisco Art Association Gallery.

According to the few personal letters still remaining, the family was a happy one whose members, each in their own way, led productive lives while enjoying each others' company. They played cards together in the evenings and took carriage rides on balmy afternoons. They spent time each summer at Idlewild, their lovely vacation home nestled between tall pines in Lake Tahoe, where Edwin hoped to regain his vigor in the clear pine-scented air. Margaret took long walks through the woods and fished on the sparkling waters of the lake. In 1873 Edwin commissioned the building of a home in Sacramento immediately south of their own, facing P Street, as a gift to his daughter Mary Norton and son-in-law Charles Scudder. At some point between 1872 and 1875, Margaret and Edwin became the legal guardians of Margaret's grandnephew Elwood Bender after the death of the little boy's parents, bringing him into their home as part of the family.

The family shared in the joyous occasion of Kate Eugenie's marriage to James Gunn on February 2, 1874. The ceremony took place in the Crocker mansion, with Reverend Dwinell of the First Congregational Church officiating. As was the journalistic style then, the newspaper merely announced the marriage with no mention of a festive wedding reception, although dozens of the sociable, hospitable Crockers' friends were probably present to make toasts and share the bridal couple's happiness. Not ten months later, Katie died of kidney disease on October 26, 1874. She was only twenty-one. Kate Crocker Gunn's funeral was held two days later in the Crocker family home.

Edwin's health had been deteriorating since before Kate's nuptials; by 1873 he was spending much of his time in bed. Fourteen months after Kate's death, Edwin passed away on June 24, 1875, aged fifty-seven. Eloquent eulogies mourned his passing in the papers, at the Sacramento Bar meeting, and his funeral on the morning of June 26, in the family parlor.

After twenty-three years happily married to a vibrant, gregarious, philanthropic man, Margaret became a widow at fifty-three. Of the children still living at home, Nellie was eighteen, Jennie fifteen, Amy twelve, and Elwood just five. Judge Crocker had provided for his family's care and protection by filing, two years previously, papers naming his brother Charles the trustee of the entire estate, with instructions on its distribution to his heirs. Margaret inherited her home, furnishings, and stables plus one half of the estate as an individual, sharing the remainder with her daughters. Charles, of course, took his responsibilities as executor and personal advisor to heart, but after the requisite one year period of mourning, Margaret began to emerge as a capable, effective civic and social leader and magnanimous philanthropist in her own right.

First, however, she was a loving mother who had fatherless children to raise and educate. Further, she was a financially well-situated woman with siblings and other relatives she could help. At her invitation, a widowed sister came to live with her. With care and affection, she provided homes for various cousins, charging them a small rent for a short time until she saw they were getting along well and then deeded the house over to them. For others, she paid for educations or started them in business. Margaret loved to plan small surprises for her family, friends, and servants, and the more unsuspecting they were, the greater was her own delight. She thoroughly enjoyed the company of young people and encouraged her daughters to invite their own friends over frequently. Her strengths during those first years of widowhood were her family, her values, and her refusal to let her kind, genial temperament be soured by her personal losses.

The fourth year of her widowhood was an eventful one. It began happily with the wedding of Jennie Louise, now nearly nineteen, to Jacob Sloat Fassett, District Attorney of Chemung

County, New York, on February 13, 1879, at the Crocker's Sacramento residence. Margaret honored the couple with a grand reception when they returned from their Los Angeles honeymoon a week later. When the newlyweds departed for Jennie's new home on the East Coast, Margaret felt a sting of sorrow over being parted from her child. Her spirits rose again when she hosted a festive sixteenth birthday party for daughter Amy on April 18. About one hundred young people converged on the mansion for an evening of dining and dancing in the ballroom.

A month before Amy's party, Margaret had purchased the city lots bounded by Ninth, Tenth, X and Y Streets across from the City Cemetery, with the thought of building an immense greenhouse to experiment with exotic plants that might aid California agriculture, and also provide the poor with free flowers to place on the graves of their departed loved ones. When completed, the Bell Conservatory was the largest hot-house in the interior and architecturally one of the handsomest in the country; a reduced-scale copy of the original conservatory in San Francisco's Golden Gate Park. Margaret also donated lands for the enlargement of the City Cemetery. Surrounded by loved ones and with her widely acknowledged sunshiny nature subdued but intact, busy with children, devoted friends, and up to now quiet charitable bequests, Margaret's resolve to aid the needy deepened. And as it did, the press began to report her larger gifts.

On October 17, 1879 under the sub-head "Handsome Donation," the *Sacramento Daily Record-Union* noted: "Mrs. E. B. Crocker yesterday presented to the Women's Aid Society of this city a quarter of a block of land at the corner of Fifth and Q Streets. The property is worth some $4,000. She also presented the society, for the purposes of erecting the needy buildings, the sum of $10,000."[6]

A handsome gift indeed, but the newspapers and Sacramento citizens were much more excited by the scheduled appearance of former president General Ulysses S. Grant and his wife on their west coast tour. Days of preparation were dedicated to planning the official greetings at the train depot, the procession to the Capitol for public speeches, the private dinners, and the quality of the light gray horses chosen to draw the more important carriages. Margaret was one of five prominent ladies who comprised the official Escort Committee for Mrs. Grant. Festive buntings and banners draped Margaret's home to honor the occasion.

Yet this year, begun with promise and continued with happy times and good works, ended with another soul-searing tragedy combined with a pulse of new joy for Margaret. In November, her daughter Nellie traveled east to visit friends and sisters Jennie Fassett and Mary Norton, now divorced from Charles Scudder and remarried to Myron Walker. By Christmas Day, Nellie was confined to bed with a mysterious malady. She died suddenly on December 27, 1879, leaving family members and her fiancé stunned. Margaret, advised by telegram, sped to New York to bring her child back home for burial in the Sacramento family plot next to her father and sister Kate. While Margaret was still on board the transcontinental train from California to claim Nellie's remains, Jennie Crocker Fassett's first child, Bryant Sloat Fassett, was born December 31, 1879 in New York. Probably as solace to both herself and her mother, Jennie Fassett and her infant came west as soon as they were able. The June 1880 Census taken in Sacramento reveals that Jennie and her baby son Bryant were living in Margaret's household along with assorted other relatives, guests, and servants. After the period of mourning for Nellie passed, Margaret resumed her plans for the public greenhouse and another project close to her heart—finding or building a home for aged women who were unable to provide for themselves. To this end she purchased the block bordered by Seventh and Eighth, P and Q Streets, for $12,000[7] in 1880.

Sometime in late 1880 or early 1881, Margaret sent her

youngest daughter abroad for a European education, but within months learned of Amy's capricious hijinks and flirtations with unsuitable young paramours. Margaret sped to Europe to personally extricate her errant child with a firm but gentle hand, and take her on a tour through Germany, Spain, and England. Amy, now styling herself Aimee, was scarcely home again when she eloped on December 16, 1882 with Porter Ashe, a wealthy San Francisco playboy and inveterate gambler. What Margaret truly felt about this match isn't known; maybe she was relieved that her daughter was safely married and therefore no longer vulnerable to opportunistic gold-diggers. One week after the elopement, Margaret threw a fancy dress party in their honor. For a wedding gift she commissioned a near-palace on Van Ness Avenue in San Francisco. After the Ashes took residence, she visited them frequently.

One of Margaret's dreams was fulfilled with the official opening of the Marguerite Home for Aged Women on Seventh and Q Streets on the evening of February 25, 1884. It was a project she had supported since 1877, when articles of incorporation for the Women's Home Association were filed naming Margaret Crocker as its first president. As the *Union* opined in 1883, much talk had circulated for some time about establishing an elderly ladies' haven but nothing definite happened until "Mrs. E. B. Crocker took the matter in hand and proceeded at her own expense to carry out the design . . . after observing several such places on her recent trip [with Aimee] in the Old World."

With architect N. D. Goodell, an associate of Seth Babson, Margaret thoroughly planned each detail and paid for the remodeling of the existing dwelling (adding an L-shaped, 65- by 36-foot wing) and luxurious furnishings of the two-storied building and its surrounding park-like grounds. The home featured twenty-four bedrooms, each containing a fireplace, and intended for a single occupant. The parlor, reception, dining room, and other public areas were elaborately frescoed, carpeted, and decorated. Pictures for the walls and books for the residents' pleasure were liberally supplied. Margaret deeded the home to five trustees, all prominent Sacramento businessmen, with day-to-day direction given to their wives, and further supplied the trustees with a liberal endowment. Three years later, the Board of Trustees reported that the home was prospering. The *Sacramento Union* proudly asserted, with accolades to Mrs. Crocker, that there was no other institution to be found in any part of the world that exceeded the Marguerite Home either in its management or the character of its accommodations.

Nine months after the Marguerite Home's opening, Aimee's daughter Gladys Ashe—Margaret's fifth grandchild (Jennie had given birth to two more children, Margaret and Newton Fassett in 1881 and 1882, respectively) arrived November 21, 1884. Sometime that year or the next, Margaret commissioned the building of another personal residence at Third and Olive Streets in Los Angeles with the intention of spending more time near another sister who lived there.

Also in November 1884, Judge and Mrs. Crocker's long-time dedication and efforts to bring culture to Sacramento were echoing in other hearts. Several prominent citizens formed an association for the purpose of scientific research, cultivation of artistic tastes, and the study of California's natural resources, calling themselves the California Museum Association. The newly-formed society began giving public lectures and debates which attracted enough interest that the association enthusiastically felt that a large hall of their own might be useful as a public concert and lecture hall. Subscriptions were procured, but not enough, and the idea to hold a public art exhibit as a fund-raiser took shape. Committees of ladies canvassed Sacramento and San Francisco's wealthy residents for the loan of curios, artifacts, paintings, and statuary, yet the question of where to hold the exhibit remained.

David Lubin, president of the California Museum Association and co-owner of Sacramento's premier department store Weinstock-Lubin, was a long-time personal friend of Margaret and Edwin Crocker. He asked Margaret if she would help by loaning her art gallery as the site for the Art and Curio Loan Exhibit. Margaret, who had been gradually opening the Crocker's private art gallery to the public more often, usually for charitable benefits, agreed. The exhibit opened March 10, 1885.

The result was a brilliant success, with more than 12,000 private collection pieces on display, valued in the aggregate at more than $1 million dollars.[8] Intended to run only for a few days, the exhibit continued for two weeks, days and evenings, visited by over 30,000 people. Very much impressed with the association's plans and sound leadership, Margaret decided to present her art gallery and its collection to the California Museum Association for the benefit of the general public. Mr. Lubin, no doubt stunned by this offer, counter-proposed—in fact, insisted—that his group should first raise $100,000[8] to be used to maintain the building, its seven hundred framed paintings, and more than one thousand master drawings. Once this idea was out, more discussions followed. In the end, it was decided that Margaret would deed her husband's gallery and art collection to the City of Sacramento with the condition that the California Museum Association would occupy the premises and become custodian of the property.

When this agreement was announced the public awe, adulation, and appreciation for Margaret Crocker scaled to new heights. Everyone, it seemed, knew someone that her largess had already touched: individuals, churches, synagogues, schools, neighborhoods. The excited, delighted city fathers determined to show their appreciation with a grand floral festival where every citizen could take part. The Festival of Flowers took place the day and evening of May 6, 1885, attended by more than 15,000 persons. The new State Agricultural Society's glass-walled pavilion overflowed with flowers of every description, from offerings of humble wildflower blossoms to wreaths, thirty-foot pedestals, arches, bowers, miniature palaces, and other displays as large as today's Rose Parade floats, all made of flowers, vines, and plants contributed from all over the state.

Three thousand white-garbed school children paraded before the dais, laying many-hued bouquets at Margaret's feet. Eulogistic addresses and poems were recited; music was played and sung. The Sacramento Pioneer Society presented Margaret with magnificent engraved gold and silver plates. The festival's organizers gave her an oak case made from relics of Sutter's Fort richly bound in silver, with the intention of placing within the case two books (that were still being made) bound in gold and silver and velvet—one containing all articles from the press about her gift, and the other filled with hand paintings from California artists. Afterward the executive committee printed a seventy-three page, beautifully bound souvenir booklet made available to the festival's guests, listing names of the contributors and a description of their floral arrangement, with the printed apology that perfect records were impossible since many magnificent pieces had no card attached.

No other private citizen had ever been so honored. As the editors of the *Sacramento Bee* asserted—in multiple full-page articles detailing the event, Margaret's personal life, previous benefactions and a very lengthy list of the Crocker Art Gallery's holdings—it was "a higher tribute than King or Kaiser ever received." Dabbing her eyes, Margaret thanked the multitude, stating she was only implementing her late husband's intention to grant his art collection to the public. The *Bee* disputed this. The donation, they insisted, was hers alone. Perhaps unbeknownst to the news editors, their list of canvas art was short a few pieces. Margaret decided to omit one series of paintings, notwithstanding that she and Edwin commissioned this work for $5,000[9] in the early 1870s: Charles Nahl's *The Romans and the Sabines.* Feeling that the depictions of muscular Roman soldiers and scantily clad women were unsuitable subjects for public view, she instead donated these to private collector M. H. de Young in San Francisco.

The grand tribute didn't alter Margaret's unassuming nature, continued interest in helping the needy, or the way she lived her daily life, although it did bring forth a fresh spate of solicitations from would-be beneficiaries of her largess. As the *Sacramento Bee* reported, one young man wanted her to send him to Hawaii for his health. A girl who didn't like living with her relatives asked for money to open a millinery store, and another young woman— having read of Margaret's gift of the gallery to Sacramento—wrote to argue the unfairness of this donation when *she* was just as deserving. Despite these self-serving presumptions on her generous purse, Margaret's renowned benevolence continued unabated. She gave her time and money to locating and providing scholarships to deserving students of the Museum Association's Sacramento School of Design, supported Sacramento's Protestant Orphan's Asylum, and gifted the Cathedral of the Blessed Sacramento on K Street with a magnificent stained glass window and other valuable glass for the entry.

By 1886, Margaret's ornate, three-story Los Angeles mansion, a turreted landmark atop Bunker Hill for many years afterward, was ready for occupancy. Margaret and Aimee Crocker Ashe, whose marriage had collapsed, were residing there in 1887 when Porter Ashe created a national scandal by kidnapping young Gladys (also known as Alma) while Margaret and Aimee were out of the house. The resultant legal uproar finally awarded custody of the child to Margaret, who raised her granddaughter while Aimee led a globe-trotting lifestyle and wed four more husbands.

Aimee was married to second husband Harry Gillig when

Margaret was called to testify in a legal action brought by the pair against their maid because the Gilligs themselves were out of town on the court date. Much to her distress, Margaret's testimony was considered insufficient evidence and the jury found for the servant. According to *The Wave*, a weekly San Francisco society magazine, this incident broke her heart and was the reason Margaret decided, in late 1891, to leave Sacramento "and never return." More than that, though, was Margaret's longing to live near her daughters and grandchildren in New York. She had already suffered the loss of two grandbabies, both Jennie's children: the short-lived twin of Truman Fassett in 1885 and months-old Mary Fassett in 1888. A surprise going-away party hosted by Museum Association members on December 10, 1891 in the E. B. Crocker Art Gallery's ballroom drew two hundred friends.

Margaret lived in New York, with brief visits to the West Coast, for the rest of her days. Her last public gift to Sacramento was the donation of her own beloved home to the Peniel Rescue Mission in 1900, as a shelter for unwed mothers and their children. In April 1900, she sold the family's stables located at Third and O Streets to Miss Ellen Bowden, who donated the land to Bishop Grace for a Catholic chapel.

Margaret Crocker died December 1, 1901 in New York. Her ashes, encased in a handsome cedar-of-Lebanon box came home to Sacramento on the train, accompanied by her family, to be buried with civic honors next to her husband and daughters Kate and Nellie. The front of the Art Gallery was heavily draped in black cashmere for the memorial service on Thursday, January 30, 1902. Inside the main room great banks of flowers reclined against the pillars. The hall was crowded to the doors with Sacramentans and their families, the sound of their footsteps softened by thick carpeting. Bouquets, plaques, wreaths, scrolls, vases, and other floral designs completely occupied all available space. The Directors of the California Museum Association prepared a memorial page published in the *Sacramento Record-Union* that read, in part: "We regard the character of Mrs. Crocker as signally lofty and distinguished by a nobility and sweetness rare in life. She was public spirited as are but few women; she was charitable without ostentatious manifestation of it; she was kind to a fault; forgiving and merciful; she was a loving mother, a model as a wife, the object of emulation and inspiration as a citizen."

Margaret's friends and neighbors remembered her as the smiling woman who stood on her porch with her arms outstretched in welcome as they climbed her stairs.

Margaret was seventy-nine when she died, having lived a long, productive, and fulfilling life through the end of one era and into another. She had survived natural catastrophes and personal losses, and witnessed the heady, turbulent days of the Gold Rush dissolve into the maturing of California's Capital City. The end of the Civil War and the completion of the transcontinental railroad in the 1860s ushered in new thought, new customs, exciting new inventions and innovations, vexing new problems, and a new generation to take charge. As this generation moved forward into the next century, Margaret Crocker's life became the grist of legend. The benefactress Sacramentans called Lady Bountiful epitomized the resolute character, resiliency, and the innumerable contributions of so many pioneer women who had brought order to a frontier.

End Notes, Margaret Crocker

[1]Without knowing the quantity or quality of lumber Edwin purchased, approximately $2500 in modern money. Today board lumber is sold by either the lineal inch, or the board foot, calculated by multiplying the surface area of the lumber by its thickness. Modern prices vary from $2.75 to $8.00 per board foot, depending on the quality of the wood. If Charles Crocker paid $115 to $225 per thousand feet, his cost was still less than today's pricing.

[2]Levee piecemeal repair costs in 1850s dollars cannot fairly be equated with modern costs because of new technology and materials.

[3]Today bricks for outer walls cost between $275 and $325 per thousand (and higher), not including installation.

[4]The gentlemen raised cash of $25,000, or $1,250,000 in modern money.

[5]Disregarding individual stock values, $1.8 million then is equal to $90 million today.

[6]Today the corner sections around Fifth and Q Streets are government-owned. Using the data from a nearby privately owned parcel affords a guesstimate of $57,000 as the current assessed value of Margaret's quarter-block gift. The additional cash she presented to the Women's Aid Society is equivalent to $500,000 today.

[7]This block is home to two multi-story state office buildings, recently extensively renovated in a $157 million dollar project.

[8]Should such a collection be gathered today, its value would likely far exceed $50 million. Mr. Lubin's $100,000, in cash, is equivalent to $5 million.

[9]The Crockers paid the modern equivalent of $250,000 for this tripartite series of oil on canvas currently valued in the low six figures.

Bibliography

The Time, the Place, the Culture

Banning, Capt. William and Banning, George Hugh. *Six Horses.* New York & London: The Century Company, 1930.

Brown, Hallie Quinn. *Homespun Heroines and Other Women of Distinction.* New York: Oxford University Press, 1988.

Davis, Winfield J. *History and Progress of the Public School Department of City of Sacramento.* Sacramento: D. Johnston & Co., Printers, 1895.

Demas, Marilyn K. *Ungraded School No. 2 – Colored: The African American Struggle for Education in Victorian Sacramento.* Sacramento County Historical Society Golden Notes Volume 45, Numbers 1 and 2, Spring and Summer 1999.

Dove, Lois A., *Wagon Trains 1849 – 1865.* Library of Congress card number 89-090329.; page 94. (St. Joseph Gazette)

Enss, Chris. *Hearts West – True Stories of Mail-Order Brides on the Frontier.* TwoDot Books, 2005.

Erickson, Carolly. *Royal Panoply – Brief Lives of the English Monarchs.* Queen Victoria, pp. 291. New York: History Book Club, 2003.

Holmes, Kenneth L., Editor & Compiler. *Covered Wagon Women, 1850.* University of Nebraska Press, Bison Books Edition, 1996.

Smith, Jessie Carney, Editor. *Notable Black American Women, Volume 2.* Detroit: Gale Research Inc., 1996

Daily Alta California
November 1, 1852; December 1, 1852
Monterey Peninsula Herald August 27, 1949 Centennial Issue
Placer Times
December 15, 1849; December 29, 1849; January 19, 1850
Sacramento Daily Union
April 18, 1851; May 5, 1851; May 7, 1851; May 26, 1851

November 5, 1852; November 6, 1852; December 30, 1852
May 2, 1853; August 15, 1853; March 30, 1854; April 11, 1854
February 3, 1855; June 20, 1855; June 13, 1855;
September 29, 1855; November 20, 21, 23, 1855
December 19, 1856
January 12, 1857; March 12, March 14, 1857; November 16, 1857
May 8, 1858; August 24, 1861; February 23, 1864
Sacramento Daily Record-Union, January 3, 1880
Sacramento Transcript
September 10, 1850; November 16, 1850
1852 State Census Data; learncalifornia.org (11/8/2010)
Federal Census 1850, 1860
Internet:
"Flood, Elizabeth Thorn Scott," blackpast.org

Jennie Wimmer

Allen, W. W. and Avery, R. B. *California Gold Book.* San Francisco and
   Chicago: Donohue & Henneberry, Printers & Binders, 1893.
Amerson, Anne Dismukes, Georgia State Historian. "Jennie Wimmer
   Tested Gold in Her Soap Kettle" article in *Gold Rush Gallery
   newsletter*; and personal correspondence.
Barry, Genie. "Biographies" issued by Sutter's Fort State Historic Park.
   Oakland, California: Sequoia Elementary School, revised
   September 2008.
Beck, Steve. History Program Lead, Sutter's Fort State Historic Park,
   Sacramento. Personal conversations and correspondence.
Dillinger, William C. *The Gold Discovery: James Marshall and the
   California Gold Rush.* California Department of Parks and
   Recreation 1990, Revised 2006.
Donaldson, Milford W., compiler, Noble Grand Historian Squibob
   Chapter #1853 E Clampus Vitus. "Elizabeth Jane 'Jennie' Wimmer
   Co-Discoverer of the California Gold." Booklet prepared for the
   dedication of the Elizabeth Jane Wimmer plaque Valley Center
   Cemetery, October 2003. Provided by Judy Lopez.
El Dorado County Recorder, 2009. Original deeds, Wimmer; 1852 –

1859 at Coloma, California.

Hittell, Theodore. *History of California Volume III.* San Francisco: N.J. Stone & Company, 1898.

Lopez, Judy (Wimmer descendant). Personal conversations and family materials from Bert Hughes collection.

Michalski, Mark. Museum Collections Manager, Marshall Gold Discovery State Historic Park. Personal correspondence, 2009.

Roby, Neil. Docent, James Marshall Discovery State Park, Coloma. Personal interview, materials and correspondence.

Shinn, Charles Howard. "Early Horticulture in California." *The Overland Monthly Vol. VI, San Francisco:* Bacon & Company Printers, 1885.

San Francisco Chronicle October 27, 1893. "His Buried Riches," Interview of J. F. Bekeart.

Sutter, General John A. Excerpts from *Hutchings California Magazine* Nov 1857; San Francisco Virtual Museum.

Vosseller, Elias. *James Marshall, the New Jersey Discover of Gold.* Proceedings of the New Jersey Historical Society Vol. VII New Series, No. 4, October 1922. Morristown, NJ: Digital Antiquaria, PDF 2004.

Winslow, Mary P. "Mrs. Wimmer's Narrative of the First Piece of Gold," *San Francisco Bulletin*, December 19, 1874.

Leaflet: "A Simple Emigrant Christmas," prepared by Sutter's Fort State Historic Park, undated.

Leaflet: "Lest They be Forgotten Again. Sutter's Burial Grounds, New Helvetia Cemetery 1845 – 1956." Published by Sacramento County Cemetery Advisory Commission.

Federal Census 1840, 1850, Virginia

Federal Census 1860, 1870, California

Internet:

Bancroft, Hubert Howe. *History of California Volume 6.* Bancroft Library Electronic Library, Library website UC Berkeley ebooksread.com (7/19/2010)

Booth, John. "Making Lye Soap," frontierfreedom.com/ (7/8/2010)

Brown, Patty. "Harlan Wagon Train to California." Harlanfamily.org/stories.htm (7/8/2010)

Harlan, Mary Ann. "History of George Harlan." Recollections of his daughter Mary Ann Harlan Smith, harlanfamily.org/georgeh852.htm (7/8/2010)

Houghton, Eliza Poor Donner. *The Expedition of the Donner Party and its Tragic Fate.* The Project Gutenberg eBook #11146, 2004

Sherman, William T. "William Tecumseh Sherman and the Discovery of Gold," from Chapter II of *Memoirs of W. T. Sherman.* The California State Military Department Museum. militarymuseum.org/sherman4.html (6/7/2010)

Treaty of Guadalupe Hidalgo, sonofthesouth.net/Mexican-war/treaty-guadalupe-hidalgo.htm (8/2/2010)

Dorothea Wolfinger Zins

Bancroft, Hubert Howe. *The Works of Hubert Howe Bancroft, Vol. VI: 1848-1859.* San Francisco: The History Company Publishers, 1888.

Carroll, Ed. *Sacramento's Breweries.* Golden Notes Volume 53, Number 1. Sacramento, California: Sacramento County Historical Society, 2010.

Fort Sutter Papers, Vol. XIV, mss. No. 42, No. 50. California Room Rare Books Collection, California State Library, Sacramento.

Gudde, Erwin G. and Elisabeth K., Editors and Translators. *From St. Louis to Sutter's Fort, 1846 by Heinrich Lienhard.* Norman, Oklahoma: University of Oklahoma Press, 1961.

McGlashan, Charles Fayette. *History of the Donner Party, a Tragedy of the Sierra.* Truckee, California, 1879. Reissued by Hard Press, 2010.

Mulvaney, Mary Carlin. "A History of Nicolaus." *Sutter County Historical Society News Bulletin, Vol. XI No. 2.* Yuba City, California, April 1972.

Nicolaus Cemetery, Nicolaus, California. Personal visit by author, 2010.

Pioneer Biography files, George Zins. California Room, California State Library, Sacramento.

Ryan, Robert L. "Sam Brannan in Sutter County." *Sutter County Historical Society News Bulletin, Vol. XIII, No. 1.* Yuba City, California, 1974.

Steed, Jack. *The Donner Party Rescue Site – Johnson's Ranch on Bear River.* Sacramento, California: Graphic Publishers, 1993.

Stewart, George R. *Ordeal by Hunger: The Story of the Donner Party.* New York: Houghton Mifflin Company, 1960.

Sutter's Fort State Historic Archives, West Sacramento, a division of California State Parks. Judy Russo, Registrar. Various papers.

1849 City or Town Assessment Roll, original ledger. Sacramento Archives and Museum Collection Center.

Census: Federal Census 1850, Sacramento; Special California State Census 1852

Daily Alta California September 3, 1853

Marysville Weekly Appeal December 31, 1875

Placer Times:

November 10, 1849; December 29, 1849

February 9, 1850; February 16, 1850

May 1, May 8, May 27, 1850

Sacramento Bee October 29, 1885

Sacramento Daily Union May 31, 1854; June 15, 1872

Sacramento Transcript November 16, 1850

Stockton Democrat February 2, 1862

Internet:

An Enduring Legacy: Volume One. (Excerpt). Ancestry.com (4/5/10)

Brief History of Brickmaking in California. Calbricks.netfirms.com/brickhistory.html.

History, El Dorado County, California esternlivingcenter.com/history/history~placerville.htm (4/5/10)

Johnson, Kristin. "New Light on The Donner Party" utahcrossroads.org; plus personal correspondence with Kristin Johnson

Sutter County History at w.suttercounty.org (7/2/10)

Terry, Carole Cosgrove. "Germans in Sacramento, 1850 – 1859. Clubs.unlv.edu/psisigama/journals/terry/2005.pdf.

Houghton, Eliza P. Donner. "Expedition of the Donner Party." Project Gutenberg eBook. Static.scribd.com/docs/9k088c5gkhif.pdf

Naturalization Records. Archives.gov/genealogy/naturalization.html (10/30/2010)

Smith, Marian L. "Women and Naturalization, ca. 1802-1940."

Prologue: *Quarterly of the National Archives, Vol. 30, No. 2 (Summer 1998).* Archives.gov/publications/prologue/1998 (10/30/2010)

Whittle, Syd. "The First Brick Building in Sacramento." The Historical Marker Database. Hmdb.org/marker.asp?marker (9/7/2009)

Mary Zabriskie Johnson

Benton, Joseph. *Journal of Reverend Joseph Benton, January 11, 1849 – December 31, 1856, Vol. I.* California Room, Rare Books Collection. California State Library, Sacramento.

City Assessor Map Book, 1851. Sacramento Archives and Museum Collection Center 551 Sequoia Pacific Blvd. Sacramento, California.

Cook, Lynn and LaDue, Janet. *The First Ladies of California.* Sacramento: Xlibris Corporation, 2007.

Haiman, Miecislaus. *Polish Pioneers of California, Vol. V*, Annals of the Polish Ro. Cath. Union Archives and Museum. Chicago: Polish R. C. Union of America, 1940.

Hollingsworth, John, M.D., personal interview November 27, 2009. Information from Doctor's private collection *Diseases and Their Cure: Fifty Years of Experience* by O.H. Crandall, M.D., published 1898.

McMahon, Lucia. "A More Accurate and Extensive Education than is Customary: Educational Opportunities for Women in Early-Nineteenth-Century New Jersey." Complete article on-line at creativecommons.org.

Melendy, H. Brett and Gilbert, Benjamin F. *The Governors of California from Peter H. Burnett to Edmund Brown.* Georgetown, California: The Talisman Press, 1965.

Pioneer files Governor J. Neely Johnson. California Room, California State Library, Sacramento.

Pioneer files Colonel James C. Zabriskie. California Room, California State Library, Sacramento.

Regan, Timothy E. *Images of America: New Brunswick.* Arcadia Publishing, 2003.

Sacramento Archives and Museum Collection Center: Charles Page & Associates Historical/Architectural Survey Form; J. Neely Johnson mansion, undated, c. 1976.

Zabriskie, George Olin. *The Zabriskie Family: A Three Hundred and one Year History of the Descendants of Albrecht Zaborowskij (C. 1638-1711) of Bergen County, New Jersey, Volume I.* Ridgewood, New Jersey: Genealogy Society of Bergen County, 1963. Selected pages provided by Peggy W. Norris, Bergen County Historical Society.

Federal Census 1850, 1852, 1860, 1870, 1900; Ancestry.com

California Special Census 1852; California Room, California State Library.

Trust Deeds 1850 – 1859, James C. Zabriskie and J. Neely Johnson. Sacramento County Clerk/Recorder, 600 Eighth Street, Sacramento, California.

Daily Alta California, San Francisco:

October 8, 1850; June 28, 1851

July 17, 1856; November 28, 1856

May 29, 1870; November 24, 1887

Morning Appeal Ormsby County, Nevada, November 24, 1887

Placer Times:

November 3, 1849; December 29, 1849

March 23, 1850; May 17, 1850

Sacramento Daily Union:

April 16 and April 18, 1851; June 12, 1851

March 22, 1852; September 25, 1852; November 2, 1852; November 7, 1852

December 14, 1855; December 19, 1855; December 26, 1855

January 5, 1856; January 8, 1856; January 9, 1856;

January 29, 1856

February 18, 1856; February 25, 1856

January 12, 1857; March 27, 1857; November 7, 1857; November 28, 1857

December 19, 1857; December 24, 1857; September 2, 1872

Sacramento Transcript:

October 21, 1850; October 24, 1850; December 9, 1850

San Francisco Call: November 24, 1887

San Francisco Daily California Chronicle: January 10, 1856
Internet:
Governors of California: J. Neely Johnson;
  Californiagovernors.ca.gov/h/biography/governor_4.html.
  (8/5/2009)
En.wikipedia.org/wiki/J_Neely_Johnson (8/2009)
"Pioneer Congregational Church/United Church of Christ, Our History."
  Sacramento.Pioneerucc.net/our_history.html (8/26/2009)
  Attribution to California State Library Sacramento.
The California Military Museum. "Sherman and the San Francisco
  Vigilantes," originally published in *The Century Magazine*
  December, 1891.Militarymuseum.org/Sherman2.html

Margaret Frink

Akahori, M. B., Editor and Publisher. *This is California –Early History
  of California and its Development Into a State.* Los Angeles: Town
  Crier Blue Book, c. 2000.
Banning, Captain William and Banning, George Hugh. *Six Horses.* New
  York: The Century Co., 1930.
California History Magazine, Vol. 9, No. 1. San Francisco, California,
  March 1930.
California History Magazine, Vol. LXXV, No. 3. San Francisco,
  California, Fall 1996.
Connolly, Elaine, and Self, Diane. *Capital Women: An Interpretive
  History of Women in Sacramento 1850 – 1920.* Capital Women's
  History Project c/o Sacramento History and Science Division:
  Sacramento, California, 1995.
Edwards, Owen. "Snail Mail." National Postal Museum, *Smithsonian
  Magazine* May, 2010.
Enss, Chris. *How the West Was Worn.* Guilford, Connecticut and
  Helena, Montana: Twodot, an imprint of The Globe Pequot Press,
  2006.
Holmes, Kenneth L., editor. *Covered Wagon Women: Diaries & Letters
  from the Western Trails, 1850, Vol. 2.* Lincoln, Nebraska, and
  London: University of Nebraska Press, 1983. Reprinted by

arrangement with the Arthur H. Clark Company.

Letters of Osgood Church Wheeler, pg 309. *California Historical Society Quarterly, Vol. 27.* March 1948.

Parker, Charles H. *The General Laws of the State of California from 1864 to 1871 Inclusive, Vol. III.* San Francisco, California. A.L. Bancroft and Company, 1871.

Pioneer Biographical Files, Ledyard and Margaret Frink. California Room, California State Library.

Sacramento County California Recorder's Office. Ledyard Frink trust deeds, 1851 – 1856.

Sutter's Fort Archives, Sacramento, California. Undated, c. 1939 *Sacramento Bee* article: "Historical Memories," letter from L. A. Winchell.

Sutter's Fort Archives, Sacramento, California. "Historic Cottage in Sacramento" article published in *Grizzly Bear* Magazine, December 1927. A publication of the Native Sons of the Golden West.

Transactions of the California State Agricultural Society. By the State Printer at Sacramento, California. For the years 1858-59; 1863; 1866-67; 1868-71; 1872-73; 1874-77; 1878-79.

Federal Census: 1850, Sacramento; 1860 Sacramento & Solano; 1870, Solano

Special California Census 1852, Sacramento

California Farmer and Journal of Useful Sciences September 28, 1855; September 11, 1863

Sacramento Daily Union:

April 22, 1851; April 25, 1851

June 30, 1852; June 9, 1852; July 7, 1852; July 31, 1852;

August 7, 1852; October 28, 1852; December 14, 1852

July 8, 1853; August 10 - 11, 1853

June 6, 7, 19, 1854; August 23, 1854

November 20, 21, 24, 25, 27, 1854

December 22, 1855

May 11, 1855; May 16, 1856

July 27, 1857; March 26, April 1, 2, 1858; March 21, 1860

December 26, 1864; December 25, 1866

Sacramento Transcript:

September 14, 1850; November 16, 1850
February 8 & 11, 1851; March 8, 1851; March 24, 1851
April 18 & April 26, 1851
The Evening Bee. June 20, 1896.

Lavinia Waterhouse

Chambers's Enclyclopaedia, A Dictionary. Vol. IV. New York: Collier,
1887.

Day, Rowena Wise. "Carnival of Lights." *Golden Notes*; Sacramento
County Historical Society, 75th Anniversary Edition, Vol. 16, No. 2
and 3. Sacramento, California. July 1970.

Heimer, Dianne. "Sacramento Women: Women of Capital Importance."
Sacramento Magazine, July 1997. Sacramento, California,
Sacramento Magazines Corporation.

Levy, Jo Ann. *Unsettling the West*. Berkeley, California: Heyday Books,
2004.

Martin, Wallace E., Editor. "The Muldrow Claim." *The Humboldt
Historian, Vol. XVIII*, September – October 1970. Eureka,
California: Humboldt County Historical Society, 1970.

McLane, Lucy Neely. *A Piney Paradise by Monterey Bay: Pacific
Grove, the Documentary History of her First Twenty-five Years*.
San Francisco: Lawton Kennedy, 1952.

Pioneer biography files, Lavinia Gertrude Goodyear Waterhouse.
California Room, California State Library Sacramento, California.

Reiter, Joan Swallow (text). *The Women*. By the editors of Time-Life
Books. Alexandria, Virginia. Time-Life Books, 1978, revised 1979.
Illustration of painting by L. G. Waterhouse.

Sequoia Chapter, Daughters if the American Revolution. *Annual
Compilation of Births, Marriages, Deaths in the Sacramento Union
1859-1886, Vol. I*. San Francisco: Mrs. G. Ernest Mott, State
Chairman, Gen. Records Committee, 1856.

Taylor, Nathaniel R. "The Rivers and Floods of the Sacramento and San
Joaquin Watersheds." United States Weather Bureau Bulletin,
Issues 37 – 44. Washington D.C.: United States Weather Bureau,
1913.

Waterhouse, Cornelia S. *Personal Diary November 18, 1856 – October, 1858;* Transcribed from the original. California Room, California State Library, Sacramento, California.

Waterhouse, Lavinia. *Original Account Book 1857 – 1859.* California Room Rare Books Collection, California State Library.

Waterhouse, L. Gertrude. "My View of San Francisco Bay." *Overland Monthly Vol. XXI – Second Series, January – June, 1893*, p. 261. San Francisco: The Overland Monthly Publishing Company, 1893.

Waterhouse, L. Gertrude. "The Sacramento." *Overland Monthly Vol. XXII – Second Series, July – December, 1893*, p. 400. San Francisco: The Overland Monthly Publishing Company, 1893.

Waterhouse, Mrs. Dr. L. G. "The Sleeping Giantess and Other Poems." (pamphlet) Sacramento: California. Globe Printing Company, 1873. Rare Books Collection, California State Library.

[no author] Golden Notes. "Smith's Gardens, Sacramento Showplace of a Century Ago." Sacramento County Historical Society, Vol. 5, No. 1. Sacramento State College, California. October, 1958.

U.S. Federal Census: New York, 1840, 1850; California, 1860, 1880.

Sacramento Bee: December 8, 1965

Sacramento Daily Record-Union: January 19, 1880; August 9, 1880

Sacramento Daily Union:

September 20, 1853

April 11, 1854; April 24, 1854; May 18, 1854;

July 15, 1854; July 14, 1854; July 17, 1854; September 26, 1854

November 22, 1855; January 5, 1856; February 23, 1856; December 5, December 6, 1856

December 9, 24, 26, 30, 1856; February 14, 1857; March 27, 1857; April 29, 1857; June 20, 1857; July 20, 1857

June 28, 1861; January 11, 1862; March 3, 1862

April 16, 1868; December 6, 1871; March 31, 1873;

February 19, 1879

Sacramento Transcript November 25, 1850

The Daily Bee June 3, 1859

Internet:

El Carmelo Cemetery, Pacific Grove, Monterey County, California. Interment.net/Cemetery records on line:

interment.net/data/us/ca/monterey/elcarmelo; and
files.usgwarchives.org/ca/monterey/cemeteries/elcarmelo

Findagrave.com/Hannah Goodyear, Find A Grave Memorial #35924445

Hosmer, Janet, Ph.D. "Spiritualism & Feminism – Changing Humanity
Together," posted July 30, 2009 on
AlternativeApproaches.com/Article5251.html

James McGaw Wagon Train 1852, Parts III & VII. biographies/company
members. freepages.genealogy.rootsweb.ancestry.com/

Hydrotherapy. "The Everyday Miracle of Water."
Library/Bookshelf/Books/21/29.cfm

Montereyhistoryfiles.usgwarchives.org/ca/monterey/history/1893/memor
ial/chapterx433nms.txt;

Monterey County Genealogy, cagenweb.com/montereybbs/

Ober, Patrick K., MD. "The Pre-Flexnerian Reports: Mark Twain's
Criticism of Medicine in the United States." History of Medicine
annals.org.

Pioneer Companies that Crossed the Plains 1847 – 1868.
w.xmission.com/~nelsonb/company.htm

Rosenberg, Charles E. "The Book in the Sickroom: A Tradition of Print
and Practice." Librarycompany.org/doctor/sickroom

Scott, Donald. "Evangelicalism, Revivalism, and the Second Great
Awakening." Essay, Queens College, City University of New York,
National Humanities Center, October 2000.
nationalhumanitiescenter.org.

Margaret Crocker

Bagley, Harry P. "A Long Honeymoon Across the Isthmus to a Pioneer
Home." Reprint, 1853 letter of Mary Deming Crocker. *Sacramento
Bee Magazine Section* November 23, 1940.

Hopkins, Timothy. *Memory of a Boyhood in Sacramento: Reminiscences
of Timothy Hopkins.* No. 3, Occasional Monographs of the
Sacramento Pioneer Association. Sacramento: The Sacramento
Pioneer Association, 1987.

Kurutz, K. D. "Sacramento's Pioneer Patrons of Art, The Edwin Bryant
Crocker Family," *Golden Notes Volume 36, Number 1, Spring 1990.*

Sacramento: Sacramento County Historical Society, 1990.

Lowney, Barbara. "Lady Bountiful: Margaret Crocker of Sacramento." *California Historical Society Quarterly Vol. XLVII.* San Francisco: June 1968.

Pioneer biographical files, Edwin Crocker family. California Room, California State Library, Sacramento.

Ramirez, Salvador A. *The Inside Man: The Life and Times of Mark Hopkins.* Carlsbad, California: The Tentacled Press, 2007.

The Festival of Flowers May 6, 1885. Commemorative booklet. Sacramento: H.S. Crocker & Co., Printers and Publishers, 1885. California Room, California State Library.

The Wave – A Journal for Those in the Swim. (magazine) San Francisco, California, January 23, 1892.

Transactions of the California State Agricultural Society, 1858 and 1859 editions, California State Archives. Sacramento, California.

Daily Alta California October 3, 1862

San Francisco Call December 27, 1889

The Sunday San Francisco Call, December 15, 1901

Sacramento Daily Record-Union October 23, 1879

Sacramento Daily Union:

April 25, 1851; September 3, 1853

February 19, 1856; April 8, 1856; April 10, 1856

August 16, 1861;October 1, 1863; April 18, 1865

August 9, 1869; February 4, 1874; October 27, 1874

May 7, 1885; August12, 1886; February 26, 1887

San Francisco Chronicle February 7, 1872

Sacramento Record Union January 31, 1902

The New York Times December 3, 1901

The Daily Bee, Sacramento, May 6, 1885

The Sacramento Bee April 18, 1900; June 26, 1956

Federal Census 1850, Indiana; 1860, 1870, 1880 California, Ancestry.com.

Internet

American Experience: Transcontinental Railroad; Pbs.org/wgbh/amex/tcrr/peopleevents/p_ecrocker.html (8/27/2010)

Bailey, William F. "The Story of the Central Pacific." *The Pacific*

Monthly, January and February 1908.
cprr.org/Museum/Bailey_CPRR_1908.html
California Supreme Court Historical Society:
cschs.org/02_history/02_a.html (8/27/2010)
Family History Library, Salt Lake City, Utah, microfilm 1503389.
Ancestry.com (8/17/2010)
fassettfamilytree.org/(Jennie Louise Crocker Fassett)
Galloway, John Debo. "The First Transcontinental Railroad." New York:
Dorset Press, 1989. Reprinted by Central Pacific Railroad
Photographic History Museum, cprr.org/Museum/Galloway4.html.
(8/29/2010)
onbunkerhill.org. Los Angeles home of Margaret Crocker. (9/20/2010)

Sacramento History, General

Avella, Steven M. *Sacramento: Indomitable City.* The Making of
America Series. Arcadia Publishing, 2003.
Barber & Baker, Engravers, Authors and Publishers. *"Sacramento
Illustrated 1855,"* a magazine. Printed by Monson & Valentine,
steam book and job printers. San Francisco, 1855.
Beck, Warren A. and Williams, David A. *California A History of the
Golden State.* Garden City, New York: Doubleday & Company, Inc.
1972.
Bryant, Edwin. *What I Saw in California.* University of Nebraska Press,
1985.
Burg, William. *Then & Now Series: Sacramento.* Arcadia Publishing,
2007.
Cole, Cornelius. *Memoirs of Cornelius Cole, Ex-Senator of the United
States from California.* New York: McLoughlin Brothers, 1908.
Digitized for Microsoft Corporation by the Internet Archive in
2007, University of Toronto.
Colville, Samuel. *Sacramento City Directory for the Year 1854-1855.*
San Francisco, California: Monson & Valentine Book and Job
Printers, 1854.
Cutter, D.S. & Co., Compilers and Publishers. *Sacramento City
Directory for the Year A.D. 1860.* Sacramento, California: H.S.

Crocker & Co., 1859.

Davis, Winfield J. *An Illustrated History of Sacramento County, California.* Chicago: The Lewis Publishing Company, 1890.

Dillon, Richard. *Captain John Sutter: Sacramento Valley's Sainted Sinner.* Santa Cruz, California: Western Tanager Press, 1991.

Draper, Robert E. *Sacramento City and County Directory for 1868.* Sacramento: H. S. Crocker & Co., Steam Printers and Stationers, 1868.

Hayes, Peter J., Editor. *The Lower American River: Prehistory to Parkway.* Sacramento, California: The American River Natural History Association, 2005.

Henry, Fern. *My Checkered Life. Luzena Stanley Wilson in Early California.* With reprint of *Luzena Stanley Wilson: '49er,* originally published by Eucalyptus Press, 1937. Nevada City, California: Carl Mautz Publishing, 2003.

Helmich, Stephen G. *Sacramento's 1854 City Hall & Waterworks.* Sacramento County Historical Society Golden Notes Series, Vol. 31, No. 4. Winter, 1985. (booklet)

Hittell, Theodore H. *History of California Volume III.* San Francisco: N. J. Stone & Company, 1898.

Holliday, J. S. *The World Rushed In – The California Gold Rush Experience.* Norman, Oklahoma: University of Oklahoma Press, 2002.

Holden, William M. *Sacramento: Excursions into its History and Natural World.* Fair Oaks, California: Two Rivers Publishing Company, 1988.

Hook, Eileen. "Suttersville: A Pipe Dream at Best." *California Territorial Quarterly Number 60, Winter 2004.* Paradise, California.

Horner, Jody and Horner, Ric, Researchers and Compilers. *The Golden Hub, Sacramento.* Pilot Hill, California: 19th Century Books, an imprint of Electric Canvas, 2008.

Hurtado, Albert L. *John Sutter A Life on the North American Frontier.* Norman, Oklahoma: University of Oklahoma Press, 2006.

Jackson, Joseph Henry. *Anybody's Gold.* San Francisco: Chronicle Books, 1970.

Jones, Guy P. "Thomas M. Logan, M.D., Organizer of California State

Board of Health." *California and Western Medicine Vol. 63, No. 1.* CMA Los Angeles, 1944.

Kibbey, Mead B., Editor. *J. Horace Culver's Sacramento City Directory for the Year 1851.* Sacramento, CA: California State Library Foundation, 2000.

Kibbey, Mead B., Editor. *Samuel Colville's Sacramento City Directory for the Year 1853-54.* Sacramento, California: California State Library Foundation, 1997.

Levy, Jo Ann. *They Saw the Elephant, Women in the California Gold Rush.* Norman, Oklahoma: University of Oklahoma Press, 1992.

Matthews, Alice Madeley, "The Great Flood of 1861." *Golden Notes Vol. 28, No. 2.* Sacramento County Historical Society. Sacramento, CA Summer 1982.

Ottley, Allan R. (introduction by). *Sacramento County California.* Original copyright 1880. Berkeley, CA: Howell-North, 1960.

Sacramento Archives and Museum Collection Center and the Historic Old Sacramento Foundation. *Old Sacramento and Downtown.* Arcadia Publishing Images of America Series, 2006.

Sacramento's Alkali Flat. Special Collections of the Sacramento Public Library. Arcadia Publishing, Images of America Series, 2010.

Sacramento City Cemetery burials 1849 – 2000 (on line)

Sacramento City and County Directory 1889-90. San Francisco: F. M. Husted, Publisher, 1889.

Sacramento City and County Directory for the Year 1907. Sacramento: H. S. Crocker & Co., Publisher, 1907.

Sacramento Directory for the Year 1880. Sacramento: H. S. Crocker & Co., Publishers, Stationers and Printers, 1880.

Severson, Thor. *Sacramento – An Illustrated History: 1829 to 1874 From Sutter's Fort to Capital City.* California Historical Society, 1973.

Stone, Irving. *Men to Match My Mountains: The Opening of the Far West 1840 - 1900.* Garden City, New York. Doubleday & Company, 1956.

Taylor, Nathaniel R. "The Rivers and Floods of the Sacramento and San Joaquin Watersheds." *United States Weather Bureau Bulletin, Issues 37-44.* Washington, D.C. 1913.

Thompson and West's History of Sacramento County, California.
Reproduction with Introduction by Allan R. Ottley. Berkeley,
California: Howell-North, 1960.

Williams, John Hoyt. *A Great and Shining Road: The Epic Story of the
Transcontinental Railroad.* New York. Random House, Inc. reprint.
Originally published by Times Books (a division of Random
House), 1988.

Winter, Carl G. Editor. "Sacramento 1853 by Mark Hopkins." *Golden
Notes Volume 1,* June 1954. Sacramento County Historical Society,
June 1954.

Index

Note: The six women who have full biographies, and their families, are not listed in the Index. See individual chapters.

28514120R00168

Made in the USA
San Bernardino, CA
30 December 2015